The Ethos of Restoration Comedy

The Ethos of
Restoration Comedy

Ben Ross Schneider, Jr.

UNIVERSITY OF ILLINOIS PRESS
Urbana : Chicago : London

152433

For
J.T.S.
and
B.R.S.

ACKNOWLEDGMENTS

My debt is great to many people, but the contributions to this book of time, patience, encouragement, and wisdom by the following people are particularly substantial.

To my erstwhile colleague, David Mayer III, the earliest encourager and advocator of my approach to Restoration comedy, I owe especial thanks. I am also obliged to my associate, Bertrand Goldgar, for reading an early version and giving material and moral support. For dropping everything to help me make last-minute decisions and prepare final copy for the press, I am forever grateful to my colleague, Elizabeth Forter.

Without the imaginative help of John Church, director of the Lawrence Computer Center, I could not have adapted the machine to the masses of unruly data I accumulated. A student, Charles Lord, gave up a summer and much time during the ensuing year to punching thousands of cards and shepherding them through the machines. To both I owe a large debt of gratitude. Thanks are also due to David Mann, who kindly shared with me information from his unpublished computer-produced concordance of Congreve's works, and to the editor of *Theatre Notebook* for permission to use in chapter 6 parts of my article, "The Coquette-Prude as an Actress's Line during the Time of Mrs. Oldfield," XXII, 4 (Summer, 1968): 143–56.

Ruth Lesselyong and Nancy Kroll have patiently converted my scraps and scribbles into a readable typescript, and Violet Walker's judicious copy-editing has removed many impurities. I thank these ladies for their care and concern for the book's welfare.

Peter Wood, Lyn Oxenford, and Sybil Rosenfeld have graciously set aside time to exchange ideas with me, and I thank them for the benefit of their wide experience with the London stage.

I have found it particularly difficult to find a way of fitting this view of Restoration comedy into the existing structure of ideas on the subject, to find the common ground and build a lucid argument on it. In this search I have been guided not only by the real contributions to our knowledge of certain scholars in the field, but also by their personal willingness to read versions of the text and wrestle with the problems raised therein. For such help I will never be able to thank enough Norman Holland, P. F. Vernon, Vernon Sternberg, Charles Shattuck, Rose Zimbardo, and Aubrey Williams.

BEN ROSS SCHNEIDER, JR.
Lawrence University
September, 1970

The Ethos of Restoration Comedy

CHAPTER ONE

The Critical Basis for an Ethical Approach

Ours is a particularly bad moment in time from which to assess a body of literature declaring moral instruction to be its main purpose. While on the one hand we have been liberated from the prudery that warped the vision of Victorian critics, our own aesthetically oriented style of criticism prevents us from seeing ethical dimensions of any sort. At the same time, we are still Victorian enough, even (or especially) the most liberal of us, to habitually restrict morality to the realm of sex. But there are certainly other virtues than fidelity and chastity and other vices than promiscuity, and perhaps some of them are more important ones, too. If it happened that some other set of values than the Victorian sexually centered ones were present in Restoration comedy, we could easily miss it. In fact Macaulay himself might have been better prepared, as a Victorian, to understand the plays than we are: "It is not the fact [wrote Macaulay] that the world of these dramatists is a world into which no moral enters. Morality constantly enters into that world, a sound morality and an unsound morality; the sound morality to be insulted, derided, associated with everything mean and hateful; the unsound morality to be set off to every advantage and inculcated by all methods, direct and indirect."[1] Though many critics have differed with

---

[1] Quoted in Norman Holland's *First Modern Comedies* (Cambridge, Mass., 1959), p. 202. This book contains an excellent survey of the criticism of Restoration comedy (chap. 16).

Macaulay's conclusion, his major premise—that the plays advocate a morality—has never been investigated, even though the playwrights themselves affirmed the proposition mightily and continually, and even though it was actually the *morality* of the plays that Collier attacked in the famous controversy bearing his name, not their *lack* of morality. The crucial error was perhaps Lamb's—to deny Restoration comedy any morality whatsoever.[2] Lamb's contention, that Restoration comedy describes a never-never land where moral judgments are irrelevant, still dominates our critical scene. "Manners" criticism, "social mode" criticism, even in some ways "wit" criticism are mere extensions of his view that Restoration comedy deals with an amoral world.[3]

The literary theories of the comic poets themselves are of course no obstacle to an interpretation of Restoration comedy that assumes a morally instructive purpose. In fact, whoever asserts a version of Lamb's position gives them the lie direct. If the critical positions of the playwrights were hard to discover, this fact would be easier to understand, but everybody knows about the neoclassical advocacy of the Aristotelian-Horatian principle of *utile dulci*, and few students of Restoration comedy could fail to notice how frequently the playwrights affirmed it in dedications, prologues, epilogues, and answers to Collier. Nor can the affirmations be explained away as responses to Collier's *Short View of the Immorality and Profaneness of the English Stage* of 1698. The comic writers, trained on Aristotle, Horace, Boileau, and Rapin, had no need to learn from Collier that plays ought to improve the morals of their audiences. In this respect, Collier was a fol-

---

[2] In Charles Lamb's essay "On the Artificial Comedies of the Last Century."

[3] As I see it, the amoral line of criticism runs from Lamb through John Palmer (*The Comedy of Manners*, London, 1913) to Kathleen Lynch (*The Social Mode in Restoration Comedy*, New York, 1926), where, on pp. 6–7, she finds her thesis in a passage from Palmer. She merely carries Lamb to his logical conclusion: if comic characters are artificial, they must be hiding something natural under the fake surface. The plays are concerned with resulting inner-outer tension. She thus opens the door to the Hobbesian-Machiavellian-hedonistic-naturalistic interpretations of Thomas Fujimura (*Restoration Comedy of Wit*, Princeton, N.J., 1952) and Dale Underwood (*Etherege and the Seventeenth Century Comedy of Manners*, New Haven, Conn., 1957), who, while trying to increase the intellectual weight of the comedies, only succeed in giving them an even more unpalatable reputation. Much more successful are Norman Holland (*First Modern Comedies*), who lets the plays speak for themselves in the new critics' manner, and Rose Zimbardo (*Wycherley's Drama*, New Haven, Conn., 1965), who at last gives full recognition to the satirical thrust of Wycherley, though without developing the moral component that satire implies.

lower, not a leader. Indeed, anyone who interprets this pamphlet war as a debate about *whether* plays should be moral misses the real issue. It is a debate about *what* morality plays ought to propagate. Despite the fact that most of the evidence for these assertions is well known, I shall review that evidence here partly for the sake of completeness and partly because it is so universally ignored in modern studies.[4]

When England restored Charles to the throne and Charles restored the theatres, he decreed that theatrical recreations ought to be "not only harmless delights but useful and instructive." Whatever we may say about the Merry Monarch, it cannot be denied that he knew a play must, as Cibber put it, "as well *prodesse* as *delectare*."[5] Although he could complain that Crowne's *Sir Courtly Nice* "wanted a little more . . . smut," he could defend Wilson's *Cheats* on sounder neoclassical grounds when it was removed from the stage in 1663 because it offended the people it satirized. After looking at some of the passages objected to, Charles sanctioned the play, charging the players "to take heed in this as in all their other plays, to expose upon the stage anything that was either profane, scandalous or scurrilous, observing which they should be protected and no longer."[6]

There is no reason to be astonished, as Montague Summers is, that such moralistic pronouncements should proceed from "Old Rowley's" mouth.[7] The king is merely affirming the critical tradition of his day as it had come down from Aristotle. According to Congreve's translation of an often-repeated passage, Aristotle defines comedy as "an imitation of the worse sort of people." Interpreting the definition, Congreve in typical Augustan fashion gives it a moralistic turn:

> He does not mean the worse sort of people in respect to their quality, but in respect to their manners. This is plain, from

[4] J. W. Krutch in his most thorough and carefully reasoned study of the controversy, *Comedy and Conscience after the Restoration* (New York, 1924), does not evade this evidence. Recognizing that instruction is indeed the "critical dogma" (chap. IV), he concludes that the comic writers were "heterodox" (p. 86). To maintain this thesis, however, he has to shrug off as defensive gestures a great deal of evidence to the contrary in prefaces, dedications, prologues, and epilogues, some of which are cited.

[5] Colley Cibber, *An Apology for the Life of Mr. Colley Cibber* (London, 1889), ed. Robert Lowe, I:lxi, 266.

[6] Montague Summers, *The Playhouse of Pepys* (New York, 1935), p. 220.

[7] *Ibid.*

his telling you immediately after that he does not mean [that comedy relates to] all kinds of vice: there are crimes too daring and too horrid for comedy. But the vices most frequent and which are the common practise of the looser sort of livers are the subject matter of comedy. . . . Men are to be laughed out of their vices in comedy; the business of comedy is to delight, as well as to instruct.[8]

By introducing the terms *instruction* and *delight* Congreve, again typically, attaches Horace to Aristotle. The following passage from the *Ars Poetica*, translated by Congreve's contemporary, the Earl of Roscommon, supplies the Horatian context of these important terms:

> Old age explodes all but morality,
> Austerity offends aspiring youths,
> But he that joins instructions with delight,
> Profit with pleasure, carries all the votes.[9]

The classical tradition is reinforced in England by influential French attitudes. Molière, at least a dozen of whose plays were copied or pirated during the Restoration, defined comedy as "une poème ingénieux qui par les leçons agréable, reprend les defauts des hommes,"[10] and Boileau restated Horace as follows (I quote from the Soames-Dryden translation of 1683):

> Authors, observe the rules I here lay down.
> In prudent lessons everywhere abound,
> With pleasant join the useful and the sound:
> A sober reader a vain tale will slight,
> He seeks as well instruction as delight.[11]

Rapin, in his *Reflections on Aristotle's Poesie*, translated by Rymer in 1694, tells us, "For no other end is poetry delightful than that it may

---

[8] William Congreve, "Amendments of Mr. Collier's False and Imperfect Citations," *The Complete Works of William Congreve*, ed. Montague Summers (Soho, 1923), III:173.

[9] Horace, *Of the Art of Poetry*, made English by the Earl of Roscommon (London, 1680), pp. 23-24.

[10] Preface to *Tartuffe* (1669), quoted in Molière, *L'Avare* (Paris, 1964), p. 15.

[11] [Nicolas] Boileau, *The Art of Poetry*, written in French . . . made English (London, 1683), pp. 58-59.

be profitable." He defines comedy as "an image of common conversation [which] corrects the public vices by letting us see how ridiculous they are in particulars."[12]

In England critics recited the same formalities. Rymer admired the Romans because they "reckoned, as the Greeks had done, that the end of poetry was as well to be profitable as to be pleasant."[13] For Dennis, "the two ends of comedy [were] pleasure and instruction."[14] In his *Complete Art of Poetry* Gildon echoed Aristotle's definition of comedy, saying that it "imitates common life in its actions and humors, laughing at and rendering vice and folly ridiculous."[15]

The opposition to and near-extirpation of the theatres by the Puritan Commonwealth made Restoration critics in reaction more conscious of the moralizing properties of the stage than they would have been without Puritan goading. For Puritans, only the pulpit was capable of improving mankind; the stage, never. Davenant, who believed it was the other way around, sneered, "Those virtuous enemies [to the stage] deny heroic plays to the gentry, [but] they entertain the people with a seditious farce of their own counterfeit gravity."[16] This statement, written before 1663 with the Civil War still fresh in memory, opens an interesting vista for the contemplation of Restoration comedy. Davenant seems to see, in a state of class war, "the people" going to church to receive a morale-stiffening display of "counterfeit gravity" while their opponents, "the gentry" in the playhouses, steel themselves to resist with heroic plays. At any rate, the stage was clearly aware that it functioned as an alternative to the pulpit as a medium of instructing the populace.

What unpalatable dose of fire and brimstone could compete with a sugar-coated pill? The Puritan divine in Wilson's *Cheats* (1662) admits that he preaches against plays only because he cannot compete with them as moral instruction (I).[17] The prologue of another early

---

[12] [René] Rapin, *Reflections on Aristotle's Poesie* (London, 1694), pp. 14, 15.

[13] [Thomas] Rymer, *Short View of Tragedy* (London, 1693), p. 24.

[14] John Dennis, *Critical Works*, ed. E. N. Hooker (Baltimore, 1939), II:243.

[15] Charles Gildon, *Complete Art of Poetry* (London, 1718), I:263.

[17] When citations are complete in the text except for bibliographical details, the play is one of the special set from which the ethos of the comedies is derived, and information about the editions is given in the appendix. Because scene divisions vary from

play refuses to see the difference between a "stage-sermon" and "a pulpit-play": "Their muse and spirit differ but in name" (*Sir Solomon*). Mrs. Behn makes use of the same equivalence in the prologue of *The City Heiress*, where she decries the moral laxity of an audience who "care as little what the poets teach / As [they] regard at church what parsons preach." In his comedy *Greenwich Park* (1691) Mountfort, the player, has a character observe cynically that at church you "learn wickedness" and at the playhouse "how to dissemble it." But Mountfort refuses to leave it there; his hero is made to reply, "Ay, but you may learn good at both, if you'll make a right construction" (III). Farquhar equates the school and the stage as media of instruction, giving the stage the advantage. In *The Constant Couple* his leading lady castigates a Puritan in these terms: "Would you be thought a reformer of the times," says she, "be less severe in your censures, less rigid in your precepts, and more strict in your example." "Right," says her partner, "virtue flows freer from imitation than from compulsion." As proof, he cites his own recent reformation by the delightful woman who plays opposite him.

> In vain are musty morals taught in schools,
> By rigid teachers and as rigid rules,
> Where virtue with a frowning aspect stands,
> And frights the pupil from its rough commands.
> But woman—
> Charming woman, can true converts make;
> We love the precepts for the teacher's sake.
> Virtue in them appears so bright, so gay,
> We hear with transport and with pride obey.
>
> (V)

The school is not the pulpit, but it has the same disadvantage. Farquhar reinforced this argument in his *Discourse Concerning Comedy*, written about the same time. He defines comedy in that essay as "nothing more . . . than a well-framed tale handsomely told, as an agreeable vehicle for counsel or reproof," comparable to "Aesop's symbolical way of moralizing."

---

edition to edition and are therefore unreliable, I locate references to plays by act only. In all quotations from plays, I have modernized spelling, punctuation, and capitalization.

The wisdom of the ancients [he continues] was wrapt up in veils and figures; the Egyptian hieroglyphics and the history of the heathen gods are nothing else; but if these pagan authorities give offence to [the] scrupulous consciences [of Puritans], let them but consult the tales and parables of our Saviour in Holy Writ and they may find this way of instruction to be much more Christian than they imagine: Nathan's fable of the poor man's lamb had more influence on the conscience of David, than any force of downright admonition. So that by ancient practise and modern example, by the authority of pagans, Jews and Christians, the world is furnished with this so sure, so pleasant, and expedient an art of schooling mankind into better manners.[18]

Because Puritans objected to the deviousness and indirectness of the literary way of teaching, Farquhar's equation of comedy and Scripture is a particularly telling blow for his side.

Engaged as they were from the start in defense of the stage against Puritan objections to it as a vehicle of instruction and fortified by neoclassical critical assumptions, Restoration playwrights did not have to learn their moral duty from Collier. Before the date of the *Short View*, Davenant, Cowley, Sir Robert Howard, Wilson, Shadwell, Wycherley, Mrs. Behn, Thomas Betterton, John Crowne, and Congreve, to name a few of the most important, had affirmed the instructive view of the function of comedy.[19] Vanbrugh, writing a year before the publication

[18] George Farquhar, *Complete Works*, ed. Charles Stonehill (Bloomsbury, 1930), II:336–37.

[19] Davenant, in verses of gratitude for the re-establishment of the theatres, gives the king credit for the reformation of morals on the stage (Leslie Hotson, *The Commonwealth and Restoration Stage*, Cambridge, Mass., 1928, p. 219). His comedy, *The Man's the Master*, begins with a prologue in which he informs the audience that he is "fain to moralize / That he might serve your mind as well as eyes." And in the dedication to the *Siege of Rhodes* (1663) he defends the stage as a source of morality. Cowley tells us in the preface of *Cutter of Coleman Street* (1661) that it is the perpetual privilege of comedy "to pluck . . . vices and follies . . . out of the sanctuary of any title." The Jonsonian predilections of Sir Robert Howard, author of the most popular Restoration comedy, *The Committee*, are well known, for it was he who as Crites in the *Essay of Dramatic Poesy* (1668) maintained the cause of Jonson and the ancients against Dryden as Eugenius. In the first edition of his plays in 1665 Howard declares the preference for Jonson in his own name. Another early Jonsonian, John Wilson, declared unequivocally in the epilogue to *The Projectors* (*Works*, Edinburgh, 1874) his conviction that "plays are but morals." Concerning the presuppositions of Shadwell, who "conforming to the rules of master Ben . . . to correct and to inform did write"

of the *Short View*, sums up the playwrights' repeatedly declared position with blazing clarity in the prologue of *The Provoked Wife*:

'Tis the intent and business of the stage
To copy out the follies of the age,
To hold to every man a faithful glass
And shew him of what species he's an ass.

Since the many reiterations of this position that occurred after Collier's attack have to be disallowed as possibly self-interested attempts to keep a good thing going, we may omit specific mention of them. But Dryden's often-quoted doubt about whether "instruction could be any part of [comedy's] employment" must be taken up because it does run counter to my thesis. Dryden's doubt must itself be disallowed because (1) in the context of the whole passage in which it occurs much of its force is withdrawn, (2) it is probably conditioned somewhat by his op-

---

(*Squire of Alsatia*, prol.), there can be little uncertainty. As far as he was concerned, "instruction is an honest poet's aim" (*Lancashire Witches*, prol.).

Wycherley declares his principles in the dedication of his *Plain Dealer* to a notorious bawd, declaring to her that "the vices of the age are our best business" and indicates his determination to cure them in his play. Dryden called this comedy "one of the most bold, most general, and useful satires which has ever been presented on the English Theatre" ("Author's apology prefixed to *The State of Innocence*"). Dennis thought it "a most instructive and a most noble satire" (*Critical Works*, I:157). Congreve admired Wycherley because he "dared to lash this crying age" (*Love for Love*, prol.). And Farquhar echoed this sentiment in the prologue of his *Beaux' Stratagem*.

In the epilogue to *The False Count* (1682) Mrs. Behn says that making people laugh is by itself an insufficient justification for comedy. Her prologue to *The City Heiress* identifies the "vices" and "follies" of the age as her subject matter, and in the dedication of *The Lucky Chance* she maintains that the stage is a veritable instrument of government. The preface to *The Amorous Widow* (1668), attributed to the celebrated actor Thomas Betterton, states that the aim of a comedy is to "amend the faults of the public." John Crowne, author of the extremely popular *Sir Courtly Nice* (1685), believed that plays should "profit" and "delight the mind," according to the epilogue of that play.

From the beginning Congreve is conscientiously moral in purpose. Southerne welcomes him on the publication of *The Old Bachelor* (1692, front matter) as the new champion of virtue, to succeed Dryden, Etherege, Wycherley, Lee, and Otway in this capacity. On the appearance of *The Double Dealer* (1693) Dryden hailed Congreve as the repository of Jonson's judgment, Fletcher's wit, Southerne's purity, Etherege's courtship, and "the satire, wit and strength of Manly Wycherley." In the dedication Congreve puts his play forward as "a true and regular comedy." One aspect of its regularity is certainly its adherence to the principle that "it is the business of a comic poet to paint the vices and follies of human kind." *Love for Love*, its prologue declares, intends in conscious imitation of *The Plain Dealer* to "lash this crying age" with satire.

position to the advocates of a more Jonsonian, heavy-handed, explicit, and obvious kind of instruction, and (3) Dryden's position is perfectly conventional in other places. Immediately after voicing his doubt, Dryden hedges: "At least [instruction] can be but its secondary end." Next comes an acrobatic passage in which he tells us how plays may instruct without instructing.

> The business of the poet is to make you laugh: when he writes humor, he makes folly ridiculous; when wit, he moves you, if not always to laughter, yet to a pleasure that is more noble. And if he works a cure on folly and the small imperfections in mankind by exposing them to public view, that cure is not performed by an immediate operation. For it works first on the ill-nature of the audience; they are moved to laugh by the representation of deformity; and the shame of that laughter teaches us to amend what is ridiculous in our manners.[20]

This language is very close to that in which Dryden's contemporaries explain how imitation produces instruction in comedy. In sum, Dryden is merely insisting, in line with his argument against Jonsonians like Shadwell, that the comic medicine must be administered indirectly. The instruction must be implicit in the dramatic action, not explicit in the lines, as it is in the labored sermons which Shadwell makes his characters preach. Dryden, we remember, preferred the fine satiric stroke "that separates the head from the body and leaves it standing in its place" to "the slovenly butchering of a man."[21]

Elsewhere Dryden's position is plainly orthodox. "Comedy is both excellently instructive and extremely pleasant," he says in the "Author's Apology" to *The State of Innocence. Marriage à la Mode* ends with an epilogue in which the husband of the play, now reconciled to his lot, states the moral to the audience:

> Thus have my spouse and I informed the nation,
> And led you all the way to reformation;
> Not with dull morals, gravely writ, like those
> Which men of easy phlegm with care compose—

[20] John Dryden, *Essays*, ed. W. P. Ker (Oxford, 1926), I: 143.
[21] *Ibid.*, II: 93.

Your poets of stiff words and limber sense,
Born on the confines of indifference—
But by examples drawn, I dare to say,
From most of you who hear and see the play.

In the dedication to *The Kind Keeper* (1678) Dryden claims that the play was written to expose to ridicule "our crying sin of keeping," and that performance of it was forbidden because it was too effective a satire. Langbaine, who is no lover of Dryden, agrees with his explanation of the episode.[22] Although the comedy has been called "one of the truly immoral works of the period,"[23] good satire is accustomed to such charges—they prove nothing. In his eulogy of Dryden, Wycherley, whose integrity, if not his versification, made him a legend in his own time, neither expressed nor implied any doubts about Dryden's intentions in his plays:

When the vulgar vice employs your pen,
How we despise ourselves in other men!
At once we grow more merry, yet more wise,
Pleased and instructed with your comedies.[24]

Another reason for our failure to consider the possibility of moral content in Restoration comedy has been uncertainty about how to deal with the satirical aspect of comic expression, particularly as it was understood during the period in question. It is no longer customary to think of Swift's and Pope's work as both satirical and immoral at the same time, as if no contradiction in terms were involved. But we have not yet come to the point of granting the Restoration comic poets the same ground of unstated but assumed and deducible positive values used as a base for the satiric attack. In fact, the word *satire*, as it is used in modern criticism of Restoration comedy, commonly has no moral content at all. Thus a recent book devoted to Wycherley as a satirist starts out on the assumption that morality is an "extraliterary concern,"[25] and the dean of theatre historians repeatedly uses the terms

[22] Gerard Langbaine, *An Account of the English Dramatic Poets* (Oxford, 1691), p. 164.
[23] Allardyce Nicoll, *A History of Restoration Drama* (Cambridge, 1928), p. 218.
[24] William Wycherley, *Complete Works*, ed. Montague Summers (Soho, 1924), IV: 64.
[25] Zimbardo, p. 1.

satirical and *immoral* as if both can hold true of the same literary work at the same time.[26] But according to its seventeenth-century definition, satire is moral. The view of the French authority Rapin, "made English" by Rymer, was that "the principal end of satire is to instruct the people by discrediting vice."[27] Dryden pronounced "the true end of satire [to be] the amendment of vices by correction."[28] We note immediately that the word *comedy* might easily be substituted for the word *satire* without violating Restoration usage of either term. In fact, even when making the effort to distinguish the genres, Dryden found little difference between them. In his *Discourse of Satire* (1793) he uses Heinsius's definition: "Satire is a kind of poetry, without a series of action, invented for the purging of our minds, in which human vices, ignorance, and errors, and all things besides which are produced from them . . . are severely reprehended; partly dramatically, partly simply and sometimes in both kinds." Commenting on the adequacy of this definition, Dryden remarked, "The clause in the beginning of it, *without a series of action*, distinguishes satire properly from stage-plays."[29] In another place he said, "Admiration would be the delight of [tragedy] and satire of [comedy]."[30] The fact that Dryden made so small a distinction between comedy and satire helps us explain why the two terms are used almost interchangeably during the period. Cowley speaks of the "perpetual privilege of satire and comedy to pluck [out] vices" (preface, *Cutter of Coleman Street*); the prologue of Shadwell's *Lancashire Witches* assumes that the corrective element of comedy is satire; Mrs. Behn believes satire to be the justification of comedy (epilogue, *False Count*); Congreve speaks of "the satire of this comedy" (dedication, *Double Dealer*); and near the turn of the century Colley Cibber is talking about "satire's rod in the dramatic school" in the prologue of a comedy (*Careless Husband*). Crowne (To The Reader, *City Politiques*), Wycherley (preface, *Plain Dealer*), Congreve (prologues, *Love for Love, Old Bachelor, Double Dealer, Way of the*

---

[26] See, for example, Nicoll's treatment of Dryden's *Kind Keeper* in *A History of Restoration Drama*, p. 218.

[27] Rapin, p. 143.

[28] Quoted in *Critical Opinions of John Dryden*, ed. John M. Aden (Nashville, Tenn., 963), p. 223.

[29] *Ibid.*, p. 222.

[30] Dryden, "Defense of an Essay of Dramatic Poesy," *Essays*, I:120.

World), Farquhar (prologue, *Beaux' Stratagem*), Steele (preface, *Funeral*), and Bullock (*A Woman Is a Riddle*, I) use the word *satire* in reference to their comedies.[31] The evidence is sufficient to justify an interpretation of Restoration comedy as satire, implying an ethical aim and a method for achieving it.

What is the satiric method of Restoration comedy? As countless prologues, epilogues, dedications, and prefaces testify, the method is to mirror society in such a way as to criticize it, that is, to present on the stage examples of recognizable human behavior,[32] some to be shunned and some to be copied. Which is which? Professor L. C. Knights in a famous *Scrutiny* essay complains of the difficulty of distinguishing "betwixt the character of a Witwoud and a Lovewit."[33] The distinguishing device at any rate is quite uncomplicated, though the distinction itself may still not be easily apparent to modern readers. The method by which the poets tag their characters for emulation or aversion is simply poetical justice.[34] The preface of *The Cheats* (1662) points out that a

[31] Professor J. H. Wilson demonstrates that Wycherley's *Plain Dealer* is moralistic satire (*A Preface to Restoration Drama*, Boston, 1965, pp. 160–66). Paul and Miriam Mueschke have shown that *The Way of the World* is satire (*A New View of Congreve's Way of the World*, Ann Arbor, Mich., 1958). Charles O. McDonald believes, as I do, that Restoration comedy in general is satirical, but I part company with him when he maintains that *all* characters in the plays are objects of satire ("Restoration Comedy as Drama of Satire: An Investigation into 17th Century Aesthetics," *Studies in Philology*, LXI (1964):522–44).

[32] Characters in the play are equated to members of contemporary society, usually in the audience itself, in the epilogues of *Rover, Marriage à la Mode, Sir Patient Fancy*, and *Wife's Relief*, and in the prologues of *Sir Martin Mar-all, Tender Husband, Provoked Wife*, and *Relapse*. In *A Plot and No Plot* a character identifies coxcombs involved in the plot with "coxcombs who are now in my eye," in the audience (II). The epilogue of *Chances* testifies to the prevalence of accusing epilogues by objecting to the practice. The idea that the stage is a mirror of the audience occurs in the prologues of *Man of Mode, Provoked Wife, The Lady's Last Stake*, and in the epilogue of *Wife's Relief*. W. R. Chetwood (*General History of the Stage*, London, 1749, p. 26) records the motto of the Drury Lane Theatre: "*Veluti in speculum*"—behold as in a glass. It was displayed over the stage.

[33] The essay, "Restoration Comedy: The Reality and the Myths," is reprinted in L. C. Knights, *Explorations* (London, 1946), p. 143.

[34] Several scholars have already noted the presence of an instructive mechanism. In "Libertine and Précieuse Elements in Restoration Comedy" (*Essays in Criticism*, IX (1959):240–41), C. D. Cecil says, "The plays are in one sense extended definitions of good behavior couched largely in terms of bad, as all satirical and hortative works apparently must be." Norman Holland (*First Modern Comedies*, p. 114) sees that "the plays tend to set off plots or characters which succeed or are ethically or socially correct (the right way) against plots or characters which fail or win only a limited success or are ethically or socially incorrect (the wrong way)."

comedy must paint "the true picture of virtue or vice, yet so drawn as to show a man how to follow the one and avoid the other." The easy way to do this is simply to adhere to the rule of an "opposite catastrophe for good and bad" that Aristotle recommends for comedy.[35] Gildon delivers the concept in great detail: "comedy instructs by laughing at and rendering vice and folly ridiculous and recommending virtue by the success it always does or ought to give it."[36] When Wycherley in the prologue of *The Plain Dealer* asks, "Where else but on stages do we see / Truth pleasing or rewarded honesty?" he is not only lashing his "crying age" but enunciating the method of his satiricomic medium.

Collier himself abstracted the moral content of Restoration comedy, in order to attack it, by assuming the operation of poetic justice. By entitling his fourth chapter "The Stage-Poets Make their Principal Persons Vicious and Reward them at the End of the Play," he shows both his understanding of the principle and his disagreement with the values it puts forward. He takes it for granted that the values of the "principal persons" or "fine gentlemen" are those advocated by the playwrights, but from his ideological position these virtues are vices. Therefore a young man whom the poets would consider high-mettled, natural, adventurous, plain-dealing, unsanctimonious, and skeptical is to Collier a "whoring, swearing, smutty, atheistical" person.

When Collier objects to the "Cavalier" in the comedies for whom "the pedantry of virtue" is "unbecoming," he accurately identifies the ideological origin of Restoration comedy's ethos and exactly states the comic poets' position on prudish hypocrisy, except that they would call it "vicious" instead of "unbecoming." When he complains that "learning, industry and frugality" are ridiculed in comedy, he is right again, except that the dramatists would use pejorative terms like *pedantry* and *stinginess* to describe two of their favorite objects of ridicule. When he objects that "rich citizens" are often presented as "misers," he again penetrates to the heart of the matter, except that the poets are making the opposite predication, that misers are too often "rich citizens." Finally, when he concludes that "the marks of honor and infamy are misapplied" by the playwrights, he means only that he thinks that "rich citizens," as he knows them, are better objects for emulation

[35] I quote from the Butcher translation of Aristotle's *Poetics*, XIII:7–8.
[36] Gildon, *Complete Art of Poetry*, I:263.

than "fine gentlemen."[37] The comic poets simply prefer the character of their fine gentlemen as they present it on the stage. But there is no disagreement over the principle that dramatists reward characters having values they approve of and punish characters having those they disapprove of. If we act on this principle, abstracting the ethos of Restoration comedy is only a matter of stating the characteristics of rewarded and punished characters.

Still, even if we know that reward and punishment are the tags, and even if we can overcome the cultural conditioning that causes us, like Collier, to read virtues as vices, it may not be easy to identify which characteristics of the great many attributed to a character qualify him for praise or blame. Popular literature like Restoration comedy, where audiences attach conventional virtues to heroes just because they are heroes, not because of what they do, presents special difficulties. If he is the hero, he must be witty, whether he demonstrates it or not, because heroes are always witty. In popular literature morality is one of the conventions *within* which (not necessarily *with* which) the artist works.

Two aspects of the method used in this study are designed to bring out the conventional properties of these comedies. First, I have sifted a large number of plays, and second, I have sifted them systematically. Using a mass of plays enables one to determine, by frequency of occurrence in all, what features are really important for each.[38] (How can critics generalize about Restoration comedy on the basis of a study of one, three, or five authors, as they so confidently do, time and again?) By sifting the evidence systematically, one reduces the subjective element of interpretation, which, granting that it cannot be removed, does seem to get in the way of a clear view of Restoration comedy.

This study is based on a survey of 1,127 characters in 83 plays (see appendix). Included are all the comedies most popular in their own

[37] Jeremy Collier, *A Short View of the Immorality and Profaneness of the English Stage* (London, 1698), pp. 140, 143-45. Professor Jean Gagen, in an article called "Congreve's Mirabell and the Ideal of the Gentleman" (*PMLA*, LXXIX (1964):422-27), has broken through Collier's "Puritan curtain" by observing how closely Congreve's hero follows recommended behavior in contemporary courtesy books. Our findings agree in several points.

[38] For this reason, perhaps, J. H. Smith's *Gay Couple in Restoration Comedy* (Cambridge, Mass., 1948) is one of the best appreciations available of the typical hero and heroine. It is based on some 200 Restoration comedies.

time (that is, those most frequently performed between 1660 and 1730); all the comedies of Etherege, Wycherley, Congreve, Vanbrugh, and Farquhar (I have excluded farces); 7 plays by Dryden, 7 by Cibber, 5 by Mrs. Behn, 4 by Shadwell, 3 by Crowne, 3 by Steele, and 3 by Mrs. Centlivre. Of the 83 plays, 53 were written before Collier's *Short View* in 1698 and 9 after Farquhar's death in 1707, the year of *The Beaux' Stratagem*. It is so difficult to determine a date for the dissolution of what we call Restoration comedy—Crowne was writing what some would call "sentimental" comedy in 1676, and Christopher Bullock and Mrs. Centlivre were writing good old-fashioned "bawdy, cynical comedies" in the second decade of the eighteenth century—that I have decided to include the point of decline rather than to find it and so have cut off at *The Conscious Lovers*, an undeniable watershed. Of the 83 plays, 44 can be considered popular in the light of the available evidence. The lesser comedies of major writers, comedies by actors, and comedies interesting because of frequent mention in books about the period constitute nearly half of the sample. The list of plays, giving the editions used, will be found in the appendix.

The method used to find the ethical common denominators in the plays was to count the frequency of occurrence of a fixed set of characteristics in the 1,127 characters. The fixed set was arrived at by guesses and expectations based on previous reading in Restoration comedy. There were, of course, certain circumstantial attributes, having no apparent moral significance, that might make a difference, like the sex of a character, his age, his marital status, his importance in the play, his social class, his profession. Then there were moral characteristics that seemed likely to be important, such as whether the character was liberal or mercenary, brave or cowardly, chaste or unchaste. There were also certain types to pin down, such as the stingy parent, the fop, the prude. Of paramount importance was the playwright's approval or disapproval of a character. The list of characteristics, which finally contained 113 different items, was mimeographed and used as a form to be filled out for each of the 1,127 characters.

The fact that all categories under consideration were chosen in advance does not mean that the cards were stacked in favor of my thesis before I began gathering data. In every case the absence or opposite of a characteristic was always a possible finding. On the contrary, choosing categories in advance made it impossible to change the rules of the game after it had started, thus calling in question the final outcome. Since only categories for which the plays could provide clear and distinct evidence were used, this method subjected my thesis to an objective test, in which a negative result was always as possible as a positive one. In accord with some definitions of scientific method, an intuitive thesis about a phenomenon was tested by an experiment capable of giving a *yes* or *no* answer as to its validity.

The information on each character was punched on an IBM card, so that a computer could do the counting. Using mechanical methods eliminated the necessity of deciding what to count; it was possible to count everything, a great advantage because it was impossible to know in advance what would be important. At first I thought that I would need to know the frequency of every correlation of any two characteristics. Eventually I found that I needed every correlation of any three characteristics. It was not enough to know how many characters with X also had Y. I more often wanted to know how many characters with both X and Y had Z; for example, not only how many *tradesmen* were *mercenary* but how many *young* tradesmen were mercenary. This meant counting the cards in about a million different assortments, but the computer did this easily and printed out the results in a tabular form that enabled me to find any particular count in less than a minute (for instance, how many female lawyers lived in the country). There were other advantages to computer use. Because the data were punched on cards, the computer could make an index of all characteristics, enabling me to find the name of every character having a given characteristic. Since my notes were filed by character, the computer also provided an index of my notes while indexing the characteristics.

Since the computer makes no mistakes, the reliability of the results obtained by it depends on the soundness of the data-processing system and the accuracy of the data. If there are flaws in the system, they should be evident in the logic of this chapter. But there is no practical way to present all the evidence and reasoning that went into the attribution of each characteristic to each of the 1,127 characters in the 83 plays. The attribution of a protagonistic or an antagonistic function to a character was perhaps the most crucial decision. No attribution in this category could be made at all for 21 percent of the characters. Except for sex, no category ever contained all characters because very often the information was simply not given. For this reason the sum of attributions for a given set of characters never adds up to the total number of characters in that set. To say, "Out of 1,127 characters 463 are protagonistic and 418 are antagonistic," makes sense only when one understands that 246 cannot be categorized at all. Another way of putting these figures might be, "Of 881 characters whose status is indicated, 463 are protagonistic and 418 are antagonistic," but this deprives us of important information—the density of attribution in the 1,127 as a whole. I have, however, used either statement, depending on which has greater significance.

Any character whose enterprises succeeded at the end of the play, whose behavior was praised by a reliable character, whose efforts were rewarded, or who (like Sir Wilful Witwoud of *The Way of the World*) participated in the victory of the protagonists in some way or other (Sir Wilful is allowed to drive the villain off the stage in the last act) were categorized as protagonistic. When opposite conditions held, a character fell into the antagonistic group. The fact that there are always two fairly clear-cut sides in a comic conflict and that nearly every character is committed to one or the other helps the categorizing process considerably. I trust that as the moral characteristics of the *dramatis personae* in these comedies are described and documented in this study my reasons for attributing characteristics will become clear. I have naturally made some mistakes, but I hope they are few. My test in case of doubt has been the question, Am I able to document this attribution in a manner that meets the standards of literary scholarship?

Some readers may feel that statistical evidence is not convincing. For this reason I hope I have supplied enough documentary support to make a convincing argument in the conventional way. But certainly there is no better way to show the prevalence of a thing than to count the frequency of its occurrence, however strong the prejudice may be against "counting things." And certainly, generalizations about literature are not less true because the instances upon which they are based are shown to be numerous. But even if the statistics were discarded entirely, my experience in getting them suggests that computer methods, because they require a systematic approach whose logic is thoroughly worked out in advance and which enables and encourages an exhaustive search of every possible locus of information, are a good way of becoming acquainted with a subject.

In some parts of England, if a photograph is taken from an airplane of a field of grass at a certain altitude at a certain time of year in a certain light, the plan of a Roman city, invisible to a person standing on the ground, will show up on the photographic plate. Using the moral angle of vision that I have defined, surveying a piece of comic territory of the size I have described, I have had the sense of seeing the ethical pattern of the plays spread out beneath me like the plan of one of those Roman cities. Other archaeologists must now judge whether that plan, as laid out in the chapters that follow, is a trick of fancy or an authentic image.

CHAPTER TWO

Generosity

At the point of resolution in Congreve's *Love for Love*, when Valentine renounces his patrimony to please Angelica, causing the icy facade she has presented to him from the first to melt suddenly, she exclaims, "Generous Valentine!" Here Congreve, in 1695, in the final moments of his most successful play, gives prominence to a term that epitomizes the ethical substratum of Restoration comedy in general. Although it is probably the same word that we would use today to characterize Valentine's act of self-denial, we would probably mean less by it than Congreve and his contemporaries did. It is doubtful that we would use the word now to suggest a quality of poetry, as Pope did in the familiar lines from the *Essay on Criticism*: "The winged courser, like a *generous* horse, / Shows most true mettle when you check his course." In what way are horses or, by implication, poems, "generous"? Nor would it probably occur to us to use it in more prosaic places, such as this passage from an eighteenth-century stage history describing the trials of a beautiful actress: "A nobleman, some few years before her death, offered her a very large settlement to live with him, which she *generously* rejected."[1] In both cases something more than simple *liberality* is intended.

In fact, some of the more precise meanings of the word in seventeenth- and eighteenth-century usage are, according to the *NED*, now obsolete or rare. Most of the word's content had already evolved in the Latin, where its root *genus*, meaning *origin* or *descent* or *race*, had also

---

[1] Thomas Davies, *Dramatic Miscellanies* (London, 1784), I:187.

the sense of *high* or *noble birth*. The adjective *generosus*, meaning "full of *genus*," had even stronger ethical connotations: *noble-minded, magnanimous*. In English as in Latin, *generous* once denoted *high-born*. According to the *NED* it describes actions "appropriate or natural to one of noble birth or spirit; hence, gallant, courageous; magnanimous, free from meanness or prejudice" and persons who are "high-spirited, gallant, courageous; magnanimous, nobleminded."

In Restoration comedy *generosity* is the word used to convey the attributes of character that make up the finished gentleman who occupies the position of chief protagonist. Its opposite, *meanness*, comprehends the cluster of ugly deeds and attitudes consistently attributed to his adversaries in the plot. A glance at the most obvious sources of moral thought in Renaissance Europe shows that the seventeenth-century concept of generosity evolves from ancient and most respected authorities on conduct. It has origins in Plato's *Republic*, Aristotle's *Ethics*, Cicero's *De Officiis*, the New Testament, and Castiglione's *Courtier*, as one would expect it to have.

From Plato come the four virtues: Wisdom, Courage, Temperance, and Justice. These are also the main branches of Cicero's moral philosophy. Aristotle's list is considerably longer, emphasizing Courage, Temperance, Liberality, Greatness of Soul, Truthfulness, and Justice. The ethical emphases in Restoration comedy, as I derive them, are also fourfold: Liberality, Courage, Plain-dealing, and Love. Only Courage is common to all these sets, perhaps for the reason that it of all the classical virtues is the one most basic to the complicated set of values I have called *generosity*.

For the ancients the courageous man was simply one who feared certain moral violations more than he feared death: "The great-souled man [says Aristotle] does not run into danger for trifling reasons, and is not a lover of danger, because there are few things he values; but he will face danger in a great cause, and when so doing will be ready to sacrifice his life, since he holds that life is not worth having at every price" (*Ethics*, IV, iii, 23).[2]

The price that one will not pay for life is honor, the highest good (IV, vii, 10–11). The fine gentlemen of Restoration comedy are al-

[2] I am quoting the translation by H. Rackham of Aristotle's *Nichomachean Ethics*, Loeb ed. (Cambridge and London, 1934).

ways understood to be and frequently are labeled "men of honor." Though in Aristotle Greatness of Soul appears as a subheading, it can be seen to foster important virtues. For instance, it provides the foundation for Liberality by freeing its possessor of attachment to worldly possessions (IV, iii, 18). A great soul "is fond of conferring benefits" (IV, iii, 24). In spending he exhibits Magnificence, "the art of expenditure." "He will spend gladly and lavishly, since nice calculation is shabby" (IV, ii, 5, 8). Greatness of Soul leads also to Truthfulness, because its possessor "must be open both in love and in hate, since concealment shows timidity; and care more for the truth than for what people will think; and speak and act openly, since as he despises other men he is outspoken and frank" (IV, iii, 28). Here, perhaps, we may see the beginnings of Restoration comedy's plain-dealer. In another place Aristotle also applauds a person who presents himself as less, not more, than he is, and whose conversation is livened by wit, also marks of the plain-dealer in Restoration comedy (IV, vii, 10–16; IV, viii, 1).

But though he may be modest, the comic hero is not humble. *Impudent* is the word that often describes him. Wycherley's definition of this term as a kind of making sure one gets what's coming to him[3] partakes somewhat of the Great Soul's attitude. Because he deserves more than ordinary men, he claims more (IV, iii, 1–16). The comic hero's wildness[4] may also relate to Aristotle's Spirit, by which he means much the same as we should mean when we speak of spirit in a horse (III, viii, 10–11).

Next to the Bible perhaps no other guide to conduct had such an influence on Western manners during and since the Renaissance as "Tully's *Offices*" had, though it is little regarded now when courtesy books are consulted, even though many of these are little more than Cicero warmed over. *De Officiis* was, in 1465, the first classical book ever to be issued from a printing press. Erasmus and Melanchthon published it with annotations in 1533.[5] There were at least nine English editions of four different translations of it between 1534 and 1684.[6]

[3] See pp. 86–87.
[4] See pp. 167–69.
[5] Cicero, *De Officiis*, tr. Walter Miller, Loeb ed. (Cambridge and London, 1947), pp. xiii, xiv.
[6] The Newberry Library has nine such editions. See Virgil B. Heltzel, *A Checklist of Courtesy Books in the Newberry Library* (Chicago, 1942).

Roger L'Estrange, who translated it in 1680, introduced it as "the commonest school book that we have, and as it is the best of books, so it is applied to the best of purposes, that is to say, to the training up of youth in the study and exercise of virtue."[7] Cicero admires above all the glorious achievements won by the "great, exalted, spirit" who has supreme contempt for the "vicissitudes of earthly life." For a Roman, military achievement is the highest kind, and of the soldier's virtues, Courage comes first (I, 61).[8] Regarding Liberality, a prominent virtue in Restoration comedy, Cicero notes that "no vice [is] more offensive than avarice" (II, 77). Material goods are the gift of nature to all men; ownership is meaningless. It is only as trustees for humanity that we control property. "Friends [have] all things in common" (I, 51).

For Cicero, there is no bond more "powerful" or "noble" than Friendship, also a great power in Restoration comedy, except where love intervenes. But Cicero gives love no place among the virtues. For a Stoic, fondness for women is a weakness; sex is a destructive appetite which must be rigorously controlled. That Odysseus is "even" courteous to women strikes Cicero as curious (I, 113). In the classical tradition Venus is the downfall of Mars, Paris is a bad soldier, and Aeneas almost swerves from his duty because of Dido.

Under Temperance, Cicero takes up much that suggests what I call Plain-dealing in Restoration comedy. It is here that he discusses the concept of *decorum*, the art of being natural. His first premise is that "if we follow nature . . . we shall never go astray" (I, 100). By following nature, we might suppose that we would all become wild animals. Not so, for *decorum* is defined as "that which harmonizes with man's superiority in those respects in which his nature *differs* from that of the rest of the animal creation" (my italics, I, 96). Thus, that *decorum* which makes our behavior *natural* derives from a deliberately imposed, hence *artificial*, discipline of disorderly appetite to prevent subhuman and ugly behavior from disturbing the "natural" harmony of self and society. Perhaps the true cause of that contradictory behavior in Restoration comic heroes, so painstakingly explained by our modern critics as the natural man at war with social fakery while he is himself a

7 Tully's *Offices* . . . turned . . . into English by Ro. L'Estrange, 2nd ed. (London, 1681).
8 I am using the Miller translation (see n. 5 above).

fake, is that these heroes are following nature according to the "commonest school book" of their day, nature in the sense of a harmony of components. It was not natural by Cicero's definition for man, the rational creature, to let his bestiality loose. Still, *De Officiis* warned against extremes of artifice and effeminacy as well as those of coarseness (I, 129): manners ought to be "simple" and "unaffected"; we must not be too neat or too slovenly; in dress "the best rule is the golden mean" (I, 130). By such Plain-dealing one may tell the wits from the "wit-wouds" and the fine gentlemen from the fops in Restoration comedy.

If the classical idea of self-control that descends from Plato militates against devotion to women, it does at the same time provide a foundation for the elevated passion that developed in Christian cultures, known as courtly love. For this kind of love required the same sort of selfless commitment that Friendship did for Cicero, the same sort of self-denial that Temperance and *decorum* did. The classical heritage joins with the Christian heritage in the Renaissance concept of Love. We can see this amalgamation taking place in Castiglione's *Courtier*, published in 1528, translated into English in 1561, and considered by Dr. Johnson "the best book ever written on good breeding."[9] Despite its reputation as a handbook of court etiquette and platonic love, Castiglione builds on a sterner foundation, always assumed but not blazoned forth on every occasion. As with the ancients, "the principle and true profession of a Courtier ought to be in feats of arms. . . . And even as in women honesty once stained doth never return again to the former estate: so the fame of a gentleman that carrieth weapon, if it once take a foyle [soil?] in any little point through dastardliness or any other reproach, doth evermore continue shameful in the world and full of ignorance."[10] Courage is the *sine qua non*, and that is that. Liberality is similarly assumed, always occurring in the several lists of virtues that one comes upon in *The Courtier*, along with the usual Wisdom, Courage, Justice, and Temperance.

When we come to consider the special quality of the Restoration comic hero that I have called Plain-dealing, Castiglione's concept of *sprezzatura* is most helpful. *Sprezzatura* is the art of making "whatever is done or said appear to be without effort and almost without any thought about it."[11] In the sixteenth century Thomas Hoby translated the word as *recklessness* and its antonyms as *curiosity* and *preciseness*. All three of these words occur frequently in Restoration comedy, the first as a word of approval and the latter two of disapproval. *Sprezzatura* also embodies the nature-art paradox that we noted in discussing *decorum*. As its definition implies, it is the art of concealing art. But its opposites are *affetazione*, which Hoby translates as *curiosity*, and *attilatura*, meaning overfastidiousness in dress, which Hoby translates as *preciseness*. By *curiosity* he probably meant "undue niceness or fastidiousness as to food, clothing, matters of taste and behavior," and by *preciseness*, "strictness in behavior, manners, morals, or religious observance; a rigid propriety, primness, fastidiousness, scrupulousness, puritanical quality" (*NED*, using this Hoby passage as evidence). It is more interesting for our purposes to observe how an Englishman attempted to translate *sprezzatura* than to decide what it really means. If *preciseness* and *curiosity* are forms of forced behavior, then *recklessness* (*sprezzatura*) must mean "easy, effortless, natural behavior." Other antonyms of *curious*, like *Careless* and *Easy*, are common proper names for the heroes of Restoration comedy. *Negligence* is the term often used to describe their behavior, obviously in an ameliorative sense. This *sprezzatura* or *recklessness*, this "verie art that appeareth not to be art,"[12] which is a self-conscious creature's only way of avoiding affectation, may be a source of the Plain-dealer's graceful informality. It was the diametrical opposite of foppery, for which *curiosity* (*affetazione*) and *preciseness* (*attilatura*) are the appropriate terms.

By the time of Castiglione, love has become a proper activity for a gentleman[13] and the form that it should take is the major concern of *The Courtier*. Granted that Castiglione's love is too platonic a variety to suit Restoration comedy, still it is perhaps a source of the distinction that Restoration comedy makes between brute lust or self-gratification

11 This is the translation of Castiglione's *Courtier* by Charles S. Singleton (Garden City, N.Y., 1959), p. 43.
12 Hoby translation, pp. 45–49; names of heroes are discussed on pp. 118–19, 167–68.
13 *Ibid.*, pp. 301–2.

and the noble self-denying passion of which the protagonists are assumed to be capable. Certainly, Restoration comedy would approve Castiglione's wisdom in allowing the courtier to love sensually when he is young.[14] Only it is marriage that ends the comic hero's hedonistic rambles, not the sterile pastimes of platonic love.

The Shakespeare play that best defines what I mean by *generosity* is *The Merchant of Venice*, where Shylock is the perfect antithesis of the qualities I seek to define. Here *generosity* is thoroughly Christianized and given the character it will have in Restoration comedy.

Reading *The Merchant of Venice* as a representation of the beauty of generous risk removes most of the ambiguity about how to understand Shylock. As Northrop Frye has observed, "If the dramatic role of Shylock is ever so slightly exaggerated, as it generally is when the leading actor of the company takes the part . . . the play becomes the tragedy of the Jew of Venice with a comic epilogue."[15] Though such a reading of the play is common enough, it is probably not the play that Shakespeare wrote. But if we properly understand the Christians' reckless generosity, Shylock's excessive caution and shifty-eyed smallness of soul gain clear and distinct proportions. His attempts at self-justification should signify to us no more than do Iago's.[16]

The fact that Shylock is a Jew makes it easy for Shakespeare to have him represent an Old Testament antithesis to the New Testament

---

[14] *Ibid.*, p. 312.

[15] Northrop Frye, *Anatomy of Criticism* (Princeton, N.J., 1957), p. 165.

[16] That he is a Jew is probably a matter of labeling more than of prejudice on Shakespeare's part. Stinginess would be a traditional part of the Jewish stereotype. Shylock's appeals for sympathy are those of a man who will say anything to gain his ends and it is significant that he rarely makes the same plea twice. In Act I he discards his arguments about the parallel between Jacob's management of Laban's sheep and his own usury when he sees it will not go down. And when, during his trial and elsewhere, he claims to have learned his sharp practices from Christians, it is such Christians who are to be ashamed, not Shylock who is to be excused. Avarice is what Shakespeare is attacking, and the vice is not restricted to Jews. Christians who practice it, of course, are Christians only in name. The true exemplars of Christian virtues are Antonio, Bassanio, and Portia, who are Christians in deed as well as in name. It is only the minor characters who meanly rejoice in Shylock's suffering. Generosity characterizes the major ones. "The conflict of values in *The Merchant of Venice* . . . is between the greed and hate of Shylock and the generosities and love of the other characters" (Bernard Grebanier, *The Truth about Shylock*, New York, 1962, p. 215). Barbara Lewalski sees the play as a conflict "between the Old Law and the New" ("Biblical Allusion and Allegory in *The Merchant of Venice*," *Shakespeare Quarterly*, XIII (1962):327–43).

characteristics of the protagonists. He stands for the old pharasaical legalism repudiated in the Sermon on the Mount, and is thus anti-Christian in ideology as well as attitude. With the increasingly commercial emphasis in Shakespeare's time, the same contract mentality must have more and more pervaded human relationships, while chivalric faith and trust waned. This mentality has many echoes in Restoration comedy, countered always by an affirmation of the chivalric reliance on Providence or Fortune. Christ enjoins his followers to "take no thought for the morrow for the morrow shall take thought for the things of itself" (Matt. 6:34), carrying the classical contempt for worldly concerns to its logical conclusion. But Shylock takes thought for the morrow in his hesitation to commit himself, his hoarding of wealth, and his faith in the power of the law. His attempt to achieve control of his world by legal means is as foolish in Christian terms as the pharasaical attempt to control divine grace by a strict literal observance of the Mosaic law. The essential conflict between Antonio and Shylock comes out in their first confrontation, when Shylock attempts to justify usury by saying it is analogous to the way in which Jacob profited with Laban's sheep:

> This was a way to thrive and he was blest;
> And thrift is blessing if men steal it not.
> ANTONIO. This was a venture, sir, that Jacob served for,
> A thing not in his power to bring to pass,
> But swayed and fashioned by the hand of heaven.
>   (I, iii, 85–89)[17]

Shylock's "thrift" is an attempt to control fortune. Antonio rejects entirely the notion that one can thrive by his own efforts alone: the power and the glory belong to God, not man. The outcome of any venture is in the hand of heaven, not our own. Shylock wrongfully and futilely attempts to usurp the prerogative of Providence.

Shakespeare makes it clear that Shylock is not *gentle*[18] (i.e., *gen-*

[17] I am quoting from the Pelican edition of *The Merchant of Venice*, ed. Brents Stirling (Baltimore, 1959).

[18] His servants have poor liveries (II, ii, 101), he abominates masques, merriment, and music (II, v, 27–36). But though Antonio is a merchant, he is a "royal merchant" (III, ii, 239), "a true gentleman" (III, iv, 6). Bassanio's only wealth runs "in [his] veins," he is "a gentleman" (III, ii, 254–55). Shylock becomes a "gentle Jew" (I, iii,

erous). Since his daughter Jessica is at the same time repeatedly characterized as "gentle" and since Antonio is himself not a member of the gentry, it is obvious that Shakespeare means the virtues traditionally associated with a gentleman rather than the class itself.

Although Shylock tries to camouflage his avarice by a smokescreen of alternate reasons for his behavior—pride, vengeance, justice, and so on—he is, as Bassanio suspects and events confirm, a fraud (I, iii, 175) and his every instinct is truly mean. He tells the real reason for insisting on the pound of flesh to his friend Tubal: "Were [Antonio] out of Venice I can make what merchandize I will" (III, i, 112–13). It is also Tubal who hears Shylock declare that he would as soon have his daughter return to him dead, as long as her coffin contained his ducats (III, i, 78–79). Shylock's passion for "barren metal" (I, iii, 130) so inhibits his humanity that he may rightly be called "dog" (II, viii, 14), "inhuman wretch" (IV, i, 4), "cur" (III, iii, 18), and "wolf" (IV, i, 73). His "Jewish heart" is the hardest thing Antonio knows of (IV, i, 78–80).

Fear of loss plagues an avaricious nature as much as lust for gain. To convey this attitude and its antithesis, confidence or trust, Shakespeare fills the play with locks, keys, bonds, and contracts. The Christians are as careless about these things as the Jew is careful. Again, the differences between the two sets of characters are signaled in the first act by contrasting moneylending scenes. Bassanio's mere mention of a need for money is sufficient to command Antonio:

> Be assured
> My purse, my person, my extremest means
> Lie all unlocked to your occasions.
>   (I, i, 137–39)

In Shakespeare as in Cicero, "Friends have all things in common." The next Venetian scene opens with Shylock responding to Bassanio's request to borrow money from him, at interest. Notice Shylock's hesitation:

173) when he offers to lend the 3,000 ducats gratis. And Jessica is always "gentle Jessica" because she rejects her birth. Shylock's gentility was only a ruse, however, and the miracle to everyone is how the "gentle Jessica" could be his "flesh and blood" (III, i, 30–35; II, iv, 33–37; II, iii, 10–19; III, v, 9–10). She herself concludes that she is "a daughter to his blood [but] not to his manners" (II, iii, 18–19).

SHYLOCK. Three thousand ducats—well.

BASSANIO. Aye, sir, for three months.

SHYLOCK. For three months—well.

BASSANIO. For the which, as I told you, Antonio shall be bound.

SHYLOCK. Antonio, shall become bound—well.

BASSANIO. May you stead me? Will you pleasure me? Shall I know your answer?

SHYLOCK. Three thousand ducats for three months, and Antonio bound.

BASSANIO. Your answer to that.

SHYLOCK. Antonio is a good man.

BASSANIO. Have you heard any imputation to the contrary?

SHYLOCK. Ho no, no, no, no! My meaning in saying he is a good man is to have you understand me that he is sufficient. Yet his means are in supposition. . . . The man is, notwithstanding, sufficient. Three thousand ducats—I think I may take his bond.

BASSANIO. Be assured you may.

SHYLOCK. I will be assured I may; and that I may be assured, I will bethink me.

(I, iii, 1–28)

One hundred lines later, he is still bethinking himself. Contrast these lines again with the following series early in Act II:

GRATIANO. Signior Bassanio!

BASSANIO. Gratiano!

GRATIANO. I have a suit to you.

BASSANIO. You have obtained it.

(II, ii, 162–65)

Shylock also bethinks himself at length on whether or not to accept Bassanio's invitation to dine. In Act I he refuses; in Act II, after decisions and revisions consuming twenty-five lines, he goes, apparently because he cannot resist the pleasure (and thrift?) of feeding upon the "prodigal Christian" (II, v, 14–15). As a result of his indecision Shylock usually acts when forced to according to whim. The "merry bond" itself is a suggestion of the moment, and it is by chance that Antonio falls into his trap, not by Shylock's taking thought.

While Antonio's "extremest means lie all unlocked" to his friend, Shylock keeps his means tightly under lock and key. "Lock up my doors" (II, v, 28). "Fast bind, fast find / A proverb never stale in a thrifty mind" (II, v, 52–53). Bonds, physical and legal, are his obsession. In the beginning he dwells on the thought of 3,000 ducats and Antonio bound. In the end, when he has Antonio in legal durance, the word "bond" becomes a fixed idea:

> I'll have my bond! Speak not against my bond!
> I have sworn an oath that I will have my bond. . . .
> I'll have my bond. I will not hear thee speak.
> I'll have my bond and therefore speak no more.
> I'll not be a soft dull-eyed fool,
> To shake the head, relent, and sigh, and yield
> To Christian intercessors. Follow not.
> I'll have no speaking; I will have my bond.
>
> (III, iii, 4–17)

Such attempts to "be assured" are extremely foolish in the world of the play. Portia's gold casket, which contains a death's head, clearly refers to Shylock's avarice. Her silver one, which contains a picture of a fool, also has a message for him. It says, "Who chooseth me shall get as much as he deserves." Like Arragon, in claiming justice Shylock "assume[s] desert," not once doubting his qualifications; that is, as Portia accuses Arragon of doing, he tries to function both as the judge and the judged (II, ix, 49–50, 58–61). Assuming desert, Shylock demands: "Justice! the law! my ducats and my daughter!" (II, viii, 17). While Portia says, "I stand for sacrifice" (III, ii, 57), Shylock insists, "I stand for judgment" (IV, i, 103). "What judgment shall I dread, doing no wrong?" (IV, i, 89). "I stand here for law" (IV, i, 143). Portia pleads with him to be merciful, but he finds it nowhere in the contract: "On what compulsion must I?" In her answer, "The quality of mercy is not strain'd," the key word is "strain'd," meaning *constrained* or *bound*. Mercy cannot be compelled any more than the gentle rain that drops from heaven (IV, i, 181–83). The man who confuses "legal" with "moral" has to learn that "in the course of justice /

None of us should see salvation" (IV, i, 197–98). And so Shylock's justice proves a false mistress, the biter is bit, the man who stands by the law falls by the law: "Thou shalt have justice more than thou desirest" (IV, i, 314). This is the fate of one who assumes desert.

The caskets are symbols of the kinds of choices men have to make. They are caskets because the outcome of any choice is hidden until the choice has been made. Shylock has chosen gold. It is barren metal which can breed only barren metal; his true offspring, Jessica, therefore leaves him (so does Launcelot Gobbo, his "family" in the sense of *household*). So this casket contains death. Frustrated here, Shylock makes a worse choice, the silver casket, standing for justice. "Judge not that ye be not judged" (Matt. 7:1). So this casket contains a fool. "They lose the world that do buy it with too much care," said the true Merchant of Venice in the opening scene of the play. What about the third casket?

The Christians in the play are reckless, prodigal, improvident, adventurous, and casual—to a fault, some producers of the play and some critics would have us believe. But of course the Christians are to blame only in terms of the Calvinistic virtue of thrift, which has come to prominence in recent centuries and now acts as a sort of historical screen between us and the seventeenth century, obscuring not only Shakespeare's outlines but those of Restoration comedy as well. In truth the Christian's "bad" habits are all attributes of a generous nature—one that never bethinks itself.

Whereas most of Shylock's wealth is locked up in his house, *all* of Antonio's is "at sea" (I, i, 177). His future rests entirely in the hand of God, but this does not worry him (I, i, 41–45). Far from taking measures to assure material success, Christians in the play take courses of action almost bound to result in failure. Antonio "lends out money gratis" (I, iii, 40). Bassanio's way of getting out of debt is to plunge deeper into it (I, i, 140–52). When, with typical gambler's optimism, he promises *this* time to repay Antonio all past debts with a big win if Antonio will provide him with one more stake, Antonio considers even this much assurance an insult to his friendship (I, i, 153–57). And he does not bethink himself two seconds about Shylock's "merry bond" because, like Bassanio, he has the Christian faith that the morrow will take thought for the things of itself (I, iii, 152–55).

The Christians spend lavishly, exemplifying the Magnificence taught by the classical moralists and suggesting the reckless spending of Restoration comic heroes. Bassanio is in debt because he has been "something too prodigal," having "disabled [his] estate / By something showing a more swelling port / Than [his] faint means would grant continuance" (I, i, 123–29). From such improvidence proceed the "gifts of rich value" by which he announces his arrival at Belmont (II, ix, 85–90). Portia, "stand[ing] for sacrifice," wishes she were "trebled twenty times herself" when she gives house, servants, and herself to Bassanio (III, ii, 153, 170–71). When she hears that for want of 3,000 ducats Antonio must forfeit a pound of flesh, her generosity is unhesitating: "What, no more? / Double 6,000 and then treble that. . . . You shall have gold / To pay the petty debt twenty times over" (III, ii, 298–307). But when money will not appease Shylock, Antonio makes almost as small a thing of laying down his life for his friend (John 15:13) as he had about laying down his fortune; and as for Bassanio, he would squander "life itself, my wife, and all the world" to save Antonio (IV, i, 263–85). Here Magnificence is enlarged to become not only Aristotle's Greatness of Soul but an analogue of Calvary.

The Christians are as careless about agreements, engagements, and contracts as Shylock is careful about them. Lorenzo comes late to his own elopement (II, vi, 3–21); Bassanio invites all his friends to a masque and then goes to Belmont instead (II, vi, 64); in spite of many oaths and vows not to part with the rings that symbolize their marriages to Nerissa and Portia, Bassanio and Gratiano generously give them up to the "lawyer" and "clerk" to whom they are indebted for Antonio's life. It is true that such "crosses" complicate most Shakespeare comedies and that they serve to symbolize the way human affairs fail of accomplishment in a world dominated by evil pursuits. But against the background of Shylock's destructive effort to enforce a contract, these events in *The Merchant of Venice* appear as constructive breaches of contract, showing how carelessness is a virtue and legalism folly. The whole point of the fifth act seems to be that among friends breaking contracts is something to joke about. *Betraying* friends, of course, is something altogether different.

Shakespeare undercuts the logic of "fast bind, fast find" (II, v, 52) in a still more devastating way. If we cannot bind the future to our will, then fortune reigns. In testimony of this fact the word *fortune* is on everyone's lips continually from the beginning to the end of the play, and the "venture" (III, ii, 10), "hazard" (III, ii, 2), "chance" (II, i, 38), or "lottery of [Portia's] destiny" (I, ii, 27; II, i, 15) is not the only objective correlative of the idea. Antonio and Bassanio are both engaged in what Restoration gamesters would call "deep play," the one having "bechanced" all his fortunes on the sea (I, i, 38) and the other throwing good money after bad because he has a hunch that he can win Portia's lottery (I, i, 175–76). The motto of the winning casket then moralizes all this "gaming" as a form of generous sacrifice: "Who chooseth me must give and *hazard* all he hath" (my italics, II, ix, 20).

In making this choice Bassanio epitomizes what I mean by Liberality, a willingness to give; Courage, a willingness to risk all he has; and Love, a willingness to throw himself away for the sake of a woman. What Antonio had done for him (and what he would do for Antonio) Bassanio is willing to do for Portia. Being romantic, the play does not provide as much scope for Plain-dealing as does a typical Restoration comedy, but the contrast between Bassanio and his self-regarding rivals, a fop and a braggart, brings home the point that affectation is also a way of taking thought and that it is as destructive of genuine human relationships as Shylock's contracts.

The Merchant of Venice was adapted for Augustan tastes by George Granville, later Lord Lansdowne, in 1701. It was performed 36 times before 1748, after which Shakespeare's own version regained the stage.[19] If the concept of generosity I have described was indeed the ethical code of Restoration comedy, one would expect Granville's adaptation to reinforce the points I have made about the play, and this is exactly what it does. Granville sees no ambiguities whatsoever in the play. Shylock is simply the villain; Bassanio and Antonio are the heroes. It is a case of black and white, not gray, and Granville does several things to simplify matters. First, he cuts out the comedy provided by Launcelot Gobbo's clowning and Bassanio's ridiculous rivals, Morocco and Arragon, probably in the interest of the classical rule of unity. The

---

[19] Christopher Spencer, ed., *Five Restoration Adaptations of Shakespeare* (Urbana, Ill., 1965), p. 29.

subject is too serious for clowning and so the play becomes a pure villain tragedy, that Restoration genre in which disaster strikes only those who do evil.[20] Granville moves Shylock's great plea for sympathy, the "hath not a Jew eyes" speech, to a place where it comes not as an answer to the lesser Christians' merciless baiting of Shylock shortly after his daughter elopes, but as salt for the wounds of the poor Antonio, in prison and awaiting execution to provide the usurer his pound of flesh. Thus Granville transfers the sympathy that always accrues to underdogs from Shylock to Antonio. Then, when Shylock finishes his great speech, the upright Antonio calls him "impenetrable cur," instead of the less reputable Solanio to whom Shakespeare had originally given the speech, and that effectively erases Shylock's eloquence. Besides blackening the character of Shylock, Granville whitens the characters of Antonio and Bassanio, whom Shakespeare had designed somewhat badly from a Restoration point of view.

Except for some exceptions that prove the rule, a merchant cannot be the hero of a Restoration play. So the play becomes *The Jew of Venice* (referring to Shylock) instead of *The Merchant of Venice* (referring to Antonio). Antonio's fleets of ships are played down and the *dramatis personae* identifies him as a gentleman instead of a merchant. W. H. Auden's intuition was sound when he suggested that Shylock's vice would be more distinct against the background of a medieval agricultural society,[21] for the virtues of Antonio are precisely those of a chivalric agrarian, not those of an acquisitive merchant. Restoration audiences would agree with Auden that a merchant differs too little from a usurer. Because the prejudice against trade was never stronger than just after the Puritan insurrection, Granville hustled Antonio away from all his mercantile connections.

To reinforce the aristocratic image of his protagonists, Granville sanctifies the friendship of Antonio and Bassanio. His intent is clear from the moment he brackets them as friends in the *dramatis personae*. And in the first scene when Bassanio asks for his loan, Antonio begins with a lecture on Friendship that sounds as if he had just put down Tully's *Offices*: "My Friend can owe me nothing; we are one, / The

---

[20] John Harold Wilson distinguishes this form of tragedy in *A Preface to Restoration Drama* (Boston, 1965), chap. 7.

[21] W. H. Auden, *The Dyer's Hand* (New York, 1948), p. 225.

Treasures I possess are but in Trust, / For him I love."[22] And so it goes throughout the play. Granville never loses an opportunity to introduce the dogmas of the religion of Friendship. It should now be nearly impossible to sympathize with the antagonist of such a virtuous pair, but still Granville is not satisfied. He must introduce a new scene in which Shylock commits the ultimate *faux pas*. Bassanio's feast does take place, a classically Magnificent affair with an elaborate masque about Peleus and Thetis. At this feast Antonio gives a toast to Friendship and Bassanio gives a toast to Love. When Shylock's turn comes, he says,

> I have a Mistress, that out-shines 'em all . . .
> O may her Charms encrease and multiply;
> My Money is my Mistress!
> Here's to
> Interest upon Interest.

To this Antonio responds with virtuous horror:

> Let Birds and Beasts of Prey howl to such Vows,
> All generous Notes be hush'd: Pledge thy self, Jew:
> None here will stir the Glass.[23]

With such deft strokes as this, Granville nailed down the theme of Love and Friendship vs. Avarice. There was nothing ambiguous about *The Merchant of Venice* on the Restoration stage.

No such heavy outlines distinguish the behavior of the heroes of Restoration comedy. Although they risk body and fortune with the same reckless *sprezzatura* that motivates Shakespeare's characters, they make no Granvillean speeches about their virtues. Aristotle observed that the best men "mostly disown qualities held in high esteem, as Socrates used to do."[24]

[22] Spencer, p. 352.
[23] *Ibid.*, p. 364.
[24] Aristotle, *Ethics*, IV, vii, 14.

CHAPTER THREE

Liberality vs. Avarice

The special emphasis on generosity in Restoration comedy is probably a form of reaction to the Civil War. It has been customary to look upon this war as a conflict between the landed aristocracy and a rising mercantile class, between those who favor land as the basis of wealth and those who favor capital. That this was actually the case, modern scholarship has seriously questioned.[1] But the seventeenth-century view of the matter seems to have been the agrarian-mercantile one, and this is the view that interests us. Perhaps the reason that Restoration theatre was attracted to the values associated with generosity was precisely that they were no longer relevant. The landed aristocracy, though apparently victorious in restoring their king, were in fact losing influence rapidly. The future belonged to the capitalists. Just as in this century we have the Fugitive movement in the American South looking back fondly to a heroic antebellum age—Faulkner writing of Colonel Sartoris in a world dominated by Flem Snopes—so in the seventeenth century Wycherley wrote of Manly in a world dominated by Alderman Gripe. In both worlds an agrarian aristocracy and its values are irrelevant but missed. In both cases irrelevance leads to romantic intensification of the irrelevant values.

On the subject of mercantile values Max Weber's *Protestant Ethic and the Spirit of Capitalism*, which traces the change in the European attitude toward money to the rise of Puritanism, is most enlightening.

---

[1] Notably in two essays by H. R. Trevor-Roper: "The Social Causes of the Great Rebellion" and "The Country House Radicals," *Historical Essays* (London, 1957).

Traditionally, as we have seen, the accumulation of money for its own sake had been condemned as avarice. It was a despicable vice for the ancients, a deadly sin for the Christians. But under a certain construction of Calvinistic principles the accumulation of money became a form of piety. Weber defines the "Spirit of Capitalism" by means of a quotation from Benjamin Franklin, "which [he says] contains what we are looking for in almost classical purity":

> Remember, that *time* is money. He that can earn ten shillings a day by his labour, and goes abroad, or sits idle, one half of that day, though he spends but sixpence during his diversion or idleness, ought not to reckon *that* the only expense; he has really spent, or rather thrown away, five shillings besides.
>
> Remember, that *credit* is money. If a man lets his money lie in my hands after it is due, he gives me the interest, or so much as I can make of it during that time. This amounts to a considerable sum where a man has good and large credit, and makes good use of it.
>
> Remember, that money is of the prolific, generating nature. Money can beget money, and its offspring can beget more, and so on. Five shillings turned is six, turned again it is seven and threepence, and so on, till it becomes a hundred pounds. The more there is of it, the more it produces every turning, so that the profits rise quicker and quicker. He that kills a breeding-sow, destroys all her offspring to the thousandth generation. He that murders a crown, destroys all that it might have produced, even scores of pounds. . . .
>
> After industry and frugality, nothing contributes more to the raising of a young man in the world than punctuality and justice in all his dealings; therefore never keep borrowed money an hour beyond the time you promised, lest a disappointment shut up your friend's purse for ever.
>
> The most trifling actions that affect a man's credit are to be regarded. The sound of your hammer at five in the morning, or eight at night, heard by a creditor, makes him easy six months longer; but if he sees you at a billiard-table, or hears your voice at a tavern, when you should be at work, he

sends for his money the next day; demands it, before he can receive it, in a lump.

It shows, besides, that you are mindful of what you owe; it makes you appear a careful as well as an honest man, and that still increases your credit.

Beware of thinking all your own that you possess, and of living accordingly. It is a mistake that many people who have credit fall into. . . .

For six pounds a year you may have the use of one hundred pounds, provided you are a man of known prudence and honesty.

He that spends a groat a day idly, spends idly above six pounds a year, which is the price for the use of one hundred pounds.

He that wastes idly a groat's worth of his time per day, one day with another, wastes the privilege of using one hundred pounds each day.

He that idly loses five shillings' worth of time, loses five shillings, and might as prudently throw five shillings into the sea.

He that idly loses five shillings, not only loses that sum, but all the advantage that might be made by turning it in dealing, which by the time that a young man becomes old, will amount to a considerable sum of money.

Weber comments,

> The peculiarity of this philosophy of avarice appears to be the ideal of the honest man of recognized credit, and above all the idea of a duty of the individual toward the increase of his capital, which is assumed as an end in itself. Truly what is here preached is not simply a means of making one's way in the world, but a peculiar ethic. The infraction of its rules is treated not as foolishness but as forgetfulness of duty. That is the essence of the matter. It is not mere business astuteness, that sort of thing is common enough, it is an ethos. *This* is the quality which interests us.[2]

[2] Max Weber, *The Protestant Ethic* (New York, 1958), pp. 48–51.

Restoration comedy fails entirely to see any value in Franklin's approach to life. First, it is sterile: money breeds only money; pure pleasure, in contrast, is a more justifiable offspring. Second, to clothe greed and selfishness in a dress of duty or piety is hypocritical. Third, the duty of making a profit conflicts with the traditional bonds of society. Fourth, the passage recommends industry, which in the eyes of Restoration comedy is mere "busyness," an aimless activity really less worthwhile than the conversation of good company. Finally, Franklin takes thought for the morrow. Restoration comedy delights in the man who makes the most of today, who is care-less about financing, magnanimous to friends, and magnificent in spending. It continues the Cavalier side of the Civil War by attacking not just Puritans but the Puritan economic philosophy.

The intimate connection between the Restoration stage and the restored king himself is well known. Charles took a personal interest in the management of theatres, in the writing and acting of plays, and in actors and actresses. With the exception of Shadwell, all the important dramatists were Cavalier in sympathy. And, in his plays at least, Shadwell's Whiggism before 1688 was so timid as to be nearly undetectable. The actors were members of the Cavalier party, too. The writer of *Historia Histrionica* (1699) recalled that of the members of the two original companies at the Restoration only one actor had sided with the Presbyterians; all the rest, including the much-applauded Hart, Colonel Mohun, and Shatterel, had been loyal to the monarchy, mostly as soldiers in the field.[3] Given such a decided bias at the start, the stage resisted the shift in political power that later drove the Stuarts from the throne. In 1683 John Crowne could say with confidence, "Wit is a Tory, ne'er with [Whigs] would join, / Wit never helped the Whigs to write one line."[4] To be sure, comedy by its very nature tends to be conservative, because it is aberrations from the traditional norms that produce the loudest laughs. So we are not surprised when Professor John Loftis, in his thorough-going *Politics of Drama in Augustan England*, concludes his chapter on the Restoration period with the obser-

[3] *Historia Histrionica*, published in the first volume of Robert Lowe's edition of Colley Cibber, *An Apology for the Life of Mr. Colley Cibber* (London, 1889), pp. xxix–xxx.
[4] John Crowne, *City Politiques*, epilogue.

vation that tragedy turned Whig much sooner than comedy: "If in comedy the Tory social philosophy was to persist through Anne's reign, in tragedy the strong Whig theme was stated fully and clearly before William's death."[5]

Thanks perhaps to "the Whig view of history" we are not accustomed to viewing seventeenth-century history from a Royalist point of view. But Restoration comedy did. On the evidence of the plays, the king and his party did not soon forget what they had suffered at the hands of the Roundheads. Defending his attack on Puritans in *Cutter of Coleman Street* (1661), Cowley affirms the rightness of deriding "the hypocrisy of those men whose skulls are not yet bare upon the gates since the public and just punishment of it." Such men, he continues, "engraft pride upon ignorance, tyranny upon liberty, and upon their heresies, treason and rebellion. These are principles so destructive to the peace and society of mankind that they deserve to be pursued by our serious hatred, and the putting a mask of sanctity upon such devils is so ridiculous that it ought to be exposed to contempt and laughter."[6] And so, on night after night, the Puritans were exposed to contempt and laughter on the stage, now not casually as before the Rebellion, but with a vengeance. In the year of his death, allowing some justice to Collier's complaints about the stage, Dryden cast a diagnostic eye over the period he had dominated as a man of letters. Admitting that Charles and his courtiers had worshipped "the naked Venus," he still thought that this frank sexuality was an innocent thing compared to the monstrous duplicity of the Puritans, for whom "nothing but *open* lewdness was a crime"; for whom "a monarch's blood was venial to the nation, / Compared with one foul act of fornication."[7] The modern tendency to look upon early Puritans as virtuous freedom fighters hides an ugly side of their nature, but this was the only side visible to the Restoration stage.

The dramatists made very much the same connection between trade and the Protestant ethic that Max Weber has observed, but without Weber's scientific detachment. About one-third (27) of the plays under discussion contain characters identifiable as Puritan, 53 in number. I

[5] John Loftis, *The Politics of Drama in Augustan England* (Oxford, 1963), p. 34.
[6] Abraham Cowley, *Cutter of Coleman Street*, preface.
[7] Vanbrugh, *The Pilgrim*, epilogue.

include in this group all those who dissent from the established church and anyone who sides with the Roundheads. If this group were to be an accurate representation of the historical distribution of Puritans and Roundheads, a large number of the Puritan group would actually be gentry, and there are a few Puritan gentry in Restoration comedy. But 80 percent of the Puritans whose métier is indicated are associated with trade. Thus, the plays convey the same connection between religion and business that Weber does. Other features of the Puritan stereotype emerge clearly. He lives in the City (21 of 22). He shows an over-whelming distaste for pleasure and an enthusiasm for business (25 of 26). He loves money (42 of 43). He is universally condemned on the stage, that is, ridiculed, disgraced, and defeated in his enterprises (50 of 50). The stock country gentleman of Restoration comedy is often stingy (12 of 21) but only 5 of 53 are Puritans. It is perhaps significant that 3 of these come from plays written in the first decade after the Restoration when the memory of the country gentry's contribution to the Rebellion was fresh.

The Weberian equivalence of piety and profit was well understood in Restoration comedy. It is clearly delineated in Cowley's very early *Cutter of Coleman Street* (1661), where the Puritan widow Bare-bottle very neatly combines the spiritual and economic meanings of the word *income* while exhorting her Cavalier suitor to emulate her de-ceased Roundhead husband's opportunism:

> Why, seek for Spiritual incomes, Mr. Colonel. I'll tell you what my husband Barebottle was wont to observe (and he was a colonel, too)—he never sought for incomes but he had some blessing followed immediately: Once he sought for 'em in Hartfordshire, and the next day he took as many horses and arms in the country as served to raise three troops; an-other time he sought for 'em in Bucklersbury, and three days after a friend of his, that he owed five hundred pounds, too, was hanged for a malignant, and the debt forgiven him by the Parliament; a third time.... (II)

The ease with which city merchants possessed themselves of Cavalier lands by legalistic maneuvers so complicated that they must be dishonest was a frequently heard complaint on the Restoration stage. John Wilson, whose play *The Cheats* was first acted in 1662, was himself a practicing lawyer and perhaps for this reason took more pains to describe the operation of city chicanery than later comic writers, who often contented themselves with merely punishing cits, not bothering to document their presumed mode of livelihood. In *The Cheats* Wilson gives us a full-length portrait of the Puritan Alderman Whitebroth at work:

WHITEBROTH.   Come, Tim, leave that and let's see how affairs stand at present. How have you done with your rotten raisins? Did they yield well?

TIM.   Troth, sir, the wine-coopers have done their part; they have made you at least sixty pipes of wine out of 'um. But they advise your worship to get your money for 'um before they stir out of the cellar; for however they may be palatable enough as long as they lie there, yet as soon as you stir 'um they'll kick up their heels.

WHITEBROTH.   Good enough to be pist against a wall an they were worse. And now I think on't, you remember the country vintner that bought the pipe of canary on shipboard and gave it to Rascal-Mark to cheat the Custom-house? See it be craned off into another pipe and filled up again with your new what d'you call it. *'Tis good enough for sinners.* If he discover it, you may tell him 'tis his own mark.

TIM.   It shall be done. But sir, Mr. Spendal was to have waited on you yesterday touching a bond of his for £500, which he says is paid and you promised to deliver up.

WHITEBROTH.   O ho! let me see. Here 'tis—[*he reads*]—'If the said Spendal shall content, satisfy and pay,' etc. Why see— the condition of the obligation, which is made for his benefit and not mine, says *if he shall content*. Pray tell him, notwithstanding the payment of the money, his bond is forfeited; for I am not contented. Does he think I can be content with six percent? I have no more to say to him; I'll take my course. Pray mind your own business. Have you received the Jew's money and sent him the pack of left-handed gloves I ordered you?

TIM. Yes sir; 'tis done.

WHITEBROTH. Put tricks upon me! Make me buy a round parcel of gloves, and now you know I have 'um by me, if I will not bate a third part of the money, you have occasion but for half of 'um, and be hanged. I'll Jew you, with a horse pox. I have received half your money, and you shall have half the gloves—that is to say, all the left-handed ones. You may truck them off with maimed soldiers; if not, I'll make you pay sauce for t'other. Reach me that book—and while I remember it, go into my chamber, and upon the table you'll find a £1000 in half crowns; pray weigh 'um one by one and lay by such as are overweight and see 'um melted down. *'Tis a hard world and fit every man make the most of his own.*—[*the bell rings*]—See who's at the door! [*exit Timothy*] [*Whitebroth reads*]—'Taken up on bottomry upon the good ship called the *Mary*, to be paid with interest after the rate of 30 per cent within ten days after her coming to anchor in the River of Thames: £1700'—So, so, that's paid: all got. She's sunk at Newfoundland. Besides, I have insured a £1000 upon her myself. *How wealth trowles upon an honest man!* The master deserves a £100 extraordinary for this and shall have it. This is the fifth ship he has sunk for me. 'Item, paid the Irish army in Peru dollars.' Ay, there's a sweet business. [*enter Timothy*] Who's that?

TIM. Sir, Mr. Afterwit desires to see you.

WHITEBROTH. Stay him a while without; I'll be for him presently.—[*exit Timothy*]—Here's a squire, too, will be worth me somewhat. Let me see his account. 'Lent his father, upon judgment, £4000. Item, more upon a statute, £3000. Item, upon mortgage, £2500. Item, upon his own account, upon bond, £500. Item, more, £300. Item, bound to me for other men, £1000.' Pox o' these bonds! I must persuade him to take another thousand and hedge all into one good mortgage. To see how the world goes round. . . . This city is like the sea—few estates but ran out of it at first and will run into it at last. Timothy! [*enter Timothy*] desire my friend to walk in!

(III)

The Cheats earned the king's approbation when its unamused enemies requested that he have it removed from the stage.[8] It then went
on to become a standard part of the repertoire of the original company
founded by Killigrew in 1660. In 1691 we hear that it still had "the
general approbation of an excellent comedy," and it was not considered
too old-fashioned for revival in 1720 and 1727.[9]

But the comedy most frequently performed on the Restoration and
early eighteenth-century stage was Sir Robert Howard's *Committee*,
even more directly aimed at the Puritans. The hilarious, bungling,
good-natured character of Teague, the "Faithful Irishman" of the
subtitle, must have had something to do with *The Committee*'s success,
but the fact that the plot concerned the efforts of two oppressed Cavaliers to save their estates and those of their mistresses from an unscrupu-
lous Puritan Committee of Sequestration must also have contributed to
its success. When the members of the committee agree that the estates
of two infants (one unborn) must be sequestered, one for the crime
of being too young to take the Covenant and the other for being en-
gendered by a Cavalier—"There's a young Cavalier in [the] widow's
belly"—Nathaniel Catch speaks up: "I move therefore that their two
estates may remain in the hands of our brethren here, and fellow-
laborers, Mr. Joseph Blemish and Mr. Jonathan Headstrong and Mr.
Ezekiel Scrape, and they to be accountable to our pleasures; whereby
they may have a godly opportunity of doing good for themselves."
When the motion is ordered, Jonathan expresses his satisfaction in
biblical style. "Now verily it seemeth to me that the work goeth forward, when brethren hold together in unity" (II). Wycherley's *Plain
Dealer* (1676) describes this sort of hypocrisy almost in the language
of Weber's *Protestant Ethic*. If you go to an alderman's house, says
Manly, "you must call usury and extortion God's blessings, or the
honest turning of the penny" (III). It is interesting to note that, although the character who calls forth this indignation is introduced as
merely a city alderman, Manly automatically assumes the rest of the
stereotype, cheating and piety.

[8] See p. 5.

[9] John Downes, *Roscius Anglicanus* (London, 1886), p. 15; Gerard Langbaine, *An
Account of the English Dramatic Poets* (Oxford, 1691), p. 513; Montague Summers,
The Playhouse of Pepys (New York, 1935), pp. 220–21; *The London Stage*, pt. 2, ed.
Emmett L. Avery (Carbondale, Ill., 1960).

Ravenscroft's *London Cuckolds* (1681), which succeeded almost as well as *The Committee*, shows a similar tendency of later comedies to take for granted the chicanery and religious cant of cits, leaving the playwright free to concentrate on the amusing process of making fools of them. The play simply assumes that aldermen are fair game. *Alderman*, of course, in the Restoration comic vocabulary, meant not *this* alderman or *that* alderman but the genus *alderman*: "Epitome of a hypocritical, avaricious, old Puritan cheat." That Ravenscroft understood it this way is proved by his epilogue, where he informs us axiomatically that there are no cuckolds but cits, and among cits, no cuckolds but Commonwealth men. Whigs, he says, are all "predestined" for horns, especially those whose wives have the most religious zeal. Here, as we would expect from reading other plays, Ravenscroft identifies his three aldermen with the City, the Commonwealth, Whiggism, and religious zeal or Puritanism. If cits make a living as does Whitebroth in *The Cheats*, if Commonwealth men behave like Nathaniel Catch in *The Committee*, and if Puritans are zealous in the manner described by Widow Barebottle in *Cutter of Coleman Street*, then perhaps cuckolding is what aldermen (super-cits) deserve. That this view was precisely that held by Augustan audiences is borne out by the fact that *The London Cuckolds* was performed regularly on Lord Mayor's Day (October 29), obviously as the Town's rebuff to the City's celebration. This vestige of the Civil War did not disappear until 1752.[10]

In *Sir Courtly Nice* (1685), also a stock play, John Crowne made some attempt to soothe political tempers of the time by balancing a fanatical Tory, Hothead, against Testimony, a standard fanatical Puritan. But in the end Crowne could not help taking sides, by having Hothead beat Testimony off the stage. This play probably owed its long continuance on the stage to the fact that it provided Colley Cibber with a chance to play the fop for which the play is named. But audiences who came to see Cibber as Sir Courtly would also see Testimony's ignominious exit.

In 1699, perhaps provoked to it by Collier's recently published *Short View*, Farquhar took his turn as a chastizer of Puritans in a play that provided the great Wilks with his most loudly and longly applauded

---

[10] Allardyce Nicoll, *Restoration Drama* (Cambridge, 1928), pp. 243–44; *The London Stage*, pt. 3, ed. Arthur H. Scouten (Carbondale, Ill., 1961).

role, Sir Harry Wildair. *The Constant Couple* devoted considerable space to a character called Smuggler, a city merchant described in Act IV as "a compound of covetousness, hypocrisy and knavery [who] must be punished," and to his uncle Vizard, whose topicality may be guessed at from some verses commendatory of Farquhar, thought to have been written by Mrs. Centlivre:

> In Vizard many may their picture find;
> A pious outside, but a poisonous mind.
> Religious hypocrites thou'st open laid,
> Those holy cheats by which our isle is sway'd.[11]

Eleven years after Farquhar's death, Mrs. Centlivre herself took up the task of lashing religious reformers. Her comedy, *A Bold Stroke for a Wife* (1717), exposes to ridicule the Quakers, Mr. and Mrs. Obadiah Prim, and Simon Pure (*the* Simon Pure), a Friend from Pennsylvania. This play was a standard item of the repertory well into the nineteenth century.

Although the number of plays during the Restoration and early eighteenth century that satirized characters clearly identified as Puritans was small compared to the number of plays staged (about one-third), because of the great popularity of some of the plays that did overtly attack Puritans, the aggregate reiterative effect must have created a different impression on the average playgoer. We are told as late as 1716, in the prologue to Addison's *Drummer*, that "Roundheads ... are standing jokes" in contemporary theatre. Addison is absolutely right. In 1716 he might have seen Puritans ridiculed in *Sir Courtly Nice* and *The Old Bachelor*, each performed six times; *The London Cuckolds*, *The Constant Couple*, and *The Plain Dealer*, each performed four times; and *The Comical Revenge*, performed once. Since records are sparse for this period, the total number of 25 anti-Puritan performances that year perhaps ought to be doubled.

Only 9 of the 83 plays have protagonists actually identified as Cavaliers. The number is small because the term *Cavalier* applies only to the king's party during the Civil War, whereas *Puritan* refers not only to combatants but also to religious zealots during the Restoration. Col-

---

[11] George Farquhar, *Complete Works*, ed. Charles Stonehill (Bloomsbury, 1930), II:262.

onel Jolly of Cowley's *Cutter of Coleman Street* (1661) is a Cavalier whose estate was confiscated during the Civil War. The protagonists of *The Committee* (1662) are Cavaliers. The heroic plot of Sedley's tragicomic *Mulberry Garden* (1668) involves Cavaliers with Commonwealth men just before General Monk's decision to recall the king. Mrs. Behn's famous *Rover* (1676), based on *Tomaso or the Wanderer*, which Killigrew wrote in exile, devotes itself to the exploits of the "Banished Cavaliers" named in the subtitle. The soldiers of Otway's *Soldiers' Fortune* (1680) are the sons of "Cavaliers," and Ravenscroft labels the horn-makers of his *London Cuckolds* (1681) "Cavaliers," though here he probably means only "gallants." Two "Tories" make fools of Shaftesbury and his crew in Crowne's *City Politiques* (1683); Young Fashion, the successful trickster of Vanbrugh's *Relapse* (1696), is called a "Jacobite," perhaps in jest. Otherwise the specific political stands of conservative characters must be deduced by implication.

The plays identify 29 characters as Cavalier. All 29 are members of the gentry. They live in the Town, not in the City (9 of 9). They are liberal in the disposition of their money and possessions (21 of 23). The playwrights generally approve of their behavior by putting them on the winning side in the dramatic conflict (26 of 28). Of the two antagonistic Cavaliers, one is the *miles gloriosus* in Sedley's *Bellamira*, his modernization of Terence's *Eunuch*. This play comes twenty-seven years after the Restoration. It appears that Sedley was frankly bored with hearing old Cavaliers tell their war stories. His *Mulberry Garden* shows him to be properly Cavalier in sentiment. The other disapproved Cavalier is a stingy parent in *Cutter of Coleman Street*, a play so decidedly pro-Cavalier as to be able to afford one less-than-perfect specimen.

To a significant degree, then, Restoration comedy corroborates Weber's thesis about the Protestant ethic and spirit of capitalism. But trade is much more widely attacked without regard to its religious connections, so much so that the bias against trade dominates the comic landscape absolutely. Those whose vocation is making money comprise one-fifth (203) of all characters. They appear in 62 of the 83 plays. Next to the gentry and servants, they are by far the largest vocational group, three times larger than all the rest put together. Furthermore, they are overwhelmingly condemned (107 of 121: 89

percent), the exceptions coming mainly from aberrant Whiggist comedies by Shadwell, Behn, and Steele. Since the playwrights favor the gentry and take no firm position on servants, the mercantile classes thus become the prime target of satire in Restoration comedy. Their crime is avarice (112 of 122, the exceptions being produced by the same sources). I identify as *avaricious* those characters who exhibit excessive thrift or whose designs are motivated exclusively by profit.

Class conflict in the Civil War may have contributed to the prejudice against trade in Restoration comedy, but its antecedents are considerably more ancient and honorable. Tully's *Offices*, that "commonest school book," under the heading of *decorum* discusses what vocations are appropriate to a gentleman:

> First, those means of livelihood are rejected as undesirable which incur people's ill-will, as those of tax-gatherers and usurers. Unbecoming to a gentleman, too, and vulgar are the means of livelihood of all hired workmen whom we pay for mere manual labour, not for artistic skill; for in their case the very wage they receive is a pledge of their slavery. Vulgar we must consider those also who buy from wholesale merchants to retail immediately; for they would get no profits without a great deal of downright lying. (I, 150)

The traditional professions are acceptable, as well as merchandizing on a very large scale, especially if the merchant retires to a country estate on his profits. "But of all the occupations by which gain is secured, none is better than agriculture, none more profitable, none more delightful, none more becoming to a freeman" (I, 151).

All sorts of trades are represented in the plays but by far the most common are the usurer and the scrivener, perhaps because their commodity is money itself. City capitalists show their grasping tendencies by their names: Scrapeall, Gripus, Moneytrap, Catch, Vulture, Sir Jealous Traffique, Sir Tristrum Cash, or Sir Francis Gripe. Their stinginess is conventionally shown by their hesitancy in bribing chambermaids or in spending money on their wives or whores. But much greater violations of liberality are committed. The alderman named in the title of Mrs. Behn's *Sir Patient Fancy* (1678) would "sooner lend . . . his wife than his money" (II), which is bad enough, but the cordwainer "set up for a gentleman" in her *False Count* (1681) would rather have his wife dead than ransom her from a Turkish pirate (IV). He eventually pleads with her to make him a cuckold with the pirate to save his own life (V). "Interest" was the only guide and "gold the god" (II) of the usurer in *The Wife's Relief* (1711); the change-broker in *A Bold Stroke for a Wife* (1717) would "outlie the devil for the advantage of stock and cheat his father that got him in a bargain" (I). A lawyer in Steele's *Funeral* (1701) tells how he deals with an unsuspecting client: "I made the only use a man of business can of a trust—I cheated him" (I). In *Cutter of Coleman Street* informing upon a friend for profit was a legitimate Puritan activity. Putting profit before wife, parent, client, or friend is an accurate reflection of the Protestant ethic, according to which once-sacred personal bonds are seen as worldly temptations to swerve from the duty of turning a penny.[12] The impersonality, the sterility of money, and the way in which individual pursuit of profit destroys family and community, are preoccupations of Restoration comedy.

Many heads used to be shaken over the profligacy and licentiousness of Restoration comic heroes. Recent critics have dignified these traits with a philosophical, if not an ethical, foundation as honest hedonism, Machiavellianism, libertinism, or Hobbism.[13] Aside from the very important fact that hedonism never has the final say in Restoration comedy, several other factors militate against the hedonistic interpretation. One of these is certainly the condemnation of the profit motive. Thrift, industry, gravity, asceticism, and all the nonhedonistic virtues are attributes of the money-makers. Thus the hedonism of comic heroes may not be so much espoused for its own sake as it is to be flaunted in the faces of the humorless, hard-working opposition.

The measurable presence of a pleasure-business dialectic in the plays supports this conclusion. Of the money-making class, 21 percent have an avowed aversion to pleasure and a love of business, as against 3 per-

---

12 Weber, pp. 106–7.
13 Dale Underwood (*Etherege and the 17th Century Comedy of Manners*, New Haven, Conn., 1957) ascribes "Machiavellian dissembling" to Dorimant in *The Man of Mode* (p. 73) and avers that the comic hero is a pleasure seeker who "insists upon man as naturally self-seeking in motivation and ruthless in his means" (p. 27). Thomas Fujimura (*Restoration Comedy of Wit*, Princeton, N.J., 1952) believes that "wit comedy was a hedonic enterprise undertaken by the wit for his diversion and for the satisfaction of his malicious, sexual, and aesthetic desires" (p. 55).

cent who do not. In contrast, the gentry make known a preference for pleasure at a rate of 30 percent and enjoy business at a rate of 2 percent (without approbation, of course). While the plays do not universally approve pleasure lovers, they never fail to condemn business lovers.

In some of his nondramatic writings Wycherley gives us the reason. His poem "Upon the Idleness of Business" calls business "circular motion" or "restlessness" and maintains that the busy "lose wealth, life, by taking for 'em care," recalling the language of *The Merchant of Venice*. They lose wealth because only by spending it can they enjoy it, life because business consumes time that could be better spent. "The wisest business," therefore, "should be none to have."[14] In *The Country Wife* Sir Jasper Fidget tells his wife, "Go, go, to your business, I say, pleasure; whilst I go to my pleasure, business." As he goes, his wife sends a couplet after him: "Who for his business from his wife will run, / Takes the best care to have her business done" (II). It is done, of course, by Horner. But Wycherley is not merely joking, because attention to business has similar consequences in plays by other authors. Ravenscroft makes it clear that it is his three London cuckolds' fear of missing a chance to turn a penny that leaves their wives open to conquest, and Congreve's alderman Fondlewife (*Old Bachelor*, 1692) leaves his wife exposed for the sake of 500 pounds (IV). What Wycherley seems to be saying is what Swift was to say later in the "Voyage to Laputa," where the "busyness" was mathematics. There unfaithful wives are an arresting symbol of the errors of specialist detachment just as they are in Restoration comedy. In both cases an impersonal and technical pursuit screens the pursuer from the important realm of human interaction. The "merely social" preoccupations of the plays— the wit duels, the idle conversation, the character analysis, the card games, the visitings, the masques and balls, even the battle of the sexes and the all-male drinking sessions—take on moral dimensions when "busyness" is the enemy of human values. Hedonism is not the whole explanation of protagonistic behavior.

If class warfare were rigorously carried on in Restoration comedy, all gentry ought to be liberal in the management of wealth. This would be so if we considered only the winners of dramatic conflict, but many

[14] William Wycherley, *Complete Works*, ed. Montague Summers (Soho, 1924), III:103–9.

gentry—mainly parents or rivals of protagonists—are blocking charac-ters. Protagonistic gentry (defined here as the opposite of antagonistic) are palpably generous with material wealth (253 of 260). In the typical comedy avarice is an optional characteristic of gentry but a necessary attribute of tradesmen and merchants. It is deplored wherever it is found, and liberality is restricted to the aristocracy.

Avarice in the gentry appears more often in the composition of a parent (32 examples) than in that of a rival, who is primarily some sort of fop (26 examples) or some sort of prude (11 examples), de-pending on the sex. The ill treatment of parents by children in Restoration comedy has from the time of Collier caused dismay. Of course, the victory of the younger generation over the older has always been the basic plot of comedy, the way in which it evokes its charac-teristic feeling of a new and better age coming.[15] The feeling of well-being is enhanced by attributing to the passing generation all the ugly things one hopes will go away and by attributing to the coming gen-eration all the beautiful things one wishes for.

For this reason, comedy never has been fair to older people, and to look upon this or that comedy as taking a stand against old people is to misinterpret. It takes a stand against whatever traits it assigns to old people. In Restoration comedy the predominant trait of old people is avarice, and not even this is peculiar to Restoration comedy. The stingy old man had been a fixture in comedy since Roman times. In *Love's Last Shift* (1696) a character of Cibber's finds "age and avarice are inseparable" (V). But in the context of the Restoration's special antip-athy toward trade, avarice is more than a stage convention and rebellion against parents is more than simple insubordination. What we see again and again is a greedy parent forcing a generous child to marry an ob-noxious person for money.

As P. F. Vernon has effectively shown, the rebellion against parents should be understood as an attack on the marriage of convenience.[16] His thesis is borne out by the fact that the playwrights commonly have parents arrange marriages in the language of trade, thus giving the

[15] For example, the new society emerging at the end of a comedy is an aspect of the "Mythos of Spring: Comedy," in Northrop Frye's *Anatomy of Criticism* (Prince-ton, N.J., 1957), pp. 169–70.

[16] P. F. Vernon, "The Marriage of Convenience and the Moral Code of Restoration Comedy," *Essays in Criticism*, XII (1962):370–81.

practice the worst possible connotations. "I must give Sparkish tomorrow five thousand pound to lie with my sister," says Wycherley's Pinchwife in *The Country Wife* (I). "Her [money] bags were contracted to his acres," explains a brother in Sedley's *Bellamira* (V). Sir William Wisewoud of Cibber's *Love's Last Shift* simply "sells" his ward (V). Even in *The Conscious Lovers*, so radical a departure in many ways, Sir John Bevil's arrangements for his son are called "bargain and sale" (I). After Collier, playwrights seem more inclined than before to justify disobedience to stingy parents, and it is perhaps this motive that prompts Steele to write the following excellent dialogue between Squire Gubbin and Banker Tipkin in *The Tender Husband* (1705):

> GUBBIN. Look ye, brother Tipkin, as I told you before, my business in town is to dispose of an hundred head of cattle and my son.
> TIPKIN. Brother Gubbin, as I signified to you in my last, bearing date September thirteenth, my niece has a thousand pound *per annum*, and because I have found you a plain-dealing man . . . I was willing you should have the refusal of my niece, provided that I have a discharge from all retrospects while her guardian, and one thousand pound for my care.
> GUBBIN. Ay, but brother, you rate her too high, the war has fetched down the price of women; the whole nation is overrun with petticoats; our daughters lie upon our hands, Brother Tipkin: girls are drugs, sir, mere drugs.
> TIPKIN. Look ye, Sir Henry, let girls be what they will, a thousand pound a year is a thousand pound a year; and a thousand pound a year is neither girl nor boy.

After a long argument about pin money, the uncle and father at last agree. "And now," says Sir Harry, "since we have as good as concluded the marriage, it will not be improper that the young people see each other" (I). Charles Johnson in *The Wife's Relief* (1711) gives equally incriminating lines to Sir Tristrum Cash, who defends his plans for his ward in these terms: "Why she is my property. I have as much right to dispose of her as my horse, or my money. I may let her, sell her, lend her, or transfer her like my bank stock. What has her will and pleasure to do in the case?" (IV).

Wards and daughters naturally resisted being treated as commodities. The horrors of their plight are graphically described in a protest against marrying for money in Killigrew's *Parson's Wedding* (1662): "Can any woman be honest that lets [such weasels as we see daily married] crawl over her virgin breast and belly, or suffer them to leave their slimy paths upon her body only for jointures? Out! 'tis mercenary and base" (V). A young lady in Sedley's *Mulberry Garden* (1668) complains, "We are not the less slaves for being bound in chains of gold" (II). Etherege's spirited heroine in *She Would If She Could* (1668) resents being displayed at the theatre like merchandise "to make the world believe it is in [her relations'] power to afford some gallant or other a good bargain" (I). His magnificent Harriet asks in *Man of Mode*, "Shall I be paid down by a covetous parent for a purchase? I need no land. No, I'll lay myself out all in love" (III). In Vanbrugh's *Aesop* a character maintains that "a lewd wife . . . is the usual effect of parents' pride and covetousness" (III), a reason often given in Restoration comedy to extenuate infidelity in wives. Shadwell was so concerned about the misuse of parental authority that the whole of the *Squire of Alsatia* (1688), his most popular play, is a labored argument against a tyrannous father, ending with the following lecture on good parenthood: "You that would breed your children well, by kindness and liberality endear 'em to you, and teach 'em by example."

> Severity spoils ten for one it mends:
> If you'd not have your sons desire your ends,
> By gentleness and bounty make those sons your friends.

In the light of such evidence the rebellion of children in Restoration comedy must be read as a comment on the marriage trade.

To judge from its frequency of occurrence, avarice is the principal vice satirized in Restoration comedy (in 238 of 418 antagonistic characters). If, then, the drama of the period holds a mirror up to nature, we can see why Dryden would write, "Our iron age is grown an age of gold: / 'Tis who bids most; for all men may be sold" (*Amphitryon*, IV), or how Wycherley's less tolerant Manly, thinking of the piety that so often accompanied buying and selling, might "rather choose to go where honest, downright barbarity is professed, where men devour one another like generous hungry lions and tigers, not like crocodiles" (*Plain Dealer*, I).

"Generous hungry lions," as a matter of fact, is a phrase that not inaccurately describes a number of comic heroes. The fact that some protagonistic characters are indeed predatory seems at first glance to undercut the attack on trade and avarice in Restoration comedy. But Wycherley's distinction between the lion and the crocodile helps to extricate us from this predicament. The lion, we note, is *hungry*, to remind us of the fact that he kills only for consumption and to remind us that those represented by the crocodile, on the other hand, kill for the love of killing. The lion is also *generous*, which in this context I take to mean *brave* and *open*, as opposed to the crocodile, who hides in the mud, takes his victim unawares, and with fake tears attempts to camouflage his motives. One is reminded that Aristotle's Great Soul insists on having what is due to a person of his own high merit (*Ethics*, IV, iii, 1–11). In this respect he is not humble. Hotspur's ability to "cavil on the ninth part of a hair" when his own deserts are involved (*Henry IV*, pt. 1: III, i, 140) is probably a comic exaggeration of this un-Christian aspect of generosity. When an impoverished hero of the Restoration comedy, also a "man of honor," tricks a merchant out of a fortune, genteel tradition probably supports him as a "generous hungry lion." If this is true, the recent Hobbesian-Machiavellian interpretations of the behavior of comic heroes are again questionable.[17] A close examination of this behavior shows how questionable.

The fact that most heroines are heiresses and that a few heroes seem to be more interested in the money than in the girl may create the illusion that the heroes of Restoration comedy are as mercenary and scheming as their antagonists, the citizens and stingy parents, but it is only an illusion. As for the heroine's fortune, I think we read the plays too literally if we assume without further evidence that because it was there, it was necessarily what the hero sought. In fairy tales the hero marries a princess not because he is greedy for wealth and power but because his exploits deserve such a reward. In these plays the girl's

[17] See n. 13.

fortune is merely part of the conclusion, "and they lived happily ever after." Although it is expressed in pounds, the girl's money is used sometimes simply as a measure of her "quality" or position in society, and we have at least one example of a gallant who likes a girl less after a sudden inheritance puts her above his station (Plume, *Recruiting Officer*, III). Another hero (Afterwit, *Cheats*, I) is advised above all to seek an "equal" marriage, to avoid the situation in which one partner has power over the other by virtue of a greater monetary contribution to the marriage. But most plays do not concern themselves with the financial compatibility of partners, and we are inclined to think of the heroine's 10,000 pounds merely as symbolizing the importance of the contest in which the hero is engaged. Aimwell's observation that "no woman can be a beauty without a fortune" (*Beaux' Stratagem*, II) holds true in Restoration comedy if not in life.

The factor of common sense is also involved. As a character in Mrs. Behn's *False Count* explains, "Our gentlemen never get but twice in all their lives; that is, when fathers die, they get good estates; and when they marry, they get rich wives" (IV). Since going into trade is not an option, it would be folly in a poor younger brother to marry for love alone. In fact, if impoverished heroes, for instance Novel of Ravenscroft's *Careless Lovers* (1673), are so hairbrained as to suggest eloping at the risk of losing the heroine's portion, their women, like his Jacinta, keep their eyes on the main chance (V). Other prudent heroines are Betrice of Wilson's *Cheats* (1662), Hippolita of *The Gentleman Dancing Master* (1672), Euphronia of Vanbrugh's *Aesop* (1696), Mrs. Lovely of Mrs. Centlivre's *Bold Stroke for a Wife* (1717), and Isabinda of her *Busy Body* (1709)—the last of whom probably speaks for all her sisters in Restoration comedy when she says that love "rarely dwells with poverty" (III). The poor but happy couple is after all the invention of a more romantic and more comfortable age, as is also the poor little rich girl who cannot find anyone to love her for herself alone.

If money is not an absolute good but merely a necessity without which one cannot lead the life of a gentleman, it follows that one marries for money only if one lacks the amount necessary to enable him to move easily among his peers. This is almost exactly the case in Restoration comedy. Of 16 young men who marry for money in the plays here under consideration, 15 are poor. Of the girls they marry, though not all of them are attractive, 8 are at least well born; and 4 more, though daughters of citizens, have wit and beauty enough to suit a higher social station. Looking at the same set of characters another way, we find that half of the unions involve love as well as money, or as one comic hero puts it, "a fine woman *and* 30,000 pounds" (my italics, *Bold Stroke*, I).

The fact that some of the best-known heroes in Restoration comedy do indeed marry unattractive girls for quite cynical reasons has had a tendency to blacken the reputations of scores and scores of disinterested lovers in the plays as a whole, so that, for example, when Dorimant in *The Man of Mode* makes something of the fact that Harriet has "a hugeous fortune" (I, IV, V), we may wrongly place this charming relationship in the same class as that of Bellmour and the vain Bellinda in *The Old Bachelor*, of Young Fashion and Hoyden in *The Relapse*, of Young Worthy and Narcissa in *Love's Last Shift*, and of Captain Clerimont and the impossible Biddy Tipkin in *The Tender Husband*. These girls had nothing to offer but money, and they deserved to be taken advantage of. On the evidence of *The Beaux' Stratagem*, at least, we see that if the girl is too fine a woman to victimize, the hero must give up his design on her fortune (V).

But even designing heroes could be generous where economic necessity was not involved; and fortune hunters, however famous some have become, are the exception in Restoration comedy. For against the 16 fortune hunters, half of whom love the girl as well as need the money, the plays offer 30 heroes who actually declare that money is no object in their pursuit of the girl; and for 8 of these, who are in financial straits, it possibly should be. Perhaps not all of these gallants are so extravagant as to say, "I'd marry you though you hadn't so much as fig-leaves" (V), as does Loveworth in Baker's *Tunbridge Walks* (1702) or state categorically with Belfond Junior of *The Squire of Alsatia* (1688) that they will not marry for money (IV). Some destitute protagonists, like Ranger of Wycherley's *Love in a Wood* (1671), can even be "sorry she is an heiress, lest it should bring the scandal of interest and design of lucre upon my love" (II), or, like Young Reveller of *Greenwich Park* (1691), lament to his mistress, "I . . . had rather serve thee for nothing" than for 15,000 pounds (II), or, like Farewell of *Sir Courtly Nice*, rejoice that his courtship is "not mercenary" because it will result if successful in his Leonora's being disinherited (IV). Words are perhaps cheap. But Mrs. Behn's penniless Rover does not even know his mistress's name, let alone her market value, until after he has promised to marry her (V). She is, of course, an heiress.

There are 17 equally disinterested women. Belinda of Vanbrugh's *Provoked Wife* (1697) would rather have "the man I love and a middle state" than "twice [Lady Brute's] splendour" (V). Mistress Pleasant of Killigrew's *Parson's Wedding* (1662) will happily marry a man of "wit and honor . . . though he has nothing but a sword at his side" (I). Leonora of *Sir Courtly Nice* will not have a big estate if it is "encumbered 'with' a fop" (I). "'Tis not profit but honor I respect," says Lucia of Shadwell's *Epsom Wells* (1672), rejecting a wealthy booby (II). And Christina of *Love in a Wood* will marry Valentine without a penny (II). These pronouncements show how much more important the character of a proposed husband is to the typical heroine of Restoration comedy than the size of his estate. There are even 3 plays in which whores would rather be loved than paid.[18]

The plays give very few examples of gentlewomen marrying for money, as Mrs. Frail tried to do in *Love for Love*, but there are several examples of women who have, much to their regret, done so before the play begins. Mrs. Brittle of Betterton's popular *Amorous Widow* (1670) is ripe for adultery because her high-born parents sacrificed her to a citizen to recoup the family fortune. And Lady Brute of *The Provoked Wife* is unhappy to find herself in a similar state because her own "ambition" led her to marry the wealthy Sir John (I). Lady Dunce of Otway's *Soldiers' Fortune* regrets in heroic couplets her marriage to Sir Davy:

> Curst be the memory, nay double curst,
> Of her that wedded age for interest first;
> Though worn with years, with fruitless wishes full,
> 'Tis all day troublesome and all night dull.
>
> (I)

There are 5 other unhappy wives of brutes and dunces, whose wit, manners, and beauty eminently qualify them for better fates, who do

---

[18] 2nd Constantia in *Chances* (Villers); Corina in *Revenge* (Betterton? Behn?); Angelica in *Rover* (Behn).

not reveal their motives for marrying, but one supposes that parental authority or their own ambition has put them in situations where adultery seems less a crime than the marriage already committed.

There are about 260 eligible protagonists of both sexes in the plays. Only 63 of these, those just surveyed, indicate anything about their financial expectations. I have no information about how many of the 260 eligible individuals actually marry by the end of the play. Most of them do. But 183 in this eligible group give definite indications that they are in love with their partners. Of the rest, except for the few pure fortune hunters noted, there is no certain evidence. So, although we can say for certain that only 47 (18 percent) *do not* marry for money, we can say on the other hand that almost everyone else *does* marry for love. Insofar as there is evidence, then, it indicates that Restoration comedy approves of marrying for money only in cases of dire necessity.

In their extravagance, Restoration comic heroes show a truly admirable contempt for money. As Cicero said, "There is nothing more honourable and noble than to be indifferent to money" (*De Officiis*, I, 68). But expenditure in Restoration comedy does not usually produce the noble "magnificence" praised by the ancients. The money often goes for mere dissipation. Archer and Aimwell of *The Beaux' Stratagem* provide a good discussion of the philosophy of spending as we know it in the comedies, just after having run through 10,000 pounds. Aimwell is not a bit dismayed: "We have lived justly, Archer; we can't say that we have spent our fortunes, but that we have enjoyed 'em." "Right," says Archer, "so much pleasure for so much money; we have had our pennyworths, and had I millions, I would go to the same market again." There follows a dissertation on the inhumanity of "murdering" one's fortune by "sacrificing all to one appetite," from which it follows that reason must always be in command of the five senses.

> Give me a man that keeps his five senses keen and bright as his sword; that has 'em always drawn out in their just order and strength, with his reason as commander at the head of 'em; that detaches 'em by turns upon whatever party of pleasure agreeably offers, and commands 'em to retreat upon the least appearance of disadvantage or danger! For my part, I can stick to my bottle while my wine, my company, and my reason, holds good; I can be charmed with Sappho's sing-

ing without falling in love with her face; I love hunting, but would not, like Actaeon, be eaten up by my own dogs; I love a fine house, but let another keep it; and just so I love a fine woman.

Various follies that allow a ruling passion to get the upper hand are discussed, and the friends agree that "keeping" is the least unpleasant one. But, "to pass to the other extremity," says Aimwell, "of all keepers I think those the worst that keep their money" (I). Farquhar, perhaps because he writes in the period affected by Collier's *Short View of the Immorality and Profaneness of the English Stage*, usually does better at explaining, justifying, or excusing the behavior of his heroes than most of his predecessors.

And the explanation is just what we would expect it to be. Archer and Aimwell's philosophy is consistent with the traditional complacency about sensuality in young men as we find it in Aristotle and Castiglione;[19] the sensuality is controlled by a temperance reminiscent of Cicero; preference for keepers of women over keepers of money is similar to Granville's preference for Gratiano's mistress over Shylock's in his *Jew of Venice*; Shylock's mistress was money, and Gratiano's, like Archer's, was "the sex in general" (*Jew of Venice*, II, ii, 23).

Whatever we may think of what they do with their money, Archer and Aimwell at least attach no value to it. They might almost have read the following item from one of the collections of edifying quotations so often printed during the period. "'Tis the infatuation of misers to take gold and silver for things really good, whereas they are only some of the means by which good things are procured."[20]

The money of comic heroes most often flows into two channels to which Farquhar has perspicuously given prominence in the title of a play: *Love and a Bottle*. Although love is the principal concern of the comedies, one gathers that every gallant has a base for amorous operations in a circle of close friends who spend their evenings in witty and winey conversation. To the end that he may always be a good companion, Rains of Shadwell's *Epsom Wells* (1672) will not "hoard" his health "like nurses" but will "lay it out" for his friends on drinking

---

[19] Aristotle, *Ethics*, VIII, iii, 5; Castiglione, *Courtier*, p. 312.
[20] Abel Boyer, *Characters of the Virtues and Vices of the Age* (London, 1695), p. 12.

(I). A good deal of amiable banter is aimed by friends at lovers for being either too often absent from or, if present, useless to their friends. "A good friend," concludes Wycherley's Horner, "cannot love money or women" (*Country Wife*, I). Certainly the young gentlemen of the comedies found it easier to satisfy the first requirement than the second.

Although friendship is relatively undeveloped as a theme, its presence is generally assumed, and occasionally one finds concrete examples of Cicero's teaching, "Friends have all things in common." It is as simple as that for Young Worthy of *Love's Last Shift*, who as a younger brother can ill afford the instant liberality that his friend's need requires of him. Rejecting the friend's offer of security and echoing Shakespeare's "royal merchant," he snaps, "Oh, sir, your necessity is obligation enough—there [the money] is, and all I have, faith; when I see you at night, you may command me further" (I). This sort of classical communism occurs in 9 plays. We might have more examples of it if playwrights had had more space left over from amorous intrigues in which to discuss friendship. They might also have felt that it was too serious a subject for comedy and that heroic drama was its rightful place. Or they might have assumed that once they had labeled a protagonist "man of honor" or "young gentleman of the town," they had already implied "true friend."

More is said about liberality toward one's beloved. Improving on the advice of Ovid, a character in Steele's *Lying Lover* tells us that "the art of love is the art of giving" (I). Wycherley strikes closer to the central conflict in the plays when a character in *Love in a Wood*, noticing Alderman Gripe's stinginess with a girl he wishes to seduce, observes that " 'tis . . . impossible for a man to love and be a miser" (III). Such remarks help to confirm one's impression that the numerous but casual acts of liberality in love affairs are to be scored as points for the protagonists in their contest with their mercenary opponents.

First of all, the lover must spend unstintingly to secure a friend within the fortress, ideally the lady's maid. For the maid is the "wicket" to her "mistress's gate," the "sluice to her lady's secrets" (*Old Bachelor*, III, V). The following episode from Dryden's *Marriage à la Mode* (1672) illustrates the way in which this wicket and sluice are commonly opened. Philotis, the maid, wants Palamede, the gallant, to know how effective a fifth column she has been:

PHILOTIS. I took occasion to commend your good qualities; as the sweetness of your humor, the comeliness of your person, your good mien, your valor; but above all, your liberality.

PALAMEDE. I vow to gad I had like to have forgot that good quality in myself, if thou hadst not remembered me of it: here are five pieces for thee.

PHILOTIS. Lord, you have the softest hand, sir, it would do a woman good to touch it: Count Rhodophil's is not half so soft; for I remember I felt it once, when he gave me ten pieces for my new-year's gift.

PALAMEDE. O, I understand you madam; you shall find my hand as soft again as Count Rhodophil's: there are twenty pieces for you. The former was but a retaining fee; now I hope you'll plead for me.

PHILOTIS. Your own merits speak enough.

(V)

Some turnstiles do not swing so easily. To gain access to Elvira in *The Spanish Friar*, Lorenzo pays 100 pounds to her priest (II). Finer women call for even more expensive stratagems. So Mirabell prepares the way to Millamant by marrying his man to her aunt's maid and promising them a fully stocked farm if all goes well (*Way of World*, II). Sometimes, however, the Liberality of protagonists shows in very small ways. The wealthy citizen's wife, Mrs. Day, alighting from a coach to begin *The Committee*, tips the coachman a groat "of more than ordinary thinness." A moment later one of the destitute Cavalier heroes gives a strange beggarly servant sixpence just because he likes his looks (I).

Because fine women are not mercenary, gallants infrequently give money to their mistresses directly, though other kinds of sacrifice are acceptable. Jacinta of Dryden's *An Evening's Love* (1668), however, agreeing with her confidante that "the two great virtues of a lover are constancy and liberality" (II), demands jestingly that Wildblood back up his claim to her affections by handing over his money. He instantly promises her 300 pistoles, all the money he has, but unfortunately he gambles it away before he can deliver it. At any rate, he does not keep the money. One can show how much one values a mistress, nevertheless, without putting the money directly into her hands. Ramble of

Crowne's *Country Wit* (1676) can offer to pay a large forfeit to Sir Mannerly Shallow so that Christina can break her contract to marry that fop (V). Clerimont of Cibber's *Double Gallant* (1707) would be happy to pay Clarinda's father 500 pounds for permission to marry her (V). Sir George Airy of *The Busy Body* (1709) pays Sir Francis Gripe 100 guineas just to talk to his daughter for ten minutes (I, II).

Ladies in love are not less liberal than the men. The penniless Loveby of Dryden's *Wild Gallant* (1663) was persuaded that he owed several large windfalls to the Devil, but his mistress was his secret benefactor. Lady Dunce of *The Soldiers' Fortune* was openly bountiful to her poor lover. Elvira of *The Spanish Friar* stole her husband's treasure for her Lorenzo (just as Shylock's daughter did for another Lorenzo), and Sir Frederick Frolic's jolly Widow Rich bailed him out of gaol in *Love in a Tub*, though it turned out that he was not really there. Pound for pound, however, no woman's generosity exceeded that of Constance in *The Twin Rivals* who was ready to give her gallant 5,000 pounds (III); but that play verges on the heroic in too many respects.

"Our gentry, how sneaking so ever they are to their creditors are most generous to [the whoring] faculty," says Mrs. Jiltup of *The Fair Quaker of Deal* (1710, III), herself a member of that body. The state of affairs she describes in this rather late play is nevertheless almost exactly what we find in Restoration comedy. For example, the scene that introduces Dorimant in *The Man of Mode* shows him first tricking a tradeswoman out of the payment he has promised her for information, and then casually giving a cast-off wench the "guinea to see the opries" she asks for, enough "to spark it in a box and do honor to her profession" (I). Few characters are eager to pay their debts to tradesmen. Whores, however, are better treated in the comedies than other characters with something to sell, perhaps because they have no possible associations with Puritanism or perhaps because they are sometimes partly motivated by something like love—"kindness," it is called.

Several playwrights, at any rate, find it necessary to provide even more permanently than Etherege does for the by-products of the hero's unrestrained youth before they can allow him to settle down to a wife and children. The writer of *The Revenge* (1680), for example, took pains to have his hero arrange for the future well-being of his whore, whom he had once "loved . . . dearly" (I, V). She had not been rescued this way in the original version of the play, Marston's *Dutch Courtesan*. The young man's charitable deed prompts the remark, "Sir, you have left her like a man of honor" (V), suggesting that being generous to cast mistresses was one of the things expected of all members of that class. Shadwell's Belfond Junior, the most virtuous libertine in Restoration comedy, leaves both his sweet whore and his bitter one with independent incomes at the end of *The Squire of Alsatia*. But the supreme act of generosity belongs to Silvia of *The Recruiting Officer*, who shows what a *woman* of honor is made of when she takes care of her own gallant's bastard by another woman while he is away at the wars (I). Similar gestures repair the damages of love in 10 other plays.

In *The Wife's Relief* (1711) a city merchant proposes to pay a young man to act the coward in a quarrel in order that his son may appear brave. "You are a gentleman," he begins. "Then you cannot think me mercenary," returns the young man (I). Actually, there are some mercenary gentlemen in Restoration comedy. But these are, as we have noted, the blocking characters—the rivals and the stingy parents. Mercenary gentlemen and gentlewomen, except for a few otherwise generous young men in search of rich wives, are condemned along with tradesmen (84 of 96). Characters approved by the dramatists (89 percent gentry) are overwhelmingly liberal in the various ways I have described (304 of 320).

These statistical measurements and random citations show us that Liberality would probably have had a certain collective impact on Restoration audiences, but they do not show us how the concept might be woven into the texture of a play as a literary theme. Extensive survey must be verified by intensive inspection of an individual sample, and this should be done for each virtue of Generosity considered. For intensive inspection I have chosen Congreve's *Love for Love* and with it I propose to illustrate how one play was affected by the ethical principles I have adumbrated. It would be possible to illustrate each virtue by a different play, but the survey I have been making proves that the ideas are widespread. Perhaps it would be a more convincing proof of Generosity's existence to show how all its features can be integrated in a single play than to appear to search for them in divers locations. *Love for Love* is, furthermore, as good a test case as any Restoration comedy;

it has as bad a reputation for immorality as any, containing two seductions and even a couple caught in the act. It is neither an early nor a late Restoration comedy but in between. It was Congreve's most popular play and 1 of the 3 most popular of the 83 plays in this sample. It was written before Collier's influence can possibly have reformed it; it was violently attacked by Collier. If I can show a strong ethical component in this play, then it will strengthen my thesis while illustrating it.

Let us suppose that Congreve constructed *Love for Love* in the same way as he did *The Double Dealer*, in the dedication of which he tells us, "I designed the moral first and to that moral I invented the fable." To what moral did he invent *Love for Love?* Modern critics have laughed at Congreve for contending that even if he and his fellow playwrights "had occasionally overstepped the bounds of propriety, the indiscretion was atoned for by the salutary moral inculcated in the conclusion." The editor of *Twelve Famous Plays of the Restoration and Eighteenth Century* hoots this statement down: "His antagonist [Collier] needed only to remind him of (what he had apparently forgotten) the morals enforced in the final lines of *The Old Bachelor* and *Love for Love!*"[21] The ambiguity of the final lines of *The Old Bachelor* may indeed confuse those who expect morality always to sound like the Ten Commandments, but it must be a very prejudiced reader who can miss the salutary element of the moral that concludes *Love for Love*: "The miracle today is that we find / A lover true, not that a woman's kind." Thou shalt be true. I postpone discussion of this moral until the chapter on Plain-dealing. But the play actually has three morals—or one moral expressed three ways. The second is the title, which I shall consider in the chapter on Love. The third moral, addressed by Angelica to Valentine's father Sir Sampson, shortly before the end of the play, is directly concerned with Liberality: "Learn to be a good father, or you'll never get a second wife." The fable that Congreve invented to this moral makes Sir Sampson fail both as father and as potential husband because he is motivated almost entirely by desire for profit.[22] Since Sir Sampson's stinginess generates all the play's action, it provides an

---

21 *Twelve Famous Plays of the Restoration and Eighteenth Century*, ed. Cecil A. Moore (New York, 1933), p. xv.

22 "The punishment of an unnatural and hard-hearted parent is the moral aim of the poet; and in this he has by a judicious conduct of his plot, fully succeeded" (Thomas Davies, *Dramatic Miscellanies*, London, 1784, III:325).

excellent background for a contrasting display of Liberality by his opponents.

When the play opens, Valentine is deeply in love with Angelica, deeply in debt, and out of favor with his father for living too expensively. Sir Sampson initiates the action by offering his son 4,000 pounds with which to pay his debts in return for his signature on a *bond* in which he obliges himself to sign a *deed of conveyance* of his birthright to his younger brother Ben. By this act Valentine will sell an estate worth possibly 5,000 pounds a year for the flat sum of 4,000 pounds. This is good business for Sir Sampson, though hardly a decent way to discipline a son, even assuming that the son needs discipline. But Valentine needs funds to court Angelica. He signs the bond. With this document in his pocket Sir Sampson can sell his less worldly and presumably more tractable sea-bred son Ben for a husband to one Foresight, owner of a marriageable property bred in the country, his daughter Prue. Although Congreve does not spell it out, we must suppose a marriage arrangement that is very lucrative to both parents in order to account for their excessive eagerness to see Ben and Prue wedded and bedded. Perhaps it works this way: if Valentine retains his inheritance and marries Foresight's niece Angelica, who has her fortune in her own hands, Foresight realizes no profit and loses control of his ward's fortune. But if the inheritance goes to someone who can be married to Prue, whose person and inheritance he controls as parent, Foresight can perhaps expect some sort of payoff for accepting a contract advantageous to Sir Sampson. Sir Sampson, on his part, may get a more favorable contract from Foresight than he ever could from Angelica. Furthermore, if Ben misbehaves, there is a clause unknown to Foresight in the deed of conveyance which enables Sir Sampson to engender a new heir by a new marriage who will displace Ben.

After receiving the 4,000 pounds which allows him to "rival the fops" in a contest for Angelica, Valentine's only possible strategy is to delay signing the conveyance in the faint hope that future events will work to his advantage. At this point, the situation that Sir Sampson has created, which already involves Valentine, Foresight, Ben, Prue, and Angelica, draws in all the other characters. Scandal functions mainly as a chorus to focus attention on the main point: will a girl with a fortune in her own hands marry a penniless wit for love? Scandal thinks not. Valentine has greater faith in her generosity. Mrs. Frail, sister of Foresight's young second wife, must marry because she "has no great stock either of fortune or reputation." Thanks to Sir Sampson's stinginess, Ben may soon be rich. The sisters set their nets to catch Ben, who, they believe, is too stupid to see through their devices. They encourage Tattle, a foppish follower of Valentine and Scandal, to seduce Prue away, and Mrs. Frail sets out to ensnare Ben. Valentine's fortune has now become the football whose position on the field determines the actions of every player.

The plotting sisters succeed. Prue, in love with sweet-smelling Tattle, spurns the "stinking tar-barrel" Ben, who bounces right into the waiting arms of Mrs. Frail, not fastidious where money is concerned. But suddenly Valentine pulls a trick out of his bag: he is mad; he is *non compos mentis*; he cannot sign the conveyance; he has the ball again. Everybody regroups for a new attack. Mrs. Frail "discharges" Ben, much to his surprise if not to ours, and begins a new campaign to capture Valentine, who she now believes is a helpless, but rich, madman. Sir Sampson falls back on his last resource, to marry and get a new heir.

But the greed of these antagonistic characters readies them for a trap. Valentine and Scandal, with the help of loyal Jeremy, have little difficulty in arranging that Mrs. Frail and Tattle shall devour one another. Mrs. Foresight bribes Jeremy to deliver the "mad" Valentine as bridegroom to Mrs. Frail, who will pose as Angelica. Tattle for his part is ambitious to marry rich Angelica. The protagonists merely deliver Tattle posing as Valentine to Mrs. Frail posing as Angelica. The crocodile closes its eyes when it opens its mouth, to elaborate Wycherley's metaphor, and thus the wits foil the cheats.

Congreve arranges the plot so that avarice, in the form of Sir Sampson, shall be vanquished by Liberality, in the form of his son. Offended because Valentine has feigned madness to her also in hopes of tricking her into a confession of love, Angelica takes matters into her own hands. She offers herself to Sir Sampson as the new wife by whom he can disinherit both sons—but only if her solicitors may inspect the deed of conveyance and Valentine's bond, to be sure that all is as he says. Flattered out of his wits by this offer, eager for revenge, and anxious to get his hands on Angelica's fortune, Sir Sampson happily hands over the trump card, Valentine's bond. Hearing of the marriage plans, Valentine, now ashamed of his fraudulent dealings with Angelica, offers to sign the deed of conveyance for her sake as his father's spouse. This was the "generous Valentine" that Angelica had been all the while hoping to uncover. She tears up the bond, she gives herself to Valentine, the mighty fall, the cynic is contradicted, and the meek inherit the earth.

Besides writing a plot that turns on Liberality, Congreve shows his hand in scores of other ways. For instance, there are in the first act the juxtaposed visits of "the nurse with one of [Valentine's] children from Twitnam" and the scrivener Trapland. Certainly as duns they help to emphasize Valentine's financial crisis. But they also objectify the conflict of values Congreve is concerned with. Just as in *The Man of Mode*, the hero stalls the tradesman while he instantly if not graciously recognizes the claims of an obsolete amorous liaison. The scene with Trapland illustrates the pleasure-business dialectic of the comedies described earlier. "Love and pleasurable expense," "coaches," "liveries," "treats," "balls," have consumed Valentine's fortune. It is thus fitting that he be dunned by someone who is all business. Valentine and Scandal try to tempt Trapland with pleasures—wine and prurient talk. But Trapland, though susceptible, manages to resist their overtures by reminding himself of his ideological position: "This is not our business. . . . We'd better mind our business. . . . Business must be done. . . . My business requires" (I). The same pleasure-business antithesis marks Angelica's entrance. Foresight, who has been studying omens relating to the marriage contract with Sir Sampson, arrives at the conclusion, " 'Tis now three o'clock, a very good hour for business." This is Angelica's cue to enter and say, "Is it not a good hour for pleasure, too, uncle? Pray lend me your coach, mine's out of order" (II). By borrowing a coach she, too, goes into debt for pleasure. Foresight, however, is so stingy that he has to be blackmailed into lending the coach. Thus the business-pleasure theme links the world of Trapland to the world of Sir Sampson and Foresight.

The connection of the antagonistic characters to the Whig or Puritan ideology is not overtly made in *Love for Love*, but to judge from some hints on the surface, it is assumed underneath. Both Sir Sampson and Foresight are worried about the dangers of popery (II, III), which may be a sign of Whiggery. In his mad scene Valentine, posing as Truth, describes the City as a place where "you will see such zealous faces behind counters, as if religion were to be sold in every shop" (IV). Trapland's piety was not emphasized in the dunning scene, but he did disapprove of wine and women in the name of business, and Valentine did remind him that he delighted "in doing good."

Congreve misses few opportunities of pointing out what motivates the acquisitive characters. In Act II Valentine asks for his father's blessing. Sir Sampson says, "You've had it already; sir, I think I sent it to you this morning in a bill of four thousand pound." Valentine pleads for leniency. His father shouts, "Why sirrah, mayn't I do what I please? Are you not my slave?" (II). Jeremy works his sleight of hand on Tattle by getting him to concentrate on Angelica's "thirty thousand pound" (V); indeed the exact figure is nowhere else mentioned. When Tattle and Mrs. Frail appear married to each other, it seems to Ben as though "a couple of privateers were looking for a prize, and should fall foul of one another" (V). Scandal warns Foresight, "Let not the prospect of worldly lucre carry you beyond your judgment" (III). Sir Sampson is accompanied by a lawyer "with an itching palm" (IV).

Against this background, Valentine, Angelica, Scandal, Ben,[23] and Jeremy represent Liberality. Valentine's allies, though they oppose his altruism, contradict themselves by their loyalty to him. It is a cliché of Restoration comedy that the impoverished gentleman is deserted by his "friends." But Valentine's man Jeremy will "die with [him] or starve with [him] or be damned with [his] works," as long as he does not turn poet (I). And Scandal clearly has Valentine's interest at heart in every action he takes. Ben has no special allegiances, but coming in off the sea, he is merely untainted by the vices of the Town or City. He does not care whether Sir Sampson marries to disinherit him or not, and when Mrs. Frail shows her true colors he tells her he would not marry her if she had her "weight in gold and jewels" (IV).

In this play Congreve understands Liberality almost in terms of the central Christian paradox that loss is gain, or in terms of the epigram in *The Merchant of Venice*, "They lose [the world] that do buy it with

---

[23] Davies read the play this way: "Ben is not a humorist" (that is, an object of satire); "Scandal is introduced as a second Manly, to satirize the vices of the age" (*ibid.*, p. 326).

much care" (I, i, 75). On the first page Valentine tells Jeremy that the wise Epictetus is "a very rich man, not worth a groat." To Scandal's mind, Valentine is a "thoughtless adventurer, / Who hopes to purchase wealth, by selling land / Or win a mistress, with a losing hand" (I). Valentine does at first try to win Angelica by "taking thought," that is, trying to convince her that her coldness has caused his madness. When she detects the trick, he tries to lie his way out by emphasizing the material advantages of his deception:

> My seeming madness has deceived my father and pro-
> cured me time to think of means to reconcile me to him and
> preserve the right of my inheritance to his estate, which
> otherwise by articles I must this morning have resigned.
> And this I had informed you of today, but you were gone
> before I knew you had been here.
>
> ANGELICA.   How! I thought your love of me had caused this
> transport in your soul which, it seems, you only counter-
> feited for mercenary ends and sordid interest.
>
> VALENTINE.   Nay, now you do me wrong, for if any interest
> was considered it was yours, since I thought I wanted more
> than love to make me worthy of you.
>
> ANGELICA.   Then you thought me mercenary.
>
> (IV)

His attempts to retrieve the situation have made it worse. In the final moments of the play Valentine performs an act of contrition for underestimating his mistress so badly. When he complains that she has deserted him for his father, she answers him like the Voice from the whirlwind:

> 'Tis true you have a great while pretended to love me;
> nay, what if you were sincere? Still you must pardon me
> if I think my own inclinations have a better right to dispose
> of my person, than yours.
>
> SIR SAMPSON.   Are you answered now, sir?
>
> VALENTINE.   Yes, sir.
>
> SIR SAMPSON.   Where's your plot, sir, and your contrivance
> now, sir? Will you sign, sir? Come, will you sign and seal?
>
> VALENTINE.   With all my heart, sir.

SCANDAL.   'Sdeath, you are not mad indeed, to ruin yourself?
VALENTINE.   I have been disappointed of my only hope, and
he that loses hope may part with anything. I never valued
fortune but as it was subservient to my pleasure, and my
only pleasure was to please this lady. I have made many
vain attempts, and find at last that nothing but my ruin can
effect it. Which for that reason I will sign to—Give me the
paper.
ANGELICA. [*aside*]   Generous Valentine!

After saving the day, Angelica reinforces the theme of Generosity:
"Had I the world to give you, it could not make me worthy of so
generous and faithful a passion." For even further emphasis *her* generosity converts Scandal: "I was an infidel to your sex, but you have
converted me."

Valentine cannot have planned this outcome because he does not
know that Angelica has the trump card, his bond. It is she that has saved
him, not he himself. She plays Providence[24] to his improvidence and is
rightly named Angelica.

[24] In a fascinating article Aubrey Williams has arrived by a different route at a
similar reading of this play's denouement. Noting that Restoration critics charac-
teristically thought of poetic justice as if it were Providence, he looked for signs of
God's hand in the plays of Congreve. He found the evidence of it undeniable, though
surprising in the light of Congreve's reputation for immorality ("Poetical Justice, the
Contrivances of Providence, and the Works of William Congreve," *English Literary
History,* XXXV (1968):540–65).

CHAPTER FOUR

Courage vs. Cowardice

In Wycherley's *Love in a Wood* another type of divine Angelica, this time named Christina, gives the character *generous* to another type of Valentine, oddly enough also named Valentine (IV). These interesting parallels probably do not indicate that Congreve's *Love for Love* was influenced by *Love in a Wood*—more probably there are enough Valentines, divine heroines, and generous heroes in Restoration comedy to assure that a coincidence of the three will occur at least once by chance—but they do serve well to point out another context of the word *generous*. For where Congreve's Valentine had risked his estate for a divine creature, Wycherley's had risked his life. The only testimony of generosity that Christina's Valentine has given us at this point is his returning to see his mistress after having been banished on pain of death for killing a man in a duel over her. Certainly Generosity in the highest sense implies a willingness to part with life as well as money if the occasion demands it. Therefore one of its components in Restoration comedy must be Courage.

Except in romantic plays, like Mrs. Behn's *Rover*, which abound in flamboyant deeds of derring-do in faraway places, the courage of protagonists is not thrust upon us, and only by observing attitudes to danger in a fairly large aggregate of plays can we sensitize ourselves enough to notice signs of it in the more familiar realistic "comedies of manners." In the standard plays love-making, foppery, and intrigue are much more in evidence than sword fights. The reasons for the obscurity of the signs of physical courage in comic characters are several.

First, and most obviously, a comedy cannot treat situations requiring a great amount of courage without being in danger of becoming a tragedy. Tragedy is the best place to deal with Courage as a virtue; and, as we know, Restoration tragedy built it up to unbelievable heights. Second, of course, is the fact that audiences knew that a fine gentleman was brave, just as they knew that an alderman was avaricious; it was useless to belabor the point. Many plots were stolen or created out of a regard for comic situations. When situation is uppermost, the writer does not have to characterize extensively, so long as he makes sure that each character behaves according to the accepted conventions for his type. If the plot does not call for Courage, the playwright will not show it. Third, a virtue may have such importance in a society as to take on the character of a taboo. Comedy, which attempts to observe the real world, must also observe the taboos of that world in its characters. La Bruyère, whose comments not surprisingly often help to explain the world of Restoration comedy, maintained that not only Courage but Liberality as well had the standing of taboos in seventeenth-century French society. "Il est vrai qu'il y a deux vertues que les hommes admirent, la bravoure et la liberalité; parce qu'il ya deux choses qu'ils estiment beaucoup, et que ces vertues sont negliger: la vie et l'argent. Aussi personne n'avance de soi qu'il est brave ou liberal."[1] In England Richard Flecknoe had noted much the same phenomenon some years earlier in *Sixty-nine Enigmatical Characters*. The "Valiant Man," he said, "has but one defect; he cannot talk much, to recompense which he does the more."[2]

The Provoked Wife provides a good instance of this reticence about Courage. Constant is no saber-rattling *miles gloriosus*. That is more the forte of his rival, the drinking, roaring, whoring Sir John Brute. Sir John's courage, however, is purely alcoholic, and it consists mainly of bullying innocent passersby in the streets or fighting the watch when he and his cronies outnumber it. Of Constant's courage we have no overt proof until the last act, when Sir John suggests that Constant has been tampering with his wife. Constant's answer is a simple denial and the quiet statement, "I wear a sword, sir." It would be easy for a mod-

---

[1] Jean de La Bruyère, *Les caractères de Theophraste . . . avec les caractères ou les moeurs de ce siècle* (Paris, 1700), II:90.

[2] Richard Flecknoe, *Sixty-nine Enigmatical Characters* (London, 1665), pp. 70–71.

ern audience to miss the fact that a challenge has been delivered, that unless Sir John can kill Constant in a duel, his wife is honest. Sir John of course decides to accept Constant's wearing of a sword as evidence of his wife's chastity and forget that he wears one, too. This scene does more than merely discomfort Sir John: it vindicates not only Constant's quest for the favors of Lady Brute but also her inclinations to grant them. She is married to something less than a gentleman—to a Brute, in fact.

Restoration comedy comes to us through a period in which Cavalier virtues declined and Puritan virtues became pre-eminent. Although we are today a notably emancipated people, our habit is to relate morality to sex and to accept the reputations of literary works as they are handed down to us. Hence, unless we can at least imagine a world in which the code of honor was more important than the code of chastity, we are in danger of reading these plays very much the way Macaulay did, even though we lack his Puritanical indignation. This is not to say that chastity is unimportant in Restoration comedy—we give so much weight to what is said that we may overlook what is done—but merely to say that it is less important than the kind of honor that goes with wearing a sword. This is not the place to argue the wisdom of such a morality. A world in which differences of opinion on important questions are settled by force must have great drawbacks. The alternative to private force is public law. But the law, as Augustan satirists never tired of pointing out, has its drawbacks, too. It is the weapon of the Shylocks, the Old Testament weapon, as well as the Calvinist, Protestant, and capitalist weapon.

It is perhaps for this reason that what we see when we look closely at Restoration comedy is the continual opposition of the sword to the law—not the lawless sword to the lawful law but the just sword to the unjust law, or the sword preferred to the law as an instrument of justice. This is exactly what it comes down to in Crowne's *City Politiques* (1683), the most overt piece of political propaganda in the 83 plays. Although the play takes place in Italy, the Podesta or leader of the City is commonly identified as Shaftesbury.[3] Crowne equips him

---

[3] This is the assumption of the editors of Crowne's *Dramatic Works* (Edinburgh, 1873). Professor John Harold Wilson (introduction to Regents edition) suggests that

with an adviser who continually recommends law as the surest means of defeating his adversary, the Viceroy (King Charles), and with an old crafty cheating lawyer named Bartoline, the type of parasite on the legal machinery with whom we are all well acquainted from the writings of Swift. He can exact exorbitant fees because he alone presides over the mysteries of the law; he understands them so well that he can cause any case to win or lose; and so he accepts fees from both sides and awards justice to him who pays the most. Two young gentlemen of the Town whom Crowne has made more dissolute than usual, perhaps to make his moral more abundantly clear, take it upon themselves to cuckold the lawyer and the Lord Mayor, whose wives have more wit and beauty than the old men are capable of appreciating. Cuckolding was then the most serious weapon that a comic writer could use, though, as always, the heroes wear swords, a silent reminder of more final forms of retribution. Once, indeed, Crowne allows himself to brandish the sword at the Whigs, if not to use it. Near the end of the play one of the town gentlemen protests that it is "better [to be] ruled by the swords of gallant men than the mercenary tongues of such rascals as you are." The speech is addressed to the lawyer.

The town gentleman's remark falls directly into the main stream of seventeenth-century history, if we read it according to G. M. Trevelyan, as an alliance of "the squires . . . the merchants and the common lawyers . . . striking down the royal powers."[4] Restoration comedy does not attack the politics of squires, but *City Politiques* attacks the merchants, represented by the Podesta, and the common lawyers, represented by Bartoline. Because history takes the side of the winners, the achievements of the great lawyers of this period have come to be venerated. Restoration comedy, committed to the side that history has left behind, took an entirely different view of the events of the century. It was a time when "the swords of gallant men" fought for survival against the "mercenary tongues" of the common law.

Although this conflict between the law and the sword is omnipresent in Restoration comedy, lawyers themselves are not often subject to

the Podesta is a composite of actual Lord Mayors. My interpretation requires only that he represent city attitudes and aspirations, which he does in either case.

[4] G. M. Trevelyan, *History of England* (Garden City, N.Y., 1953), II:146.

such extensive attacks as in *City Politiques*. Like Sir Sampson's Buckram in *Love for Love*, they only trail along behind major characters to supply the papers on which so many plots depend. At any rate, 13 men of law have some part in 13 plays, and most of them are held up to contempt. There are two exceptions. Lovewell, the second hero of *Love and a Bottle*, is a wealthy gentleman studying law at an Inn of Court, but he is far from enthusiastic about it. And although Pounce in Steele's *Tender Husband* gaily takes fees from both sides—one side being credulous enough to believe "he must have cheated t'other side for I'm sure he's honest" (V)—he helps the protagonists, and Steele rewards him with a rich husband for his sister. Though Dennis tried to explain it to him, Steele always underestimated Restoration comedy, with the result that when he tried to imitate it as in this play, he rewarded vicious characters, and when he tried to reform it as in *The Lying Lover*, he corrected faults it did not have. Not until *The Conscious Lovers* did Steele truly understand Restoration comedy. He demonstrated his grasp by striking at the heart of it. The whole play was written, he said, "for the sake of the scene of the fourth act, wherein Mr. Bevil [the hero] *evades* the quarrel [duel] with his friend" (my italics, preface).

The antipathy to law with which Restoration comedy appears to have been endowed by its Cavalier ancestors is more often expressed in attacks on the Shylocks who rely on law for safety or gain than on those who practice it. In the plays law takes on the qualities of a tool for securing personal goals, whether good or evil, rather than serving as a standard by which the good or evil of a goal may be decided. As such it has no more moral meaning than a sword has, and like a sword its virtue depends entirely on the virtue of the man who wields it. Though this law-sword parallel is implicit in plays from 1660 onward, it is explicitly stated in Christopher Bullock's *A Woman Is a Riddle* (1716). The time had perhaps come when such things needed to be said because they were no longer generally understood. In Bullock's play a city usurer named Vulture boasts to his mistress that he never fights with the sword. But, says he, "I can fight you out all my weapons at law as clean as any man."

> WIDOW. What do you mean by your weapons at law?
> VULTURE. There be several: as your writ of delay, that is

your long-sword; *scandalum magnatum* is back-sword; *capeas et quominus*, case of rapiers; a writ of execution, sword and dagger; a good conscience, sword and buckler, but that is a weapon we seldom nowadays make use of in Westminster Hall; indeed it is quite out of date. [With these weapons] I took Sterling Castle once.

(II)

When his rival, with a slap, challenges him to a duel, Vulture sues him for assault. The historical sensitivity of this passage is quite remarkable, particularly in the allusion to Sterling Castle, which implies a consciousness of the fact that feudalism supported by the sword has given way to capitalism supported by the law.

Whether or not the mock struggle for power played out night after night on the Restoration stage is indeed a simulacrum of the real struggle fought out in seventeenth-century history, the frequency with which antagonistic characters call for the law when protagonistic characters indicate that they wear their swords is testimony to the affirmative proposition. The pattern appears early and persists late. It is found in Wilson's *Cheats* (1662) when Tyro, an affected squire who rivals the hero for the hand of the heroine, gets into a situation where he must fight the hero or take a beating from him. He takes the beating, and in front of his mistress, too. His excuse is, "I am a man of the law." Instead of going to law, however, he goes into his pocketbook and hires bravoes to fight for him (IV). *The Committee*, as may be remembered, uses law against Cavaliers through the agency of the Committee of Sequestration referred to in the title, whose sham proceedings are ridiculed in the pompous legal jargon of their clerk, Obadiah. Possibly this play's attack on law also contributed to its great popularity.

In Shadwell's early *Epsom Wells*, where fights and challenges are recounted in such detail that it sometimes seems more like a textbook on the code of honor than a play, the principal fool, Clodpate, is asked to lend the heroes a hand in fighting off a gang of bravoes set on by their rivals. No, thank you. "I will give you law," says he righteously, ignoring the fact that it would not come in time (III). *The Way of the World* produces a slight but delightful variation on the same theme. Fainall has a legal document signed by his wife, which he refers to as an "instrument," in which she agrees to settle her estate on him. In the last act he produces this "instrument" and proposes by means of it to force everyone to do his bidding. Law is brandished and it is countered by a sword, thus reversing the usual pattern. Sir Wilful Witwoud will have none of these legal shenanigans. " 'Sheart, an you talk of an instrument, Sir, I have an old fox by my thigh shall hack your instrument of ram vellum to shreds, Sir! . . . Therefore, withdraw your instrument, Sir, or by'r Lady I shall draw mine." Congreve, perhaps realizing that it is too late in the day for such measures, fights fire with fire: Mirabell produces a legal document that predates Fainall's.

Although there is a certain poetic justice in beating villains with their own weapons, this is not the usual way of defeating a legal offensive. More commonly the protagonists counter in the old predatory feudal way by merely seizing the key document (as did Angelica in *Love for Love*) and rendering the legal spell powerless. This tactic may not be good in law, but it is good in Restoration comedy. It works, for example in such prominent plays as *The Beaux' Stratagem*, *The Committee*, and *The Plain Dealer*.

In a world governed by a code of honor a refusal to fight or any attempt to evade fighting by legal or other subterfuges is a mark of cowardice. If my historical explanation of the basic conflict in Restoration comedy is correct, one would expect to find gentlemen courageous and citizens cowardly, and with certain limitations this is what one does find. Again one discovers that somewhere in the 83 plays occurs an exact statement of what one feels to be true from observations of behavior. In *Greenwich Park* (1691) a grocer says, "I can pay those that fight and that's as much as was ever required of a citizen" (V). And in *Sir Solomon* (1669) we hear that such a one "is a landed man and will fight" (II). These generalizations, though they state the principle, do not quite fit the facts of Restoration comedy. One or two citizens will fight. A large number of gentry—chiefly blocking characters—will not. Of 41 of the 115 citizens that the plays contain, 39 are cowardly. Sassafras, a drugster in *Greenwich Park*, is one of the brave ones, but we are assured that he is exceptional when a character comments, "If thou art so hot upon fighting thou art no citizen" (III). The other, appearing in Mrs. Behn's "recantation play," [5] *The False Count*, is thereby

---

[5] So she says in the prologue of the play in which she indicates an intention of giving a more tolerant than usual view of cits, trade, and so forth.

acknowledged to be an exception. The proportion of cowards among gentlemen is somewhat higher. Of 346 gentlemen, 157 are brave, 58 are cowards, and the rest have no opportunity to show either quality. The cowardly gentlemen include 35 fops, 6 stingy parents, 2 *milites gloriosi*, 7 boobies, and 2 pinchwives—totaling 52. There are 186 exemplary gentlemen in the comedies. Of them, 126 give evidence of a willingness to risk life; none are cowards. These figures are based on overt acts of courage or of cowardice.

This analysis shows that cowardice is often a secondary vice of characters already aberrant in some other way, something added to the attributes of standard antagonistic types as a sort of *coup de grace* to any claims for our sympathy that they might have, much as it concluded what Vanbrugh had to say about Sir John Brute at the end of *The Provoked Wife*. It is an especially effective way of puncturing the facade of fops, witwouds, and roarers like Sir John, who affect a bravado that they have no right to. After all, fops are the sophisticated descendants of the ancient *miles gloriosus*. The plays contain 19 classic braggart soldiers from the various classes of society. Needless to say, they are all cowards in the end.

The emphasis in plays on the code of honor apparently had a curious effect on the lives of actors that provides some historical corroboration of these statistics. We know that actors, because they continually appeared in similar roles, became so well known for certain type characters that they could not deviate from them even if they would. When, for instance, Cibber, Doggett, and Sandford made the attempt, audiences tried to stop the plays.[6]

One rather astonishing consequence of this state of affairs, though certainly a logical one, is that in order to maintain the role of a man of honor on stage an actor apparently had to perform it off stage as well. William Mountfort died by the sword when he attempted to rescue Mrs. Bracegirdle from an abductor. When Jack Verbruggen came on stage to apologize for calling an illegitimate son of Charles II "a son of a whore," he admitted his rudeness in an ambiguous statement that was more of a challenge: "It is true and I am sorry for it." Verbruggen, we hear, would draw his sword "on the least occasion, if he thought his

---

[6] Colley Cibber, *An Apology for the Life of Mr. Colley Cibber*, ed. Robert Lowe (London, 1889), I:132–33, 179n; II:309.

wife insulted." The actor Horden was killed in a duel with a Captain Burgess. One Williams fought a duel in 1692. We hear that Powell wounded a gentleman. Powell challenged Wilks, chief actor and manager of Drury Lane, in hopes of frightening Wilks into giving him better parts. When he found out that Wilks was willing to fight, he went to another theatre. At one time Wilks had to challenge and fight "several amongst the ringleaders" of disorders at his playhouse. Ryan was tried for killing a man in his own defense. Bowen was killed by Quin when the former refused to accept the latter's allegation that Benjamin Johnson was better in one of Bowen's parts. At one time dueling was so frequent among players that the House of Lords was asked to make them stop wearing swords. Of these fighters, Mountfort, Verbruggen, Williams, Powell, Wilks, and Ryan normally played men of honor on the stage. Quin often did. Bowen did not. The only part of Horden's I know of was that of a man of honor; Cibber says Wilks replaced him. These facts would be less remarkable if any other actors had created a reputation for fighting sufficient to earn them notice for it in the sparse records of Restoration and eighteenth-century stage history. Perhaps more remarkable is the fact that the only actor who has come down to us as totally unwilling to fight is Colley Cibber, who usually played a coward on stage.[7]

If the behavior of protagonists is considered in the light of the fact that both actors and audiences wore swords and accepted the consequences of wearing them, then certain aspects of it acquire greater importance than they might otherwise have. There were of course a large number of comedies, taking place mainly in Spain or Italy, of which Mrs. Behn's *Rover* may serve as an example, which consists of one duel after another. Since some swashbuckling in faraway lands is to be expected, not much importance need be attached to the offhand courage of Mrs. Behn's dissolute hero Willmore. For contemporary audiences, however, Willmore's imperturbability in the face of cold steel may well have been the best thing about him. The Wildblood of Dryden's *An Evening's Love* and the Don John of several plays, but particularly of Buckingham's *Chances*, also display much skill in swordsmanship.

[7] *Ibid.*, I:239, 302–3; II:314, 344–45; Thomas Davies, *Dramatic Miscellanies* (London, 1784), III:335–36, 420–21, 452; Leslie Hotson, *The Commonwealth and Restoration Stage* (Cambridge, Mass., 1928), p. 305.

We should perhaps also give more weight to the fact that Manly of *The Plain Dealer* had been so fearless a naval captain as to have his ship sunk under him and to the equally honorable military records of a number of other comic heroes. Nor should we forget that when one character beats another or kicks him, as happens in so many plays, he engages at the same time to fight that man on the field of honor if he is not the kind who can accept such a beating or kicking. Cuckolding, of course, was a dangerous activity, but one even risked his life when he courted a girl on whom some other man felt he had a prior claim. This was an age in which girls of merit might say, when considering a husband, " 'Tis not profit but honor I respect" (*Epsom Wells*, II), or perhaps more bluntly, "All that I know is, the man that would not fight for me, should do nothing else for me."[8] Even friendship had its dangers, because it obliged a man to act as a second in his friend's quarrels and fight the other second if need be. Whoever kicks a man, cuckolds a husband, courts a girl, or declares a friendship in Restoration comedy, then, thus commits himself to fighting if the need arises. But by actually fighting or offering to fight, 99 protagonists in 51 plays indicate their readiness unequivocally.

It was natural that a society which valued physical courage would appreciate a certain amount of nerve in women. We usually explain the large number of "breeches" parts for women in Restoration comedy as excuses, in an age of long dresses, for actresses to show their legs. But in a context that gives such emphasis to manly virtues and attacks effeminacy in fops, a woman strutting about in breeches gives playwrights an opportunity, which they seldom miss, to suggest that some women can be better men than some men. When the heroine puts on breeches, she also wears a sword, and it is almost inevitable that her creator will invent a situation in which she will be required to use it. The comic possibilities seem to be too great to resist. At the same time the young lady always surprises us by being less timorous when challenged than her sex has conditioned us to expect, so that dramatists are severely taxed to find devices that will prevent her from being killed by her experienced opponent. The extreme example of female courage is Lucia of Southerne's *Sir Anthony Love* (1690), an English courtesan

---

[8] Mrs. Witwoud in Thomas Southerne's *The Wife's Excuse* (London, 1721), Act III.

who carries off her disguise as a typical loving and fighting male so well that she not only gets into numerous duels but wins them all (I, II). No other girl comes near her. Fidelia of *The Plain Dealer*, whose role as Manly's cabin boy at sea has required her to face all kinds of terrors, has the reputation of a cowardly male (I); but for a woman she has much more than enough physical courage, enough in fact to be able to fight in Manly's defense (V). Sylvia of *The Recruiting Officer*, who also loves a military man, has nerve enough to draw on a constable who comes to arrest her (V). Bellamira, the courtesan of Sedley's play of that name, is in breeches such a convincing swordsman as to be able to frighten the *miles gloriosus* of the play into accepting a beating (III, IV). Hippolita of Mrs. Behn's *Dutch Lover* straps on a sword and goes out to fight with the full intention of killing her man (IV). Girls in breeches face cold steel in 16 plays.

In skirts, the women could show their courage, too. One believes Aimwell's Dorinda in *The Beaux' Stratagem* when she wishes for a sword with which to help fight off the highwaymen (V); her sister-in-law, Mrs. Sullen, prevents her husband from murdering a suspected adulterer by drawing a pistol on him (III). Hippolita of *The Gentleman Dancing Master* entertains a forbidden suitor upon peril of her life. Sir Novelty Fashion's cast mistress becomes desperate enough to attack him with a sword in *Love's Last Shift* (IV). The heroic women of Howard's *Surprisal*, Durfey's *Don Quixote*, Dryden's *Spanish Friar*, and Farquhar's *Twin Rivals* make us believe that they really do prefer "death before dishonor," as one of them so aptly puts it (*Surprisal*, V).

For the writer of comedy it is perhaps easier to say what Courage is not than to say what it is. In these plays comic characters violate propriety in matters of honor in four principal ways: by submitting to a beating or other insult; by running from a fight or from real or imagined danger of another sort; by evading a fight; or by taking unfair advantage of an opponent. Beatings are a time-honored form of slapstick humor, but in the context of a code of honor they must have a special meaning. Dangerfield, the *miles gloriosus* of Sedley's *Bellamira* brags of his past military exploits and maintains, "I scorn the slow-paced revenge of law; 'tis blood I'll have." Against this background, his beating by a girl, even if she is disguised as a man, is more than just a beating (IV). The texts of several plays demonstrate that beatings are to be construed in terms of the code of honor. Sosia, a lackey in Dryden's *Amphitryon* who claims to be "a man of honor in everything but just fighting" (III), is beaten by nearly everybody. On the other hand, a fine gentleman in Wycherley's *Gentleman Dancing Master* replies—when the question arises whether he and his friends intend to fight another party—by rejecting the dishonorable alternatives: "Our company was never kicked, I think" (V).

A gentleman should not submit to verbal insult either, although it is easy to overlook the significance of verbal affronts given or taken when good friends may rail at each other with impunity. However, when Manly of *The Plain Dealer* finds his Olivia entertaining the foppish Novel and Lord Plausible, these two obviously evade their obligations to the code by interpreting his insult as raillery. Manly objects to Olivia's "esteem or civility for these things here."

> NOVEL. Things!
> LORD PLAUSIBLE. Let the captain rally a little.
> MANLY. Yes, things! Canst thou be angry, thou thing?
> NOVEL. No, since my lord says you speak in raillery; for though your sea-raillery be something rough, yet, I confess, we use one another, too, as bad every day at Locket's and never quarrel for the matter.
>
> (II)

It is not quite so clear that one function of the long scene between Mirabell, Fainall, Witwoud, and Petulant in Act I of *The Way of the World* is to show the yellow streak in the latter two. Before they enter, Mirabell tells us that Witwoud "will construe an affront into a jest," and Witwoud proves him right a few lines later. He has bemoaned the fact that his brother, who is coming to visit him, is a fool.

> MIRABELL. A fool, and your brother, Witwoud!
> WITWOUD. Ay, ay, my half-brother. My half brother he is, no nearer upon honor.
> MIRABELL. Then 'tis possible he may be but half a fool.
> WITWOUD. Good, good, Mirabell, *le drole*! Good, good!— hang him, don't let's talk of him.——Fainall, how does your lady?

A few minutes later, when Petulant says insultingly that two whores and a bawd in a coach outside are Witwoud's two cousins and his aunt, Witwoud thinks it a great joke. "Ha, ha, ha! I had a mind to see how the rogue would come off. . . . Gad I can't be angry with him, if he said they were my mother and sisters." But soon the ferocious Petulant has his comeuppance, too. This spark pretends to rival Mirabell for the favors of Millamant. When Mirabell threatens, "I shall cut your throat, sometime or other, Petulant, about that business," Petulant attempts a feeble reply in kind:

> PETULANT. Ay, ay, let that pass—There are other throats
>   to be cut—
> MIRABELL. Meaning mine, Sir?
> PETULANT. Not I—I mean nobody—

Congreve lets these hints of cowardice pass without bringing them to fruition in kickings or beatings. But cowards are beaten or kicked in 25 plays.

Taking an unfair advantage of one's opponent is another common sign of a coward. One way for nonfighters to get even is to hire people that will fight. Hiring bravoes is dishonorable not only because one evades the responsibility of fighting one's own battles, but because the bravoes always outnumber one's opponent. This practice occurs most often in plays with a foreign setting like *The Surprisal, The Feigned Courtesans*, or *Sir Anthony Love*, which fact suggests that it is an un-English practice as well. English merchants who develop a fondness for Spanish ways, like Don Diego of *The Gentleman Dancing Master* (V) or Sir Jealous Traffique of *The Busy Body* (V), have little standing armies in their own households. But so does Sir Tunbelly Clumsy of *The Relapse* (III), who is decidedly homebred. Tyro, the foppish antagonist of Wilson's *Cheats* hires "hectors" (*dramatis personae*) to do his bloodletting (IV). A hector appears to be a sort of gentleman footpad who subsists by frightening harmless nonbelligerents. The hectors of *Epsom Wells* themselves hire a gang of "bullies" when faced down by the protagonists of the play (III). Sparkish, the Witwoud of *The Country Wife*, tries not to understand that his rival Harcourt is insulting him, but when the fact is unavoidable, takes comfort in the knowledge that Pinchwife is on hand, with a mind to be an ally. "I may draw now," he says to himself, "since we have the odds of him. 'Tis a good occasion, too, before my mistress" (II). Drawing before one's mistress has the double advantage that one may not only impress the lady with one's courage but may even rely on her to prevent the fight, as Alithea does in this instance.

One could also increase the odds on one's side by attacking in the dark behind a lantern, like Vernish of *The Plain Dealer* (V), or with a pistol, like Doctor Wolf of Cibber's *Non-Juror* (V). Squire Sullen of *The Beaux' Stratagem* took advantage of the fact that his rival was an unarmed French prisoner of war (III). Marplot of *The Busy Body* was a professed coward, but nevertheless had courage enough to "bully" a helpless old man (III). Beyond this, drawing on women is so far beneath what is to be expected of a gentleman that playwrights used it often to make the final comment on a knave or a fool. When a cuckold like Pinchwife is enraged to the point of trying to murder his wife, his character is completely demolished. And when Brancadoro, the cowardly citizen of Howard's *Surprisal*, draws on a woman, a character comments, "He ne'er struck anybody in his life and now would flesh himself upon a woman," as if he could go no lower (IV). A similar censure is evoked by the cuckold Bubble when he draws on his wife in Durfey's *Fond Husband*. "No swords against women in my company," says the gentleman who rises to stop him (V).

The various ways of avoiding duels described in the plays must have been highly amusing to people who lived under the constant burden of a code of honor. One could, with Keepwell of *Bellamira*, arrange to have one's self jailed so as to be unable to keep an appointment on the field of honor (IV). If one's opponent were mercenary, one could merely pay him 1,000 pounds to forget the quarrel, which was Sir Nicholas Cully's way out in *The Comical Revenge* (III). Or if one's rivals for a mistress were too fierce, one could plot to have them kill each other, as Vizard tried to do in *The Constant Couple* (II). Once in a duel, one could still "fight retiring" like Kick and Cuff of *Epsom Wells* (II); or, like Lord Foppington in *The Relapse*, end the fight before it began by pretending to be mortally wounded at the first scratch (II). If one knew the man was a coward like one's self, as Cutter and Worm did in Cowley's *Cutter of Coleman Street*, one could stage a mock fight with him, thus satisfying the letter if not the spirit of the code (II). It was a simple matter merely to drop one's sword, as if by mistake, in the early passages of a duel, and so at least gain credit for meeting the challenge, though losing the fight. This was the device of Sir Amorous Vainwit in Bullock's *A Woman Is a Riddle* (II). Or, if one must have a reputation for courage, one could quarrel in a place where fighting was against the rules—in the presence of ladies or in the park (Captain Bluffe, *Old Bachelor*, IV). Better, one could draw in a crowd, where someone was sure to stop the fighting, though perhaps one should not be so obvious about it as Sir Timothy Shacklehead of Shadwell's *Lancashire Witches*, who draws and shouts to bystanders, "Hold me fast, or I shall kill him" (V). The same ruse worked for Sir Oliver Cockwood in Etherege's *She Would If She Could* (IV) and Squib, the bragging coward of Thomas Baker's *Tunbridge Walks* (1702, I).

Protagonists of these plays did not stoop to such evasions of the responsibilities that go with wearing a sword. They showed their contempt of danger sometimes in actual sword fighting, sometimes by facing down the Novels, Witwouds, and Sparkishes that peopled their world. But not all courage is physical. The comic hero of the Restoration shows his generosity also in a willingness to take risks, to gamble. He has a Ciceronian contempt for the vicissitudes of fortune. He prefers Portia's leaden casket to her gold and silver ones, the one which says, "Who chooseth me must give and hazard all he hath."

Sometimes this willingness is manifested not so much by overt acts as in the hero's style of address. The contemporary word for this style was *impudence*, a sort of self-confidence that sweeps away difficulties, a brazen refusal to be cowed by circumstances, not unlike Bassanio's shameless readiness to throw good money after bad in the first act of *The Merchant of Venice*. Though the word is often used to describe the behavior of comic heroes, the user generally intends it pejoratively. Indeed, it could even attach to a fop. A remark which shows the typical ambiguity of the term is that of Widow Outside in *A Woman Is a Riddle*, who has mixed reactions to a suitor: "I never met with anything so impudent—He's a charming fellow, Faith [*aside*]" (II). In his nondramatic writings Wycherley writes pieces both for and against this vice-virtue. In "An Address to Impudence" he describes in elevated terms the bold recklessness so often projected by the protagonists of Restoration comedy.

> Thou great support of courage, fame and sense;
> Hail to thee, bold and prosperous impudence! ...
> As best thou draw'st our virtues out to sight,
> And Sett'st them in the strongest point of light: ...
> Thou, warrior-like dost scour the dangerous field,
> While [modesty] to every bugbear doubt does yield.
> Almanzor-like thy bold disciples are,
> And all things *do*, because they all things dare.
> Thus impudence, which most unjustly we,
> The shame of all the virtues think to be:
> Mistakingly we their dishonor call,
> Which is the cause and the support to all:
> For ne'er could honor, courage, virtue, wit,
> Be brought into example but for it;
> All undistinguished, but for her would lie
> Unknown, unpractised, in obscurity.[9]

This analysis puts *impudence* in the same category with the *rugged individualism, gumption, initiative,* and *commitment* of later societies, as the name for that quality necessary to the realizing of one's potential. It also partakes of Aristotle's *greatness of soul.*

The word is used to describe young protagonists in at least 12 plays. In addition to those actually labeled *impudent,* there are Colonel Fainwell of *Bold Stroke for a Wife,* who has "assurance," and Charles of *The Busy Body,* who maintains that "fortune generally assists the bold." These instances of the use of the word or the concept have been picked up at random. Certainly the plays would yield many more if subjected to a systematic search.

Farquhar, who is always a more thoughtful writer than he is generally given credit for, tells us that "impudence in love is like courage in war; though both blind chances because women and fortune rule them" (*Love and a Bottle,* I). In Restoration comedy the battle of the sexes

<hr />

[9] William Wycherley, *Complete Works,* ed. Montague Summers (Soho, 1924), IV:198.

is more available for the display of impudence than is the battlefield.
The typical hero assumes that every fine woman is just dying to make
love with him and proceeds as if he is sure to win the last favor. A classical example is Dorimant's first sortie against Harriet in *The Man of
Mode*, which exploits the potential for double entendre in the parallel
between love and gambling.

> DORIMANT.   You were talking of play [gaming], Madam.
> Pray, what may be your stint?
> HARRIET.   A little harmless discourse in public walks, or at
> most an appointment in a box, barefaced, at the playhouse;
> you are for masks and private meetings, where women en-
> gage for all they are worth, I hear.
> DORIMANT.   I have been used to deep play, but I can make
> one at small game when I like my gamester well.
> HARRIET.   And be so unconcerned you'll have no pleasure
> in it.
> DORIMANT.   Where there is a considerable sum to be won,
> the hope of drawing people in makes every trifle consider-
> able.
> HARRIET.   The sordidness of men's natures, I know, makes
> 'em willing to flatter and comply with the rich, though
> they are sure never to be the better for 'em.
> DORIMANT.   'Tis in their power to do us good, and we despair
> not but at some time or other they may be willing.
> HARRIET.   To men who have fared in this town like you,
> 'twould be a great mortification to live on hope. Could you
> keep a Lent for a mistress?
> DORIMANT.   In expectation of a happy Easter and, though
> time be very precious, think forty days well lost to gain
> your favor.
>
> (III)

Dorimant's use of gambling as an analogue of love is typical. Fortune,
in fact, is a goddess more frequently invoked by comic heroes than
Venus, since success with the latter so often depends on success with
the former. But war, not love, demands the greatest risk, and for this
reason a hint of military prowess increases a comic hero's attractiveness to women. "The noble sense [our soldier lovers] show of the sad

fate / Of their dear country, sets a higher rate / Upon their love," argues a heroine of Sedley's *Mulberry Garden* to a doubting sister (I), as if thinking of the Cavalier poet Lovelace's famous line: "I could not love thee, dear, so much, / Loved I not honor more." Love, like war, involves daring. In every encounter with the opposite sex, people risk falling in love; they face death of self.

In comedy, intrigue takes the place of battle; stingy parents, cits, and fops take the place of the enemy; stratagem takes the place of force; resourcefulness and presence of mind take the place of skill with weapons. But the same careless self-confidence, the same readiness to "die," and the same trust in forces beyond one's control are necessary for success in either love or war. The comic scene is not the place to display heroic virtues, but the "bold and prosperous impudence" of the comic heroes of the Restoration is a desirable quality, especially when legal, financial, and physical safety are the dominant concerns of sterile antagonistic characters. The world of Dorimant may have had some moral blind spots, but there was not room in it for Prufrockian "decisions and revisions which a moment will reverse."

Persons whose life is at stake by virtue of the fact that they wear swords will naturally not appreciate any dangers faced by persons who make their fortunes by risking capital. The citizen in Restoration comedy is never, therefore, the daring speculator he may actually have been. He is instead the cautious, careful type of person who is always laying up stores against imagined catastrophes, the man to whom security is more important than conquest of any kind. Old men with young wives provide the best opportunities for developing this trait in antagonists. So Ravenscroft makes Alderman Wiseacre comb the country for a perfectly innocent young wife and then proceed to teach her a set of rules for wifely conduct more suited to a slave, which he thinks will prevent her from having any thoughts of a paramour. He also sets an Argus-eyed old aunt to watch over her. The innocent wife, the false education, and the duenna are familiar to us as harbingers of horns because they appear also in *The Country Wife*. Wycherley's Pinchwife plot, originally French, had also been used by John Caryl in *Sir Solomon or the Cautious Coxcomb*. Other husbands whose care to avoid cuckolding is the cause of it are Sir Solomon Sadlife of Cibber's *Double Gallant* (1707), Francisco of Mrs. Behn's *False Count*, Foresight of

Love for Love, Fondlewife of *The Old Bachelor*, and Gomez of *The Spanish Friar*. Of the 8 husbands, 5 are citizens. No one penetrates the folly of their elaborate precautions better than Alithea of *The Country Wife*, who sums up that play and perhaps the whole of Restoration comedy when she says, "Women and fortune are truest still to those that trust 'em" (V).

With his elaborate precautions to prevent his daughter from marrying any other than the person he chooses, Sir Tunbelly Clumsy of *The Relapse* is typical of another large group of characters who take too much thought for the morrow—stingy parents and guardians. For the same reason Don Diego of *The Gentleman Dancing Master*, Lord Bellguard of *Sir Courtly Nice*, Sir Jealous Traffique of *The Busy Body*, and Don Manuel of Cibber's *She Would and She Would Not* (1702) turn their houses into armed camps. We should add to these the watchful keepers, the timid lovers, and the tame husbands whose fear of taking risks reduces them to immobility rather than to precautionary measures. As might be expected, 65 percent of antagonistic characters have this quality in the various forms described here. Some fops have a certain gay abandon. On the other hand, 98 percent of protagonistic characters would say with Rashley of *The Fond Husband*, "Damn consideration. 'Tis a worse enemy to mankind than malice" (V); or with young Worthy in *Love's Last Shift* exclaim, "Let's avoid consideration; it is an enemy both to love and courage. They that consider much live to be old bachelors and young fighters" (II).

Physical courage, then, manifested in a tacit but careful adherence to the code of honor, and moral courage, manifested in a willingness to take risks, play a large part in determining the behavior of protagonistic characters in Restoration comedy. These persons move against a contrasting background of physical and moral cowardice, which is reflected in the violations or evasions of the code of honor by antagonistic characters and their elaborate defensive precautions. Returning to Wycherley's metaphor, we might say that the "generous hungry lions" are surrounded by mice, puppies, and tortoises.

In *Love for Love*, where we now turn to consider again what effect a knowledge of recurring patterns in the genre at large may have on our interpretation of an individual member of that genre, there is no dueling and there are no applications of the code of honor. That Scandal and Valentine will fight and that Tattle will not are facts that seventeenth-century audiences would have taken for granted, however, because these are the "fine gentlemen" of the play. Betterton played Valentine and Smith played Scandal; both actors specialized in fine gentlemen and therefore neither of them was "often kicked" on stage or off. On the other hand, audiences were accustomed to seeing Bowman, who played Tattle, being kicked in foppish roles like that of Trim in *Bury Fair* (1689). Having unconsciously associated Bowman with his other cowardly parts, they would agree with Ben's judgment of Tattle when he tells Prue, who is offended by the tongue-lashing he has given her, not to expect a redress from her "fair-weather spark" (III). Ben's daring her to make Tattle fight in this scene also settles the somewhat ambiguous matter of Ben's moral status in the play. Is he a sea-booby or, as Angelica has suggested, "an absolute sea wit" (III)—a man of sense in disguise? This indication that he will fight should remove all doubts as to the soundness of his character. Sir Sampson's little lawyer Buckram, the only character who fears Valentine in his feigned madness, is easily identified as a coward. Since law is the coward's weapon, it is natural that lawyers should run from danger.

But Congreve is not interested in flamboyant, ususual, or impossible heroics in this play, or indeed in any of his comedies. He deals with more ordinary if more subtle kinds of courage that may be called for in the everyday lives of the men and women in his audience, or in any audience. *Love for Love* is, on one plane, a conflict between those who will sacrifice love, loyalty, and honesty for security and those who will sacrifice security for these goods—a conflict between those who dare to take risks and those who do not.

If we approach the play from this direction, the reason for Foresight's existence is immediately clear. Almost immobilized with fear of what the future may bring, Foresight seeks safety in occult methods of prediction or control of events. He is a sort of Shylock who seeks security not through the law, but through the laws of nature.

> I tell you I have travelled, and travelled in the celestial spheres,
> know the signs and the planets, and their houses. Can judge
> of motions direct and retrograde, of sextiles, quadrates, trines,

and oppositions, fiery trigons and aquatical trigons. Know whether life shall be long or short, happy or unhappy, whether diseases are curable or incurable. If journeys shall be prosperous, undertakings successful; or goods stolen recovered, I know. (II)

Angelica tells of his past extravagancies: "What a bustle did you keep against the last invisible eclipse, laying in provision, as 'twere for a siege? What a world of fire and candle, matches and tinderboxes did you purchase! One would have thought we were ever after to live underground" (II). Scandal calls attention to Foresight's "consideration and discretion and caution" (III). But fortune is beyond human control, and Congreve proves it comically by causing Foresight not only to know less about what is going on than anyone else, but also to make his efforts to control events the cause of his undoing. Because he has "consulted the [stars] and all appearances are prosperous" (III) for the marriage of Ben and Prue, he is not prepared for the very real possibility that they will not abide each other. Angelica tells him that it is his preoccupation with the occult that sends his wife astray. Scandal, as if to prove this proposition, clears him out of the way to his wife's bed by giving him the idea that his health is in danger. Taking occult measures to counteract his imagined illness so preoccupies his mind that he fails to notice Scandal courting his wife in front of his eyes (III). So much for "consideration and discretion and caution."

Sir Sampson is as brash as Foresight is circumspect, but just the same he lacks enough self-reliance to face life without bonds, conveyances, deeds, and his little lawyer. He is probably not the kind of weakling who calls for the law when the sword is indicated but, as we have seen, use of the law for any purpose is reprehensible on the Restoration stage, especially so when used by a gentleman to rob his son. Instead of the responsibilities of wearing a sword, he shirks the responsibilities of being a father—an office that demands a certain amount of courage, too. His opinion that parenthood obliges the offspring but not the father— "Are you not my slave? Did I not beget you?" (II)—may be true in law, but it violates the traditional human tie that obliges the father to cherish and the son to obey. But as Angelica proves when she tears up Valentine's bond in the final scene, personal relationships are stronger than legal ones. Even when, as Sir Sampson insists, "there is not the least cranny of the law unstopped" (V), there is no more safety in scraps of paper than there is in astrology.

The two sisters, Mrs. Frail and Mrs. Foresight, and their friend Tattle seek security by hiding themselves from the world. As the antagonistic characters strengthen the walls around themselves, they come to depend more and more on them. Sir Sampson must have his Buckram. Foresight is at the mercy of every omen he invents. And the counterfeits are only as safe as their secrets. Instead of achieving greater freedom for themselves, they fall into a greater dependence on forces outside their control.

The principal protagonistic characters in *Love for Love* throw "consideration and discretion and caution" to the winds. They toil not, neither do they spin. With the exception of Prue and Jeremy, who are somewhat equivocal on this point, Congreve has made the attitude toward safety an absolute line of demarcation between his characters. Prue and Jeremy, though the first is remarkable for indiscretion and the second for impudence, are both prone to "consideration" in certain ways. Jeremy, like 83 percent of the servants in Restoration comedy, likes to eat. In the first scene of the play he threatens to quit if his master turns poet. Once he is satisfied that Valentine has given up the notion of starving, he returns to his loyal ways and participates in several mettle-testing adventures without any second thoughts. It is difficult to ascertain what we are to learn from observing Prue. Her lively and engaging impulsiveness gets her into trouble. Perhaps she has to learn that for a woman in the war between the sexes, the better part of valor is discretion. Ben's lack of caution and discretion places him in a class with Prue, but his unselfish good will removes him from it. He rejects an appeal to his self-interest as soon as he comes on stage. He asks Sir Sampson, "You ben't married again Father, be you?" "No," says Sir Sampson, "I intend you shall marry, Ben; I would not marry for thy sake." (A new wife would decrease Ben's inheritance.) Ben is unmoved: "Nay, what does that signify? An you marry again—why, then, I'll go to sea again, so there's one for t'other" (III). A man who wants nothing has nothing to lose, so Ben plunges heartily into Mrs. Frail's trap. "Will you venture yourself with me?" she says. "Venture, mess, and that I will, though 'twere to sea in a storm" (III). He would have married her, too, if she had not broken off the match when his estate failed to materialize. Fortune is truest to those who trust her.

Scandal's special form of risk is indicated by his name. The dangers of his habit of telling the ugly truth are clearly stated by Valentine when a remark of Scandal's touches too close to the quick. "Scandal, learn to spare your friends and do not provoke your enemies: this liberty of your tongue will one day bring a confinement on your body" (I)—confinement in a coffin, probably, rather than in a prison. There is, just the same, one sort of risk that Scandal will not take. He can be a loyal friend, but he cannot love a woman. In his low opinion of the female sex he is, as we have noted, a foil to Valentine. But after having used him in this capacity, Congreve allows him to be converted by Angelica's generosity. This change of heart occurs here as in other plays because, as will be seen, a capacity to admire a fine woman is an important distinguishing mark of a protagonistic character. Scandal would be incomplete without it.

Angelica, though she does not go into breeches, has valor equal to her principles. In the battle of wits with Valentine, Scandal, and Jeremy, she manifests impudence. Valentine "has a mind to try, whether his playing the madman won't make her play the fool, and fall in love with him" (IV), thinking that love of her has caused his mental collapse. When she comes on an exploratory visit to the man she is supposed to have driven mad, Angelica is wary. "I fancy 'tis a trick! I'll try." She then sets a trap for Scandal by saying to him, "I would disguise to all the world a failing which I must own to you. I fear all my happiness depends upon the recovery of Valentine." This apparent confession of love throws Scandal off his guard, and in the belief that his side has won, he unintentionally divulges the trick to her: "Be not too much concerned, madam, I hope his condition is not desperate: an acknowledgment of love from you, perhaps, may work a cure." This slip convinces her that Valentine's madness is a sham, and she forthwith denies having made any admission of love. Scandal, totally mystified by her about-face, is forced to admire her brass: "Hey, brave woman, i'faith!" When Scandal starts to leave her alone with Valentine to give her an opportunity for "the free confession of [her] inclinations," she plays dumb:

> Oh Heavens! you won't leave me alone with a
> madman?
> SCANDAL. No, Madam, I only leave a madman to his remedy.
> [*exit Scandal*]
> VALENTINE. Madam, you need not be very much afraid, for
> I fancy I begin to come to myself.
> ANGELICA. [*aside*] Ay, but if I don't fit you, I'll be hanged.

And fit him she does, by insisting on the truth of his fictional madness: she might once have loved him sane, but unfortunately she cannot love him mad. The more he tries to persuade her that he is sane, the madder he seems. Finally he calls in Jeremy to testify. But Jeremy, obeying previous orders, insists that Valentine is "as absolutely and substantially mad as any freeholder in Bethlehem." Indeed, right at this point Valentine has a true lapse of sanity. In this manner, just at the point where she is most hard-pressed and her surrender seems most imminent, Angelica calls upon all her reserves of wit, skill, and nerve and coolly turns Valentine's own weapon against him (IV). "Hey, brave woman," indeed.

Through Valentine, Congreve strengthens his total indictment of "consideration and discretion and caution," by having him, as chief protagonist, recognize them in himself, reverse his behavior, and receive a reward in consequence. After having started out to "win a mistress with a losing hand" (I), he denies this principle by recourse to the trick of madness. Angelica punishes him for this lack of faith by her "trick for trick" (IV). In despair, he makes a final leap into nothingness and gives himself up to fortune. "Generous Valentine!" His angel accepts this act of faith and translates him into heaven. "Between pleasure and amazement, I am lost," he says, "but on my knees I take this blessing" (V).

What Congreve appears to have done in Valentine's case is to elevate the conventional impudence of Restoration comic heroes from a pagan contempt for danger and trust in Fortune to a nearly Christian faith in Providence. Scandal, for instance, was an "infidel," but he is "converted" by Angelica. The lesson of Valentine appears to apply to a wider field of experience than courtship alone. It seems to be "Take no thought for the morrow, for the morrow shall take thought for the things of itself."

CHAPTER FIVE

Plain-dealing vs. Double-dealing

The third area of meaning comprehended in the term *generosity* as it was used in Restoration comedy is the complex of ideas surrounding the word *plain-dealing*, a term often used in the plays and always with favorable connotations. That Plain-dealing was indeed a part of the content of *generosity* may be supposed from the fact that several comic heroes specifically labeled *generous* are notable for the plainness of their dealings as well. For example, Congreve's "generous Valentine" poses as "Truth" in his mad scene; Wycherley's "generous Captain" Manly is the title character of *The Plain Dealer*; Farquhar's "generous creature," Silvia, is "too plain" in speech. Plain-dealing may be the form that the classical virtue of Wisdom or Truth takes in Restoration comedy.

In a letter of 1718, cited as an illustration of *generosity* in the *NED*, Lady Mary Wortley Montagu says, "It is a degree of *generosity* to tell the truth." Telling the truth is generous because it is dangerous, as it proved to be for Socrates. Drawing on the same example, it is also generous because it is a graceful gift of one's talents for the welfare and well-being of one's friends. In Restoration comedy we are sometimes reminded of the courageous aspect of Plain-dealing when the things said are true but unpopular; that is, when the plain-dealer is principally a satirist, and at others we are reminded of his charm, when his gift of sincerity, wit, and good manners enlightens and enlivens his social milieu. Wycherley's Manly can serve as a type of the more heroic variety, almost at times too heroic for comedy, and Congreve's Mirabell for the type of the congenial wit. They are not, however, mutually exclusive, because, as we have seen, swordplay was always a threat even in *The Way of the World*.

But here I must digress to defend Manly from modern criticism's charge that he is a surly brute and an object of Wycherley's satire. This mistake arises because of the wrong turn that criticism took with Charles Lamb's essay on "The Artificial Comedy of the Last Century," considerably helped out by the fact that Wycherley's plot is borrowed from Molière's *Misanthrope*. But a misanthrope is not a plain-dealer and Restoration comedy is not artificial.

A misanthrope is not a plain-dealer. The never very sound theory that Wycherley adopted Molière's ambivalent attitude toward his hero when he borrowed Molière's plot has been clearly, systematically, and, I hope, finally put to rest by A. M. Friedson in a recent article.[1] His main points are that the term *plain-dealer* is frequently used in English and never pejoratively, that Wycherley himself was often praised by his contemporaries as "Manly" and as the "Plain-dealer," and that Wycherley's alterations of Molière's story line all indicate his different attitude toward the hero. For example, Wycherley does not present the hero's bitter commentary on human life and pretensions until *after* he has contrasted him favorably with fops in an earlier scene. Then he emphasizes truth telling as the heroic virtue it often is in Restoration comedy in a dialogue with Freeman.

> FREEMAN. Don't you know, good captain, that telling truth is a quality as prejudicial to a man that would thrive in the world as square play to a cheat or true love to a whore? Would you have a man speak truth to his ruin? You are severer than the law, which requires no man to swear against himself. You would have me speak truth against myself, I warrant, and tell my promising friend, the courtier, he has a bad memory?
>
> MANLY. Yes.
>
> FREEMAN. And so make him remember to forget my business? And I should tell the great lawyer, too, that he takes oftener fees to hold his tongue than to speak?

[1] A. M. Friedson, "Wycherley and Molière: Satirical Point of View in *The Plain Dealer*," *Modern Philology*, LXIV (1967):189–97.

MANLY.   No doubt on't.

FREEMAN.   Ay and have him hang or ruin me when he should come to be a judge, and I before him. And would you have me tell the new officer, who bought this employment lately, that he is a coward?

MANLY.   Ay.

FREEMAN.   And so get myself cashiered, not him, he having the better friends, though I the better sword? And should I tell the scribbler of honor that heraldry were a prettier and fitter study for so fine a gentleman than poetry?

MANLY.   Certainly.

FREEMAN.   And so find myself mauled in his next hired lampoon. And you would have me tell the holy lady, too, she lies with her chaplain?

MANLY.   No doubt on't.

FREEMAN.   And so draw the clergy upon my back and want a good table to dine at sometimes. And by the same reason too, I should tell you that the world thinks you a mad man, a brutal, and have you cut my throat, or worse, hate me? What other good success of all my plain-dealing could I have than what I've mentioned?

(I)

Although Manly suggests several possible good results, the risks of Plain-dealing are undeniable. Manly's disinterest is aimed at here, not his misanthropy.

Restoration comedy is not artificial. The view here espoused that these plays recommend Plain-dealing is irreconcilable with any view which assumes that protagonistic characters are affected or artificial in their behavior. It would exclude the classic "comedy of manners" approach generated by Charles Lamb and passed on to Kathleen Lynch by John Palmer: "In the comedy of manners [says Palmer, quoted in Lynch] men and women are seen holding the reality of life away or letting it appear only as an unruffled thing of attitudes. Life is here made up of exquisite demeanour."[2] The "manners" approach to *The*

---

[2] Kathleen Lynch, *The Social Mode in Restoration Comedy* (New York, 1926), p. 6. Thomas Fujimura, whose recent study of the element of Hobbes-inspired wit in the plays (*Restoration Comedy of Wit*, Princeton, N.J., 1952) reveals a hitherto unappreciated stratum of seriousness in them, is led to undercut much of what he has achieved

Plain Dealer therefore requires that honest Manly be an object of satire, not of admiration.

Internal evidence supplied by these critics that Manly is unheroic ceases to have great significance when it is regarded from the standpoint of the fundamental conventions of Restoration comedy as I have been describing them. Norman Holland alleges that Manly cannot be the hero because he is "blundering, blustering, and self-deceived"—in short, a "fool."[3] Yet it is this very foolishness that establishes Manly's superiority. Wycherley makes this point abundantly clear in the prologue, in which Manly proudly admits that his stubborn honesty will pass for folly with a self-interested audience.

> I only act a part like none of you,
> And yet you'll say it is a fool's part too:
> An honest man who, like you, never winks
> At faults; but, unlike you, speaks what he thinks:
> The only fool who ne'er found patron yet,
> For truth is now a fault as well as wit.

Manly is accused by "manners" critics of inability to control his passions, of "extreme misanthropy," and of lack of polish. These alleged shortcomings derive from a failure to register the conventional meaning of Manly's words and deeds. His "obscene lust," which according to Mrs. Zimbardo[4] shows his morality to be a pose, is actually generous love in terms of dramatic formulas, and *love* is the word used for it in the text. His inability to control his passion for Olivia after he discovers she is unworthy of it is presented by Wycherley as testimony

by an emphasis on beauty of style or decorum in which he comes dangerously close to the "manners" approach he professes to deplore. His affinity with Miss Lynch, whose "social mode" he rejects, is clearest when he comes to deal with Wycherley's Manly. Bonamy Dobrée (*Restoration Comedy*, Oxford, 1924) soundly refuses *The Plain Dealer* admittance to the manners category. But Fujimura, who finds Manly lacking in decorum, finds himself rather strangely in agreement with Miss Lynch, who finds Manly lacking in social modishness. They have been joined by (1) Norman Holland, whose very perceptive interpretation of the play (*First Modern Comedies*, Cambridge, Mass., 1959) would be even more satisfying if he had accepted Manly as the hero without complications; and (2) Rose Zimbardo, whose most enlightening discourse on the parallels between classical satire and *The Plain Dealer* (*Wycherley's Drama*, New Haven, Conn., 1965) does not require the rejection of Manly as hero either.

[3] Holland, p. 100.
[4] Zimbardo, p. 87.

of his constancy, as proof that his passion is a generous one. Anyone acquainted with the heroic drama of this period will recognize his aberrations as the sort only a Great Soul is capable of, an Almanzor. It partakes of that "heroical love," seated in the liver, that Robert Burton speaks of in his *Anatomy*, which is the particular affliction of "generous spirits."[5] As I intend to show in the next chapter, this madness is a common feature of comic heroes also. That Manly suffers from a constitutional inability to be inconstant rather than from an uncontrollable lust is clear from the language in which he blames himself for continuing to love: "Damned, damned woman, that could be so false and so infamous! And damned, damned heart of mine that cannot yet be false, though so infamous! What easy, tame, suffering, trampled things does that little god of talking cowards make of us!" (IV). Because it is dishonorable to love a whore, which Olivia's infidelity virtually makes her, Manly hides his true motives for continuing to court her from those who must participate in the enterprise. It is for Fidelia's benefit that Manly says he will "lie with [Olivia] out of revenge" (III). And it is to her that he makes the excuse, "Call it revenge, and that is honorable" (IV). Wycherley's more private writings also declare the doctrine that love is irrational. In "A Song against Reason in Love" he makes love and reason antithetical in the same way as faith in God and reason are antithetical.[6] Manly's generous passion is of course also the cause of his being easily deceived by Olivia. A worse person would be less easily fooled because less capable of risking all.

As to Manly's preferring his false friend Vernish to his true friend Freeman, this blindness is also a result of generosity. As Manly says, "A true heart admits but of one friendship, as of one love" (I). A loyalty to Vernish as strong as his love of Olivia prevents his full commitment to Freeman, though Freeman is undoubtedly right in believing of Manly that "though I could never get you to say you were my friend, I know you'll prove so" (I).

A further reason for Manly's being unable to tell the false people

---

[5] Robert Burton, *Anatomy of Melancholy* (New York, 1948), sect. 2, member 1, subsect. 1. For an excellent and, I should think, definitive exposition of the heroic character of Almanzor-like "naturalistic drives," see Arthur C. Kirsch's chapter on "The Heroic Hero" in his book *Dryden's Heroic Drama* (Princeton, N.J., 1965).

[6] William Wycherley, *Complete Works*, ed. Montague Summers (Soho, 1924), III:41.

from the true is the conventional design of the play which calls for the conversion of the hero in the last act. The typical hero is an unbeliever in the fair sex, like Congreve's Scandal, who "runs at" all women because he trusts no individual of the species. In the course of the play he meets a girl who apparently can be trusted, and he becomes a believer. Thus most Restoration comedies move from doubt to faith. Manly's conversion implies no special criticism of him. There is a tinge of misanthropy, perhaps leaning toward misogyny, in all heroes of Restoration comedy.

If the argument by appeal to conventions of drama is not granted, the case for Manly's misanthropy still has grave flaws in it on the basis of *The Plain Dealer* in isolation. How much of a misanthropist is Manly, really, in the face of his confidence in Vernish and Olivia? Here he departs radically from his suspicious original in Molière's play. Manly is simply a man of honor incensed at a corrupt world. Like many heroes of Restoration comedy he is the satirist within the satire, showing us his author's collection of fools and knaves. When he transfers his loyalties to his true friend and mistress, his false friend and mistress serve to remind us that his low opinion of humanity does, after all, have some foundation in experience. Rightly understood, Vernish and Olivia are only two more characters in the satirist's gallery of fools and knaves. Fidelia loves Manly from beginning to end. Is *she* a fool, too?

Manly, one grants, does not have the polish of a Dorimant or a Mirabell, but he is by no means the only "blunt" hero of Restoration comedy. One of his most illustrious ancestors must be the appropriately named Colonel Blunt of Howard's *Committee*, in its own time the most popular Restoration comedy of all. This Cavalier is above all an uncompromising man of honor, unable even to think of taking the Puritan Covenant in order to save his estate. The Committee of Sequestration in fact charges him with making "an idol of that honor." To this he replies, "Our worships then are different. You make that your idol which brings you interest; we [Cavaliers] can obey that which bids us lose it." "Brave gentlemen," remarks one heroine, falling in love (II). Standing up for his principles is no problem for Colonel Blunt, but he lacks polish in the presence of ladies. When Arbella, with whom he has been smitten, rescues him from jail, it becomes necessary for him to thank her in the presence of a second pair of lovers, Careless and

Ruth. The scene gives Howard a good opportunity to expand on Blunt's lubberly bigheartedness.

> ARBELLA. You are free, Sir.
> BLUNT. Not so free as you think.
> ARBELLA. What hinders it?
> BLUNT. Nothing, that I'll tell you.
> ARBELLA. Why, Sir?
> BLUNT. You'll laugh at me.
> ARBELLA. Have you perceived me apt to commit such a rudeness? Pray let me know it.
> BLUNT. Upon two conditions you shall know it. . . . First, I thank ye, y'have freed me nobly: pray believe it; you have this acknowledgment from an honest heart, one that would crack a string for you; that's one thing.
> ARBELLA. Well! the other.
> BLUNT. The other thing is that I may stand so ready that I may be gone just as I have told it you; together with your promise not to call me back: and upon those terms I give you leave to laugh when I am gone. Careless, come, stand ready, that at the sign given we may vanish together.
> RUTH. If you please, Sir, when you are ready to start, I'll cry one, two, three and away.
> BLUNT. Be pleased to forbear, good smart gentlewoman: you have leave to jeer when I am gone, and I am just going; by your spleen's leave, a little patience. . . . Careless, have you done with your woman?
> CARELESS. Madam—
> BLUNT. . . . Stand ready, man. So, now my misfortune that I promised to discover is, that I love you above my sense or reason. So farewell, and laugh. Come, Careless.
>
> (IV)

Colonel Blunt has a number of senseless, irrational descendants like Manly, as we shall see in the next chapter. He also has a number of blunt descendants besides Manly. Dryden's Bellamy in *An Evening's Love* is embarrassed by having to imitate an astrologer because he hates lying. He tells his mistress, who is Spanish, "I am plain and true, like all my countrymen" (V). In *The Mulberry Garden*, Jack Wildish is so graceless that his mistress complains he tells of his love as if he asked "how I slept last night" (II). Vanbrugh's Heartfree in *The Provoked Wife* is the same sort of fellow, but his mistress forgives him because "a little bluntness is a sign of honesty" (III). In *Sir Patient Fancy* and *The Fond Husband* Wittmore's and Rashley's honesty is an impediment as it was for Bellamy. "Stout" Merryman of *Bellamira*, who like many protagonists prefers drinking to love-making, is nevertheless attractive to women because of his "blunt way" (III). Wycherley's Manly is described in the same language. He is complimented for "manly bluntness and honest love" in one place (II) and for "sullen bluntness and honest love" in another (I). He bemoans "how hard it is to be a hypocrite" (III) when hypocrisy becomes a strategic necessity. Wycherley himself, whose nondramatic verse is rather crude and blunt, won plaudits from Lord Lansdowne for its manliness. "His muse is not led forth as to a review, but as to a battle; not adorned for parade, but execution; he would be tried for the sharpness of his blade and not by the finery: Like your heroes of antiquity, he charges in iron and seems to despise all ornament but intrinsic merit. And like those heroes, has therefore added another name to his own; and by the unanimous assent of the world, is called the *Manly Wycherley*."[7] It would be a pity if by the help of literary scholarship, Plain-dealing, the quality for which both Wycherley and his hero were admired in their own time, should be interpreted as a flaw in that hero's character and ignored as a salient feature of the whole class of plays which Wycherley's *Plain Dealer* in this respect epitomized.

Indeed, when one considers the magnitude of the attack on hypocrisy of all sorts in Restoration comedy, it is difficult to understand how the reverse could be missed. Yet Miss Lynch has said, and many agree, "We laugh at Dorimant because his assumed affectation admits of so poor and incomplete an expression of an attractive and vigorous personality."[8] But, "Lord, Madam! all he does and says is so easy and so natural" (III), objects his friend Young Bellair in the play itself. Nature is a relative term. The style of a Dorimant may strike a later age as artificial only because it is different from its own. Compared to

[7] Quoted in *ibid.*, I:58.
[8] Lynch, p. 181.

Wordsworth's verse, Pope's seems artificial, but without Wordsworth for comparison, Pope, for whom nature was "the source, end, and test of art," probably would have sworn that he wrote "in the language really used by men," barring meter, as Wordsworth did. And, listening to Sir Fopling Flutter, Dorimant would undoubtedly have sworn the same thing about himself if Etherege had thought it necessary. "Manners" critics make the mistake of judging Restoration comedy by modern standards of naturalness.

Nature is a relative term. During the time of Restoration comedy, as we have noted, being natural was an art. Cicero's *decorum* and Castiglione's *sprezzatura* lead to this paradox.[9] For Pope, the function of art was to bring out nature. All three looked upon nature as the harmonious and beautiful "informing soul" behind the surface of things. It was the function of art to bring forth this harmony. Instead of being raw material as it is for us, nature was a refinement of raw material. Robert Frost is supposed to have said, when asked to define realism, "You can have your potato peeled; or you can have your potato with the skin on and washed; or you can have it just as it comes out of the ground with the dirt still on it. All three of these objects are real potatoes." Restoration audiences preferred the more marketable varieties.

When social arts, or manners, are a refinement of nature rather than a replacement of it, they can be a form of generosity. For Pope, "True wit is nature to advantage dressed." The person who presents himself unbathed, uncombed, and unwashed is certainly not "to advantaged dressed." He may be said to exhibit an ungenerous lack of consideration for those with whom he associates. When Pope compares poetry to "a generous horse," which "shows most true mettle when you check his course," he assumes that regulation and restraint enhance rather than stultify natural beauty.[10] The person who shows a degree of restraint in his manners, who clearly has greater potential than he releases, shows a generous deference toward the merits of others in his company. Whether nature is enhanced by embellishment or by restraint, the motive may be generous. But at a certain point embellishment becomes

---

[9] See pp. 24–26.

[10] Alexander Pope, *Essay on Criticism*, pts. I, II. The neoclassical requirement that instruction be presented in delightful form becomes, when applied to the social realm, a demand for good manners.

disguise and restraint becomes formality. At this point art becomes artifice and takes the place of nature. This point, I propose, divides plain-dealers from double-dealers in Restoration comedy.

The "manners" or "social mode" approach to the plays is partly built on protagonists' use of strategic deception to gain their ends. But deceit of this kind loses its negative meaning as soon as the plays are viewed as contests between "good guys" and "bad guys." We do not call detectives dishonest when they use duplicity to catch crooks. The same duplicity can be considered deceit if used by one side and strategy if by the other. Perhaps this thought occurred to Sedley when he made Young Lionel in *Bellamira* say, it cannot "be wrong to cozen those that cozen all the world" (II). In Baker's *Tunbridge Walks* (1703) the hero remarks disingenuously, as if he were writing the play, "To gain a mistress we're allowed deceit; in all things else you will find me a man of honor" (V). Since he is deceiving his mistress's father and not her, he may be said to speak for comic heroes of the Restoration in general. Contrary to a common assumption, one may not use deception against one's mistress, as Valentine learned in *Love for Love*.

Just as artifice becomes art when its motive is generous, deception becomes strategy. Farquhar seemed to understand this distinction in *The Recruiting Officer*, when he has Plume explain a somewhat underhanded method he uses to gain recruits for his regiment: "Some people may call this artifice, but I term it stratagem, since it is so main a part of the service" (IV). Some such thought may have crossed his mind again when he called his next play *The Beaux' Stratagem* instead of *The Beaux' Cheat*, which it might have been named if antagonistic characters had perpetrated the hoax referred to. The plot of the trickster tricked is a staple of comedy. Comic peripety requires that fakes be "faked out," as we might say today. "Manners" critics simply misread a dramatic convention when they call strategy insincerity.

Furthermore, the notion that protagonists in Restoration comedy use deception to seduce women is simply incorrect. It probably arises from the nineteenth-century code of ethics that assumes men are always responsible when women fall. No woman in Restoration comedy could ever doubt the intention of a Jack Careless or a Tom Ranger. His reputation was sufficient warning, and if that were not enough, his point-blank way of putting his business on her agenda would certainly suffice.

We have seen how even Dorimant, the "social mode" critics' champion exemplar of artifice, asks Harriet for the last favor at the first interview.[11] What he said to her on that occasion well illustrates a plain-dealing aspect of impudence that Wycherley referred to in his poem on that subject: "Scorning on truth t'impose a farded dress, / Thou shew'st her in her primal nakedness."[12] If Dorimant uses artifice in this dialogue, it is not to disguise his frank proposition but to make it attractive—and it is. Like Dorimant, comic heroes of the Restoration make their intentions clear. It is true that oaths of constancy may sometimes be broken, but this does not mean that they were false when given. Even the Beau Strategist Archer, for example, makes it abundantly clear to Mrs. Sullen that his intentions are dishonorable, though he conceals his true identity from her.

The pattern of calling "for the last course first" (II), as one Arabella describes it in Charles Johnson's *The Wife's Relief* (1711), is often repeated. Wildblood of Dryden's *An Evening's Love* (1668) confesses frankly in his first interview with his mistress, "I am not one of those unreasonable lovers that propose to themselves the loving to eternity" (II). Other heroes who ask for everything while promising nothing are Careless (*Committee*), Sir Frederick Frolick (*Comical Revenge*), Woodall (*Sir Martin Mar-all*), Ranger (*Love in a Wood*), Palamede (*Marriage à la Mode*), Bevil and Rains (*Epsom Wells*), Careless (*Careless Lovers*), Alonzo (*Dutch Lovers*), Willmore (*Rover*), Lorenzo (*Spanish Friar*), Roebuck (*Love and a Bottle*), Sir Harry Wildair (*Constant Couple*), Captain Plume (*Recruiting Officer*), Atall (*Double Gallant*), Sir George Airy (*Busy Body*), and Volatil (*Wife's Relief*). How is a girl to be deceived about the intentions of persons with names like most of these?

In a play like *The Man of Mode* we may easily miss such exemplary qualities in protagonists as Plain-dealing because, of course, fine gentlemen do not say, "Look at me—I tell the truth," any more than they say, "Look at me—I am brave." Aristotle's list of basic character types may help us to identify them. In a world of *alazones* or boasters they are the *eirones* or self-depreciators. One may be less of a person than he pre-

---

[11] See p. 88.
[12] Wycherley, *Works*, IV:198.

sents himself to be, or more of a person. In the *Ethics* Aristotle recommends the latter course, to appear as less of a man than you really are (IV, vii, 10–16). Because protagonists depreciate their virtues, such virtues are more apparent against a contrasting background of their antagonists' vices than they are when we look straight at them. Before inspecting the plain-dealing characteristics of protagonists, therefore, I shall study the forms of double-dealing in Restoration comedy, which I have classified as zeal, prudery, formality, and impertinence.

Zeal is the citizens' foppery. His clothes are plain and drab to show his seriousness, and he mouths grave sentiments to match his dress. If one could show that Puritan religious hypocrisy is the basis of the general attack on hypocrisy in these plays, the demonstration would surely round out my hypothesis that Restoration comedy is largely a protest against the Protestant ethic. But the antipathy to hypocrisy in the plays is perhaps not so much a result of their anti-Puritan bias as were the attacks on cowardice and avarice, which had stronger foundations in class prejudice. Puritans are as hypocritical in the plays as they are mercenary, and they are either of these more than they are anything else. But only a small amount of the hypocrisy in the plays is the religious form affected by Puritans. Reaction against Puritan sham assuredly might encourage Plain-dealing among victorious Cavaliers, but did the dramatists recognize in genteel foppery the same kind of enemy? Perhaps not until Swift in *A Tale of a Tub* satirized errors in religion in terms of fashions in clothes was the inevitable connection actually made. The comic writers hated foppery and they hated canting religion, but though there may have been a connection between these hatreds, they did not make it in their plays.

We have already seen how the dramatists pick apart the Puritans' pious camouflage of their shady business practices. But, despite their protestations to the contrary, Puritans were, according to the plays, as prone to sin as other mortals, if not more so. The dramatists' usual way of puncturing the facade of the grave moralist of either sex was to uncover a vein of unbridled lust in his composition. Smuggler's disgusting overtures to Lady Lurewell in Farquhar's *Constant Couple* (1699) are typical of the way in which such revelations are made. He owes Lady Lurewell some money, but he is so slow in producing it that she feels she must bring pressure to bear.

LADY LUREWELL.   Sir, I'll blast your reputation, and so ruin your credit.

SMUGGLER.   Blast my reputation! he, he, he!—Why, I'm a religious man, madam! I have been very instrumental in the reformation of manners. Ruin my credit! Ah, poor woman. There is but one way, madam,—you have a sweet leering eye!

LADY LUREWELL.   You instrumental in reformation! How?

SMUGGLER.   I whipped all the whores, cut and long tail, out of the parish.—Ah! that leering eye!—Then I voted for pulling down the playhouse.—Ah, that ogle! that ogle!—Then my own pious example.—Ah, that lip! that lip!

Smuggler's proposal, in short, is that he will give Lady Lurewell the money he owes her if she will lie with him. "Here's a villain now," she says, "so covetous that he won't wench upon his own cost, but would bribe me with my own money" (II). There are many other interesting examples of prurience too thinly covered by zeal. In *Love in a Wood* Mrs. Joyner, described as a "bonfire of devotion," turns out to be a bawd who helps Alderman Gripe, "a bellows of zeal," debauch a young girl (I). Testimony, Crowne's specimen of religious enthusiasm in *Sir Courtly Nice*, absolves himself from attempted rape by thanking God he has a "sense of sin" that sets him apart from other men (IV, V). There are 52 religious hypocrites altogether, in 29 of the 83 plays under consideration. More than half demonstrate an inability to restrain their appetites.

In protagonists religious zeal is conspicuous by its absence. Is a dramatic medium that attacks corruption in religion atheistical? Certainly not necessarily so. As Collier's answerers pointed out, a sincere concern for religion could motivate such an attack.[13] If a comic hero did happen to have Christian faith, he could not decorously reveal it, especially in a world where protestations of religious faith were the province of zealots.

Zeal has affinities to prudery, the principal foppery of gentlewomen. This vice is so often tangled up with coquetry that it is perhaps a mistake to attempt to treat it in isolation. But it must be glanced at now

[13] See, for example, William Congreve, "Amendments of Mr. Collier's False and Imperfect Citations," *Complete Works* (Soho, 1923), III:189–91.

because it is another way of presenting one's self as more than one really is. The word *prude* seems not to have entered common usage until after the period covered by these plays. Pope, as we know, gave the word a central position in *The Rape of the Lock*, first published in 1712, but a character in Mrs. Centlivre's *Bold Stroke for a Wife*, staged five years later, reacted to *prudery* as a new word (II). The first instance of its use cited by *The New English Dictionary* is in Cibber's *Careless Husband* of 1704, but Etherege's Sir Fopling had long before given a brief dissertation on the varieties of prudes in *The Man of Mode*. To be sure, he was showing off his knowledge of French. At any rate, it is apparent that the concept was current in England long before the word, because our set of plays provides 75 females who may be called *prudes* according to early definitions of the word. The *Encyclopédie* of 1757 gives the meaning, "femme qui affecte la sévérité des moeurs dans ses propos et dans son maintien. Qui dit *prude* dit assez communement *sote*, *hypocrite*, *laide*, ou *mauvaise*. On peut être *prude*, coquette, ou galante." Other entries show that a *coquette* leads men to hope for "un bonheur qu'elle n'a pas resolu de leur accorder." A *galante*, on the other hand, is just as kind as she leads men to think she may be. Reducing these definitions to their essentials, the *prude* pretends to be cruel but is kind, the *coquette* pretends to be kind but is cruel, and the *galante* does not pretend. For this reason the writer of the entry on *coquetterie* in the *Encyclopédie* prefers the *galante* to the other two.

The prude affects to be superior to, contemptuous of, or not subject to the sexual drive. Ruth, the governess in Shadwell's *Squire of Alsatia*, is a good example. She discovers her two charges, the heroines, enjoying a book of poetry. One of the girls says, " 'Tis sweet poetry. There is a pleasing charm in all he writes."

> RUTH. [*she snatches the book*] Yea, there is a charm of
> Satan's in it. 'Tis vanity and darkness. This book hateth
> and is contrary to the light; and ye hate the light.

The other girl complains that Ruth has just now made them come away from the light of the window.

> RUTH. Look thee . . . thou are wanton. . . . Ye seek tempta-
> tion; you look out of the casement to pick and cull young
> men whereby to feed the lust of the eye.

If they may not look out of the window, may they at least read the book?

> RUTH. No, it is wanton, and treateth of love. I will instantly
> commit it to the flames.
>
> (III)

Of course Ruth turns out to be highly inflammable herself, in the end.

In the light of the Cavalier sympathies of Restoration comedy the connection between prudery and Puritanism that we see in Ruth is to be expected, but the religious association is not a necessary or usual part of the word's meaning. It refers especially to that exaggerated concern for chastity, honor, or reputation represented by such characters as Mrs. Squeamish, Mrs. Fidget, and Lady Dainty Fidget, the "virtuous gang" of Wycherley's *Country Wife* who cry, "Do not use that word naked," when someone inadvertently refers to "the naked truth" (II). Others "nauseate" at the thought of a lover, or claim to, as does Olivia of *The Plain Dealer* (II); or, like Mrs. Marwood of *The Way of the World*, they unconvincingly boast of "an aversion" to mankind (II). The plays take special pleasure in proving that such people, because they deny nature, are sure to have their pretensions contradicted. Of the 75 prudes who boast of their invulnerability to male charms, 36 prove the contrary conclusively.

Heroines are the reverse of prudes in both speech and action. As Collier correctly notes,[14] they are as frank as men about sex. But they do not bestow the last favor. Of 114 unmarried young ladies who have the approbation of their authors, 82 of 90 reject illicit offers. Those who do not are sadder but wiser cast mistresses or foreign girls like those in several of Mrs. Behn's plays with Spanish settings. Willing young ladies are punished (52 of 53) unless they are honest whores, hoydens, or young wives of old men. The young wives' case has been discussed.[15] The hoydens and honest whores provide an enlightening contrast to the prudes.

The comedies supply us with 37 whores in 22 plays. Because these

---

[14] Jeremy Collier, *A Short View of the Immorality and Profaneness of the English Stage* (London, 1698), p. 146.

[15] See pp. 54, 58–59, 89.

plays set such a high value on Plain-dealing, one might expect that they would favor whores, and to some extent they do. But although no one can accuse a prostitute of prudery, she is not entirely without hypocrisy, either; for it is money, not love, that motivates her kindness. Nevertheless, the plays are more sympathetic toward common and kept women than they are toward any others engaged in commerce. Of the 37 whores, 13 are rewarded with settlements or husbands and 7 have no moral status at all, but are merely introduced to serve as comment on the moral status of other characters. On 3 others, the plays equivocate. Almost as many whores as are rewarded are held up to contempt, but on close inspection it appears that whoredom is not the cause of their being shamed: 6 of these 11 exhibit ill humor when they do not get their way, a breach of decorum that the plays always punish; 3 others help cheats who must be exposed; and the remaining 2 are the only straightforward prostitutes who are disapproved of. As usual it is a late play which gives the best explanation of this sympathetic treatment of prostitutes. In *Fair Quaker of Deal* a character asks Mrs. Jiltup, a member of the profession, "You make degrees in whoring?" "Oh ever," she replies. "She that is a bastard-bearing whore is the most notorious; she that lies with half the town and does it privately, is a prudent whore; she that gets money by it, is a mercenary whore; she that does it generously and bare-faced is a whore of honor" (III). What is interesting here is the connection of generosity and honor with barefaced whoring. The preceding types help to isolate the generous and honorable elements of the final type. The bastard-bearing kind is a public scandal merely because she is unable to keep her secret. There is something of a hypocrite in the prudent kind who, unlike her unfortunate sister, enjoys the sin without the shame. The third kind shams love for money. Only the barefaced whore is generous. Although no bastard forces her sin into the open, she owns up to whoredom freely. Although she has everything to lose and nothing to gain, she gives herself unconditionally. The barefaced *and* generous whore does not, however, occur in Restoration comedy. Girls like Bellinda of *The Man of Mode*, Berinthia of *The Relapse*, and Mrs. Fainall of *The Way of the World* do transgress purely for love, but they transgress in secret. On the other hand, whores like Bellamira, "Sir Anthony Love," and Betty Frisque (*Coun-*

try Wit) are barefaced enough, but they are kept. Apparently, then, although the combination of generosity and openness does not occur, the plays can still approve the generosity of the Bellindas and the openness of the Betty Frisques.

Through his "Sir Anthony," who was actually the kept Lucia in breeches, Thomas Southerne furthers the doctrine that plain-dealing whoredom has much to be said for it. In his play a character points out that after the first slip some women by circumspect behavior "live themselves into a second reputation." "Sir Anthony" continues, "And other women, who by a natural negligence never setting up for any, from the freedom of their behaviour have passed uncensured in those public places and pleasures which would have undone ladies of sprucer reputations." From these premises, Ilford concludes, "So, 'tis not what they do but not doing all of a piece that ruins their character" (IV). Wycherley, we recall, dedicated *The Plain Dealer* to a notorious bawd because "no one can charge [her] with that heinous and worst of women's crimes, hypocrisy." "Sir Anthony Love" was so fine a woman that when the hero, with full knowledge of her past, offered to marry her, she generously refused, belying her mercenary mode of livelihood (IV). The youthful keeper in *The Revenge* (actually Marston's *Dutch Courtesan* brought up to date) did not find that his payment of money made his mistress mercenary. On the contrary, he observed with special reference to her that women "are no ungrateful persons; they'll give love for love" (I). One kind of merchant, it appears, gets better treatment than the rest: the kind that exhibits neither religious hypocrisy nor prudery.

The comedy of the hoyden stems from her liberation through ignorance from the decorum which the prude overstates and the plain-dealing heroine understates. But affectation by those who have some knowledge of decorum is perhaps worse than ignorance. Furthermore, nature unenhanced by art may still be preferable to affectation. It seems logical that Restoration comedy would tend to approve of hoydens, who are so lacking in guile that they could not be double-dealers if they tried. A hoyden is a country girl with an ill-concealed enthusiasm for the opposite sex. Her plain-dealing frankness about her sexual desires might partly account for her favorable treatment, though her

innocence and impulsiveness get her into trouble. In a literature dominated by males, ladies who could be kind might always be welcome.
But for some playwrights the honesty of hoydens appears to be more
important than their kindness.

Horner, for example, praises Margery Pinchwife's crude love letter
to him because "'Tis the first love letter that ever was without flames,
darts, fates, destinies, lying and dissembling in it" (IV). Indeed, without Margery, Wycherley's task of ridiculing the hypocrisy of Mrs.
Squeamish and her gaggle could not have been at all as effectively ac-
complished. This contrast accounts for the ladies having so much
difficulty, as the play ends, in preventing Margery first from blurting
out that she loves Mr. Horner "with all my soul" and then, after Pinchwife is assured that Horner is physically incapable of cuckolding him,
of insisting "to my certain knowledge" that he is as perfect a man as any
lady could wish for. The full enormity of the prudes' way of life comes
home to us when Margery, strongly objecting, is taught to lie. Other
country girls who find it difficult to lie are Peggy of *The London
Cuckolds* and Prue of *Love for Love*, who differs in being happy to get
rid of that "old-fashioned country way of speaking one's mind" (II).

Are these girls honest *because* they come from the country or are
they honest *and* they come from the country? In spite of Restoration
comedy's obvious zest for town life, the concept of country honesty
and simplicity in contrast to town artifice and corruption had strong
classical support, as for instance in the "O fortunatus nimium" passage
of Virgil's *Georgics*. When we read of country Betty in Caryl's *Sir
Solomon* (1669) that "her wit and her love flow from the clear fountain of nature without the least tincture of artifice" and that she has
"so perfect a soul, and so capable of the highest improvement" (IV), it
is somewhat difficult not to think "She dwelt among the untrodden
ways." John Crowne also required the fountain metaphor to describe
his hoyden Lucinda in *City Politiques* (1683). Her lover says, "I am
strangely taken with this sweet young creature! 'Tis so pleasant to
drink at such a fresh spring, which never brute defiled nor muddied.
. . . 'Tis so much wholesomer to love [her] than the sophisticated
beauties of this town, which sicken and kill an intrigue in a few days"
(V). These hoydens stand in contradiction to the widespread belief

that Restoration comedy despises country life and its bumpkinly ways. The encouragement they are given supports the attack on prudery in the plays.

Among town gentlemen foppery takes the form of forced, obtrusive, ostentatious dress, bearing, and speech. Because of its fastidious, preening, self-regarding, precious quality, it strikes one as effeminate. The idea that Restoration comedy presents socially prominent people who uncharitably snub well-meaning but gauche outsiders does not die easily. In his most excellent recent survey, *The Idea of Comedy*, William Wimsatt unfortunately perpetuates this myth. The dramatists' "unsympathetic derision was directed against the social misfit, the climbing bourgeois or city merchant, the country Tory, the chilly 'prude,' the conventional prig, the obtuse gull. They ministered to the vanity of the smart aristocratic audience."[16] Anyone who thought much about it would immediately realize that most of the fops, prudes, and coquettes who fill the comedies are themselves members of the aristocracy: 59 or 70 percent are gentlemen; the rest consist of 17 tradesmen, 2 servants, and 6 well-born country boobies. Although the attack on the rising middle class is pervasive, it is based on the firmer ground of religious hypocrisy and avarice, not on social pretension. The outsiders from the country, as we have noted, often have the approbation of their creators. Far from "ministering to the vanity of the smart aristocratic audience," the dramatists said over and over again what Dryden says in his epilogue to *The Man of Mode*: "Sir Fopling . . . represents ye all." We are told that Cibber very cleverly increased the satiric effect of his various fops by keeping them up to date. "As the fashion of the times altered, he adjusted his action and behaviour to them and introduced every species of growing foppery."[17] There must have been a chance, at any given performance, that some of the smarter members of the audience would find themselves dressed like the stage fop. The satire of Restoration comedy is in fact quite democratically distributed: each sex has its favorite vices and follies; no class is spared.

Like the prude and the Puritan, the genteel fop attracts attention to himself by a certain rigidity or preciosity. He bows too low, his com-

---

16 William Wimsatt, *The Idea of Comedy* (Englewood Cliffs, N.J., 1969), p. 89.
17 Thomas Davies, *Dramatic Miscellanies* (London, 1784), III:425.

pliments are too extreme, his walk is overly studied. "A pox on 'em . . . that force nature," rails Horner in *The Country Wife* (I). When the forms of social intercourse take the place of that intercourse altogether, when manners become more important than the intimacy they are supposed to facilitate, intercourse and intimacy are both destroyed. Social groups must always fight formality to preserve the form of their interaction from decay. When manners are working well, "you cannot tell the dancer from the dance," to borrow Yeats's metaphor.

In Restoration comedy overformal behavior is designated *precise* or *curious*, as it was by Thomas Hoby in his translation of *The Courtier* in 1563, as well as *pinched, ceremonious, civil*, and *formal*. The terms were somewhat loosely applied to the many different ways of "forcing nature." A Puritan prude, objecting to the amount of bosom her niece exposes, is thus answered: "Are the pinched cap and formal hood the emblems of sanctity? Does your virtue consist in your dress, Mrs. Prim? . . . I know you have as much pride, vanity, self-conceit and ambition among you, couched under that formal habit and sanctified counte-nance as the proudest of us all; but the world begins to see your prud-ery" (*Bold Stroke*, II). An English version of La Bruyère's *Caractères* (1699) translates the French word *prude* as "one that is precise or formal" and translates *pruderie* as "formality." In 1665 Richard Fleck-noe used *precise* as the antonym of *libertine* in a discussion of school-mistresses.[18] The *dramatis personae* of *The Squire of Alsatia* (1688) describes the character Ruth as a "precise governness." *Preciseness* clearly must derive from the French *preciosité*.

The same vocabulary describes foppish mannerisms: "No man living more studies and adores all manner of forms," announces Sir Courtly Nice (V). The words describing Trim of *Bury Fair* were often used of other fops: he was "all ceremony, no sense," full of "breeding" and "civility" (I). Sir Mannerly of *Country Wit*, as his name suggests, took great care to observe decorum. From this kind of fastidiosity it is a short step to other kinds: the "nice conduct" of a snuff box (Clodio, *Love Makes a Man*; Mockmode, *Love and a Bottle*); sensitivity to bad odors

---

[18] Jean de La Bruyère, *Les caractères de Theophraste . . . avec les caractères ou les moeurs de ce siècle* (Paris, 1700), I:157–58, 160; *Characters of the Virtues and Vices of the Age* (London, 1699), pp. 65, 67; Richard Flecknoe, *Sixty-nine Enigmatical Characters* (London, 1665), p. 50.

and the use of perfume (Sir Courtly, *Sir Courtly Nice*; Sir Fopling, *Man of Mode*; Clincher Senior, *Constant Couple*); the use of cosmetics (Apish, *The Quaker's Wedding*); chastity (Trim, *Bury Fair*; Maiden, *Tunbridge Walks*; Sir Courtly, *Sir Courtly Nice*); and drinking milk (Trim, *Bury Fair*). Eventually male formality shades into downright effeminacy, perhaps because delicacy of manner is more a female than a male trait. Sir Fopling's "head stands, for the most part, on one side, and his looks are more languishing than a lady's" (*Man of Mode*, I). The younger Shadwell's "finical sea fop" decorates the cabin of his man-of-war like a lady's chamber, with china displayed around the walls (*Fair Quaker of Deal*). Finally, Maiden of *Tunbridge Walks*, described as "an effeminate coxcomb," claims to be kept by a gentle-man and likes to wear dresses to the theatre (II).[19]

Finical costume is a definitive element of foppery, and the plays are full of style shows, dressing scenes, and mirror inspections that show off the fop in his full regalia. Concerning the dress and bearing of male protagonists, little is said, but the keynote of good manners would seem to be informality and masculinity in dress. What other behavior is possible to a set of characters bearing names like Careless, Manly, Ramble, Wilding, Airy, and Easy? Compared to the usual modern production of a Restoration comedy in which everyone on the stage, male or female, behaves like some sort of fop[20] (the recent Peter Wood production of *Love for Love* at the National Theatre in London is a most welcome exception), seventeenth- and eighteenth-century productions must have shown clear distinctions between fops and their antagonists in the dramatic conflict. Perceiving such a difference, in fact, may be necessary to understanding the play. It seems apparent, first of all, that the costume of protagonists was more plain and simple than that of fops. In *Love in a Wood* the wits love the dark because

---

[19] Kissing men appears to be a foppish aberration. Protagonists (e.g., Rhodophil and Palamede, *Marriage à la Mode*; Horner, *The Country Wife*) kiss men when they are actually girls in breeches. This seems to be part of the joke; and when Old Coupler makes apparently homosexual advances on Young Fashion (*The Relapse*), it must be realized that Young Fashion was originally played by a girl. "Sir Anthony Love," actually a courtesan in breeches, carried the joke as far as it could go when she actually disappointed a homosexual old abbé by revealing her sex. Old Coupler, this abbé, and Maiden (*Tunbridge Walks*) are the only clearly homosexual charac-ters in the 83 plays.

[20] At least in the dozen or so productions I have seen, chiefly in England.

their inattention to dress will not be observed (II). The fact that Roe-buck's old clothes "demonstrate him a wit" (I) in *Love and a Bottle* is some confirmation of that rule. According to lines in the plays, Careless and Wild (*Parson's Wedding*, III), Gerard (*Gentleman Dancing Master*, I), Manly (*Plain Dealer*, II), Elder Worthy (*Love's Last Shift*, II), Carlos (*Love Makes a Man*, I), Clerimont Senior (*Tender Husband*, V), and Colonel Fainwell (*Bold Stroke for a Wife*, V) dress plainly. Otway's wits, Beaugard and Courtine, appear in dirty worn-out clothes. Dorimant may be more "the man of mode," but he clearly rejects Sir Fopling's extreme. When his man Handy fusses too much with his cravat, he says, "Leave that unnecessary fiddling."

> HANDY.   You love to have your clothes hang just, Sir.
> DORIMANT.   I love to be well dressed, Sir, and think it no scandal to my understanding.
> HANDY.   Will you use the essence or orange flower water?
> DORIMANT.   I will smell as I do today, no offense to the Ladies' noses.
> HANDY.   Your pleasure, Sir.
> DORIMANT.   That a man's excellency should lie in the neatly tying of a ribbon or a cravat!
>
> (I)

Three acts later Sir Fopling is complaining, "I never saw [Dorimant] have a handsome cravat."

It is probable that most protagonists were well dressed by the standards of the age, but not overdressed. From Cicero to Lord Chesterfield, the accepted moralists recommended a style of dress that was neither too elegant nor too coarse. According to Chesterfield,

> Any affectation whatsoever in dress implies . . . a flaw in the understanding. . . . A man of sense carefully avoids any particular character in his dress; he is accurately clean for his own sake; but all the rest is for other people's. He dresses as well, and in the same manner, as the people of sense and fashion of the place where he is. If he dresses better, as he thinks, that is, more than they, he is a fop; if he dresses worse, he is unpardonably negligent. But of the two, I would rather have a young fellow too much than too little dressed; the excess on

that side will wear off, with a little age and reflection; but if he is negligent at twenty, he will be a sloven at forty, and stink at fifty years old. Dress yourself fine, where others are fine; and plain where others are plain; but take care always that your clothes are well made, and fit you, for otherwise they will give you a very awkward air. When you are once well dressed for the day think no more of it afterward; and, without any stiffness for fear of discomposing that dress, let all your motions be as easy and natural as if you had no clothes on at all.[21]

Contemporary descriptions of actors may give us some idea of how they dressed and carried themselves. Wilks, who played characters named Wilding, Rover, Easy, Careless, Frolic, Rashley, and Airy, appears to have been somewhat more dressy on stage than such names would imply. He "was so genteely elegant in his fancy of dress for the stage that he was often followed in his fashion, though in the street his plainness was remarkable," says the stage historian Chetwood.[22] Wilks's most famous character was Sir Harry Wildair of *The Constant Couple* who gained Farquhar a compliment because the character showed that "a man of sense may dress and be a beau."[23] This statement, by making Sir Harry exceptional, shows that men of sense do not *normally* overdress. It is possible either that Wilks was simply more "genteely elegant" than his predecessors or that Chetwood remembered him chiefly for the dressy Sir Harry. Suffice it to say that a man whose private tastes ran to plainness must have known how to distinguish himself on the stage from the fops. There was nothing showy about Wilks's manner, according to John Downes, the Drury Lane prompter during Wilks's early days at that theatre. Wilks, he records, was "proper and comely in person, of graceful port, mien, and air; void of affectation. . . . The emission of his words free, easy, and natural. . . . He is indeed the finished copy of his famous predecessor, Mr. Charles Hart."[24] Hart played Wildblood, Ranger, Jolly, and Manly.

[21] Philip Dormer Stanhope, Lord Chesterfield, *Letters to His Son* (Washington, D.C., 1901), Letter LXI, December 30, 1748, p. 151.

[22] W. R. Chetwood, *General History of the Stage* (London, 1749), p. 236.

[23] George Farquhar, *Complete Works*, ed. Charles Stonehill (Bloomsbury, 1930), II:261.

[24] John Downes, *Roscius Anglicanus* (London, 1886), p. 51.

Another specialist in fine gentlemen (Careless, Rambler, Ranger, Rover) was Jack Verbruggen, described as an "unpolished hero" who, in Colley Cibber's opinion, portrayed "nature without extravagance." Davies records that Verbruggen "had a roughness and a negligent agreeable wildness in his manner, action, and mien which became him well." Speaking of Mountfort, another specialist in this line (Wildish, Reveller, Rover), Cibber emphasizes naturalness again. When he played the fine gentleman, "the wit of the poet seemed always to come from him extempore."[25] Though there is not specific reference to clothes in these accounts, the dress of actors would have to be part of the image they projected and which these commentators received.

Hints here and there in the plays suggest that leading ladies were also more conservatively dressed than their antagonists. Gertrude of *Bury Fair* does not paint, on principle (II). Hippolita of *The Gentleman Dancing Master* calls herself a "homebred simple girl" (II). Etherege's Harriet will not allow her maid to set a curl in order, remarking, "Women ought to be no more fond of dressing than fools should be of talking" (*Man of Mode*, III). Mrs. Behn's Isabella of *Sir Patient Fancy* also complains of her maid's fussing with her hair (III). Amanda of *The Relapse* maintains she is "a plain unpolished thing" (IV), and Sylvia of *The Recruiting Officer* thinks that she, too, is "plain" (I).

A recent essay by Miss N. W. Henshaw[26] on Restoration acting technique, based on the study of contemporary French and English graphics, reinforces this hypothesis that protagonists' dress and manners avoided foppish excess. Miss Henshaw has established that French manners and dress, though widely adopted by the English *beau monde*, were at the same time looked upon as the epitome of affectation. Evidence from the plays I have studied corroborates Miss Henshaw's conclusion. Just as foppery meant Greek fashions to the Romans, it meant French fashions to the English. Lady Fantast of *Bury Fair* maintained that one's conversation should be "larded" all over with French phrases, and Melantha of *Marriage à la Mode* in a session with her maid gives a pretty demonstration of how to construct a French facade.

[25] Colley Cibber, *An Apology for the Life of Mr. Colley Cibber*, ed. Robert Lowe (London, 1889), I:128; II:311, 312; Davies, III:424.

[26] N. W. Henshaw, "Graphic Sources for a Modern Approach to the Acting of Restoration Comedy," *Educational Theatre Journal*, XX (May, 1968):157–70.

MELANTHA. O, are you there minion? And, well, are not you
a most precious damsel, to retard all my visits for want of
language, when you know you are paid so well for furnish-
ing me with new words for my daily conversation? Let me
die, if I have not run the risk already to speak like one of
the vulgar, and if I have one phrase left in all my store that
is not threadbare *et usé* and fit for nothing but to be
thrown to peasants.

PHILOTIS. Indeed, madam, I have been very diligent in my
vocation; but you have so drained all the French plays and
romances that they are not able to supply you with words
for your daily expense.

MELANTHA. Drained? What a word's there! *Epuisée*, you
sot you. Come, produce your morning's work. . . . Four-
teen or fifteen words to last me a whole day? Let me die, at
this rate I cannot last till night. Come, read your works:
twenty to one, half of them will not pass muster neither.

PHILOTIS. *Sottises.*

MELANTHA. *Sottises: bon.* That's an excellent word to begin
withal; as, for example, he or she said a thousand *sottises*
to me. Proceed.

PHILOTIS. *Figure*: As, what a *figure* of a man is there! *Naïve,
naïveté.*

MELANTHA. *Naïve!* as how?

PHILOTIS. Speaking of a thing that was naturally said, it was
so *naïve*; or such an innocent piece of simplicity 'twas such
a *naïveté.*

MELANTHA. Truce with your interpretations. Make haste.

PHILOTIS. *Foible, chagrin, grimace, embarrassé, double entendre, équivoque, éclaircissement, suite, bévue, façon, pen-
chant, coup d'étourdi,* and *ridicule.*

MELANTHA. Hold, hold; how did they begin?

PHILOTIS. They begin at *sottises* and ended *en ridicule.*

(III)

The great fops all aped French ways. Etherege's Sir Fopling "went
to Paris a plain, bashful English blockhead and is returned a fine,
undertaking French fop" (IV). Sir Courtly Nice, Sir Novelty Fashion
of *Love's Last Shift,* and his sequel Lord Foppington of *The Relapse*
also affected French ways. However much Restoration comedy may

be indebted to French criticism, drama, or culture, it consistently scorns
exhibitors of French speech or manners (23 of 26); 10 in 11 protagonists who state a preference are overt Anglophiles. On the evidence of
contemporary graphics, Miss Henshaw reaches much the same conclusion as I do: "The English prints are always a little looser and freer,
a little more careless in atmosphere, a little less formal in execution.
. . . Dorimant and Mirabel . . . put on French forms without French
politeness, without French emphasis on complaisance at all costs. They
made a point of maintaining their English propensities for idiosyncrasy,
understated directness and a certain deprecating common sense. In
short, the fancy new French sauce did not essentially alter the robust
flavor of the roast beef of old England."[27]

It is not a large jump from foppery in dress and bearing to foppery
in words. Clothes were something you added to the naked body to
present it effectively; wit was something you added to the naked truth
for the same reason. Both Wycherley and Cibber (in his first play)
recognized the family relationship between false wit and foppish dress,
Wycherley by having his fop say, "A man by his dress, as much as by
anything, shows his wit and judgment, nay, and his courage too"
(*Plain Dealer*, II); and Cibber by informing us that the fop "in his new
suit . . . is as full of variety as a good play . . . a very pleasant comedy
indeed . . . and dressed with a good deal of satire" (*Love's Last Shift*,
II). Later, in *A Tale of a Tub*, Swift ironically maintained that "embroidery is sheer wit," intentionally making the mistake of all fops and
witwouds, which is to substitute manner for content.

The modern reader of Restoration comedy may distinguish two
types of aristocratic fake: the *fop*, whose affectation took the form of
fancy dress, and the *witwoud*, who specialized in verbal pretension.
Actually the plays seem to have lumped these two types together under
the name of *fop*, with the understanding that affectation in language is
a simple extension of affectation in dress. So Witwoud of *The Way of
the World*, most notable in the text for his "similitudes," is referred to
as a *fop*, suggesting that the word did not then signify specifically ostentation in dress as it does now but ostentation in general. Further, the
part of Witwoud belonged to Colley Cibber, the actor famous also for

[27] *Ibid.*, p. 170.

his renditions of Sir Courtly Nice, Sir Fopling Flutter, Sir Novelty Fashion, and Lord Foppington. We should probably imagine Witwoud's lines delivered by an actor displaying all the foppish accoutrements and mannerisms. Of Cibber's 16 foppish parts, 5 contain only verbal affectation, but affectation in dress must certainly have been added by the actor.

"Natural wit," says Hobbes, "consists principally of two things: *celerity of imagining* (that is, swift succession of one thought to another) and *steady direction to some approved end.*" Dryden's definition of wit as "a propriety of thoughts and words . . . elegantly *adapted to the subject*" places the same emphasis on direction. *Sheer* wit and *embroidery* have no direction—they are ends in themselves. No "use [is] to be made of them," to quote Hobbes again.[28] It was easy enough to acquire metaphors, similes, buttons, and bows, but it was not so easy to find an appropriate way to use them. The witwoud, owning a large collection of memorized witticisms, was always in search of suitable occasions; the true wit, who was really inventive, thanks to his "celerity of imagining," could always find similitudes to fit occasions. It was not the very *use* of figurative language itself that constituted artificial wit, as "social mode" critics assume, but the *mis*-use of it. Depending on its pertinence to what concerns the company, wit, like attractive and unobtrusive dress, could be a generous contribution to mutual enjoyment and enlightenment, or a jarring distraction. Again, it is easier to define true wit in terms of Restoration comedy by a survey of the don'ts than by a search for the do's.

Impertinence is the word most commonly used for the various violations of verbal decorum that occur in the plays. The word itself emphasizes relevance, as Hobbes and Dryden do. False wit is above all not pertinent. Wycherley's Novel was an excellent false wit: "Pshaw! talking is like fencing, the quicker the better; run 'em down, run 'em down, no matter for parrying; push on still, sa, sa, sa! no matter whether you argue in form, push in guard or no." "Or hit or no," concludes Manly significantly (*Plain Dealer*, V). Among fops in Restoration comedy, the hits were few and far between. They missed the mark because of pretentious diction, irrelevant similitudes, puns, and railing.

---

[28] Thomas Hobbes, *Leviathan* (Oxford, 1909), chap. 8; John Dryden, *Essays*, ed. W. D. Ker (Oxford, 1926), I: 190.

This list is probably not exhaustive, but I believe it does illustrate the principal emphases in the plays.

Pretentious diction is our term for language in which highfalutin words are substituted for sense. The compliment, a sort of set piece in conversation, which encourages competition, brought out the worst in some of Congreve's characters, as in this expression of gratitude from Sir Joseph Wittol: "Hem, hem, sir, I most submissively implore your pardon for my transgression of ingratitude and omission; having my entire dependence Sir, upon the superfluity of your goodness, which, like an inundation, will, I hope, totally immerge the recollection of my error, and leave me floating in your sight upon the full-blown bladders of repentance, by the help of which I shall once more hope to swim into your favor" (*Old Bachelor*, II). Complete nonsense results when Congreve's Lady Plyant, noted for her "excellence of phrase," returns a compliment from a young man to whom she is much attracted: "Mr. Careless, if a person that is wholly illiterate might be supposed to be capable of being qualified to make a suitable return to those obligations which you are pleased to confer upon one that is wholly incapable of being qualified in all those circumstances, I'm sure I should rather attempt it than anything in the world . . . for I'm sure there's nothing in the world that I would rather" (*Double Dealer*, III). When this sort of double-talk is done intentionally as a sort of put-on, known as *banter*, it is still false wit. Shadwell gives a good example of its use and form in *The Squire of Alsatia*, when the booby servant Lolpoop questions the proceedings of a sharper named Cheatly, who he thinks is cheating his master. Cheatly then attempts to "banter" Lolpoop into acquiescence: "Your master being in this matter, to deport his countenance somewhat obliquely to some principles which others but out of a mature gravity may have weighed, and think too heavy to be undertaken; what does it avail you if you shall precipitate or plunge yourself into affairs as unsuitable to your phys'nomy as they are to your complexion?" (I).

Pretentious diction also turns up in the form of jargon or cant: terminology of a particular trade, profession, or intellectual enterprise. Samples of the religious variety have already been given.[29] In comedy all attempts to conduct one's affairs on the heroic level are ridiculous, so

[29] See pp. 42–45.

that any approach to the style of Restoration tragedy consequently becomes another form of cant. The tirades of Etherege's Loveit and the many other "injured" ladies of the comedies were probably received as hilariously pretentious heroic cant when originally acted. It is interesting to notice, in reference to this shift of meaning when tragic style is transferred to the context of comedy, that Mrs. Barry, who was most famous for her tragic roles, also played Loveit and 10 other heroically impassioned ladies in the comedies, among them Mrs. Marwood of *The Way of the World* and Angelica of *The Rover*. Sensible heroines never trusted protestations of love in the heroic vein. Platonic lovers Constant and Sadd in Killigrew's *Parson's Wedding*; Modish and Estridge of *The Mulberry Garden*, with their "flames and pity"; Sir Mannerly Shallow of *The Country Wit*, reading tragedies as a guide to manners and phraseology; Lord George Brilliant of Cibber's *Lady's Last Stake*, to whose sentiments "not blank verse but rhyme" was more appropriate—all such (I have counted 12) earned laughter for their pains. Olivia (*Mulberry Garden*), Belinda (*Parson's Wedding*), Cynthia (*Double Dealer*), Harriot (*The Funeral*), Angelica (*The Gamester*), and Annabella (*Quaker's Wedding*) reject the "whining" type of lover, as this type is generally called. Gertrude in *Bury Fair* is eloquent in her contempt for such suitors: "'Tis all alike. 'Madam, your beauties! your excellent accomplishments! your extraordinary merits! Divine, etc. The lustre of your eyes! and the rest. The honor to kiss your fair hands! etc.!' All this we have in romances and love and honor plays. Trust me ... 'tis tedious." Not only is it tedious, but it is not to be credited: "I mind vows in love no more than oaths in anger," asserts Gertrude (III). Equally vociferous in her contempt of elegant courtship is Diana of *The Revenge*. "Heavens, what a long, tedious tale of faiths and troths here! Could I once see the man I liked, I'd have done a thousand fine and more material things by this time" (II). For her part she prefers a plain-dealing lover and will be one herself. "'Tis not those that talk roguishly that are to be suspected: You shall have a hypocritical holy sister mince that publicly that she'll receive with opens arms privately" (III). One of the pleasantest moments in Steele's dramatic works is that in *The Funeral* (1701) when plain-dealing Harriot and Campley observe the blank verse rhapsodies of the other pair of lovers:

HARRIOT.   Ay, marry, these are high doings indeed; the greatness of the occasion has burst their passion into speech.
Why, but Mr. Campley, when we are near these fine folks,
you and I are but mere sweethearts. . . .

CAMPLEY.   Prithee, why dost name us poor animals? They
have forgot there are such creatures as their old acquaintance Tom and Harriot.

(V)

Legal, medical, commercial, and academic cant also came in for their
share of ridicule. It was very silly, as we have noted, to display one's
knowledge of French.[30] Novelty in language was also a good way to
attract attention. In *Cutter of Coleman Street* (1661) Puny, who
"scorns to speak anything that's common and finds out some impertinent similitude for everything" (II), sets a style that persists (IV). Sir
Mannerly Shallow (*Country Wit*) looked for "out of the way" similes.
Wycherley's Dapperwit accompanied his laboriously assembled wit
with the remark, "That's new again, the thought's new," but he was
accused all the same of retailing "last year's sonnets" (*Love in a Wood*,
I, V). Quite often the fop's search for novelty in speech took the form
of an uncommon oath that he repeated *ad infinitum* and which could
serve as a sort of tag for his character. "Let me die" was Melantha's
continual refrain in *Marriage à la Mode*. "Let me perish" announced
the presence of Sir Fopling Flutter. "Split me" also had a certain distinction. But perhaps the most curious fate a man ever wished upon
himself was Sir Novelty Fashion's "Stap [stop] my vitals," although
the "finical sea fop" Mizen in the younger Shadwell's *Fair Quaker of
Deal* introduced several interesting variations on "May I be keel-
hauled." Gallicisms like Sir Martin Mar-all's "You have reason" or
Monsieur Parris's often-repeated willingness to "do you reason" (*Gentleman Dancing Master*) also helped to give a fop an "out of the
way" air.

Pretentious diction is always with us, and its forms do not change a
great deal. Impertinent similitudes and pointless railing are more peculiar to the period of the comedies. According to Hobbes, wit originates

[30] See pp. 119–21.

in the observation of "similitudes" between "things that pass through the imagination."[31] Sir Mannerly Shallow, Crowne's *Country Wit*, thought that "a witty man's head is a simile bed" (IV). Wycherley's Dapperwit in *Love in a Wood* was nicknamed "Mr. or as" (III). But the mere production of similes did not qualify one as a wit. No one, as the eighteenth-century stage historian Thomas Davies recognized, excelled Congreve in the actual demonstrations of the misuse of figurative language.[32] We have seen how the high-flown compliment became a major disaster in the hands of Sir Joseph Wittol in *The Old Bachelor*. In *The Double Dealer* Congreve shows Lady Froth in the throes of demolishing the epic form with the help of her friend Brisk, as the two compose an episode about her coachman.

> BRISK. Being an heroic poem, had not you better call him a *charioteer*? *Charioteer* sounds great; besides, your ladyship's coachman having a red face and you comparing him to the sun; and you know the sun is called *Heaven's charioteer*.
>
> LADY FROTH. Oh, infinitely better! I am extremely beholden to you for the hint; stay, we'll read over those half a score lines again. Let me see here, you know what goes before—the comparison, you know. [*reads*]
>
> > For as the sun shines every day,
> > So, of our coachman I may say—
>
> BRISK. I'm afraid that simile won't do in wet weather; because you say the sun shines every day.
>
> LADY FROTH. No, for the sun it won't, but it will do for the coachman: for you know there's most occasion for a coach in wet weather.
>
> BRISK. Right, right, that saves all.
>
> LADY FROTH. Then, I don't say the sun shines all the day, but that he peeps now and then; yet he does shine all the day too, you know, though we don't see him.
>
> BRISK. Right, but the vulgar will never comprehend that.
>
> LADY FROTH. Well, you shall hear. Let me see. [*reads*]

[31] Hobbes, chap. 8.
[32] Davies, III:355.

> For as the sun shines every day,
> So, of our coachman I may say,
> He shows his drunken fiery face,
> Just as the sun does, more or less.

BRISK.   That's right, all's well, all's well!—"More or less."[33]

(III)

But "more or less" is *not* "well." Clearly what outrages Congreve, apart from the dilettante and pretentious self-satisfaction of this woman, is the gross inaccuracy of her language, actually its impertinence. The same thing bothers Crowne, whose Sir Mannerly admires the following couplet by himself:

> How do the nimble glories of her eye
> Frisk and curvet, and swiftly gallop by?

"There's a fine comparison, to compare a lady's eye to a horse." His friend Lady Faddle agrees: "Ay, and *nimble* is a fine, odd, out of the way epithet for *glories, nimble glories*" (IV). John Dennis was perhaps better at criticizing bad writing than in imitating it, for certainly it is difficult to believe that even such a dunce as his Bull Junior of *Plot and No Plot* (1697) could "sigh like a gun of largest bore" in a poem addressed to his mistress (III). "Odious comparisons" were the hallmark of fops so widely separated in time as Cowley's Puny (IV) of *The Cutter of Coleman Street* (1661) and Dorante (III) of Mrs. Centlivre's *The Gamester* (1705). Sosia of Dryden's *Amphitryon* (1690) used "villainous tropes and figures" (III).

Shrewd criticism of falsehood and corruption in the world, an attribute of true wit, can under certain circumstances be confused with ill humor. Therefore we also have fops who think railing and detraction are wit. In 1700 Congreve objectified this nasty kind of false wit in Petulant of *The Way of the World*, but aimless railing had been attacked before. In 1676 Wycherley's Novel made the basic error of assuming that "railing, roaring and making a noise" were "wit" (*Plain Dealer*, V). *The Revenge* contained a fop who could do nothing but contradict, and *Greenwich Park* had one who could only insult. De-

---

[33] Brisk's final "more or less" is added in Congreve's *Works* of 1710.

traction, the destruction of the characters of friends and acquaintances in order to appear a witty critic of humanity, was the most malicious foppish aberration from true wit. Wycherley's Dapperwit wrote "mouldy lampoons" (*Love in a Wood*, I). When, in *The Plain Dealer*, Novel and Olivia assassinate one by one the characters of most of their acquaintances and then conclude by damning one of them for "detraction," the point is that they have been doing just that themselves (II). With Brisk of *The Double Dealer*, Congreve pursues the same theme. Sir Fopling was willing to "sacrifice all [his friends] to [the company's] diversion" (*Man of Mode*, III). To some, as to Witwoud of *The Way of the World*, a detracting fellow like Petulant might appear to have "fire and life" (I), but the malice of a little man is not the *saeva indignatio* of a satirist, despite the few superficial resemblances.

It has been possible to show, in the earlier pages of this chapter, that comic heroes and heroines deal plainly in matters such as dress and manners, in which blocking characters do not. But because true wit is a relative thing, it is impossible to show that protagonistic characters have absolutely true wit. How can they, when some of their creators do not? False wit imitates true wit. How can we be sure that we are dealing with the real thing? We can say only that the heroes of Restoration comedy are true wits only to the extent that their creators are.

The test of Plain-dealing, like that of Liberality and that of Courage, divides the characters in *Love for Love* into the same two protagonistic and antagonistic groups as before. In his mad scene Valentine identifies himself as "Truth" and like a prophet castigates the age he lives in. Scandal says, "I love to speak my mind," and on the next page of the play, so does Ben (III). But Tattle prides himself on being a good "counterfeit" (V). Mrs. Frail "would make an admirable player." Prue learns how to make her "words . . . contradict [her] thoughts" (II). But these are only superficial signs of a much deeper exploration of hypocrisy that is imbedded in the plot structure itself.

To dramatize hypocrisy, Congreve simply gives his antagonistic characters two faces, one false and the other true. When actions built on the assumptions created by the false face are nullified by the appearance of the true face, the audience sees hypocrisy in terms of concrete action: what it looks like, what it does, and what it causes. The moral of the play in this stratum of meaning is to be found in the final couplet, where Congreve has told us to look for it:[34] "The miracle today is, that we find / A lover true: not that a woman's kind." The lines just previous to these tell us that Valentine is exceptional because he has "the constancy" to love until "the reward of love" becomes his due. Constancy of behavior is an outward sign of an open or plain-dealing personality, because one's actual face is one's true face. Hypocrisy manifests itself as inconstancy when the two faces are not congruent, when the true face can replace the assumed face. "I am Truth and hate an old acquaintance with a new face," says "mad" Valentine in one of the play's many references to faces (IV). Congreve shows us this hated sight over and over again.

Tattle (played most often by Cibber) is a form of fop. He is "all over sweet," Prue says of him. "He oozes out false generosity." He speaks of having a "tendre" for Mrs. Frail and professes himself ready to give her his "soul." To complete the picture of a finished ladies' man, he sets himself up as a "mender of reputations," a "keeper of secrets." "I thank heaven," he says, "it has always been a part of my character to handle the reputation of others very tenderly indeed" (I). The outer face—considerate, sweet, discreet, tender Mr. Tattle—conceals the inner man—mean, little, lying Mr. Tattle-tale, whose protestations of secrecy are a way of boasting that he has secrets to keep, and whose real desire to be known to the wits as a deflowerer and adulterer takes precedence over any lady's mere reputation. "For the rogue will speak aloud in the posture of a whisper and deny a woman's name while he gives you the marks of her person: he will forswear receiving a letter from her, and at the same time show you her hand in the superscription. And yet perhaps he has counterfeited the hand, too" (I). No one but an innocent country girl like Prue could have taken Tattle at face value. As a result she soon finds herself in his power. But when the nurse discovers them together, Tattle makes no attempt to handle her reputation tenderly. On the contrary he departs in a hurry, telling her to "come off as you can" (III). Truly, as Ben says, "a fair-weather spark" (III). But Prue's eyes are still not opened, and in Act V she confronts Tattle with the good news that her marriage to Ben will not take place and that she is

[34] See p. 65.

free to marry him. She is more than a little surprised at his lack of interest. Thus we see, through Prue, two faces of Tattle.

To expand the face motif Congreve makes Foresight a physiognomist. In the second act Sir Sampson asks Foresight to analyze Valentine's face:

> Has he not a rogue's face? Speak, brother, you understand physiognomy. . . . He has a damned Tyburn-face, without benefit o' the clergy.
>
> FORESIGHT. Hum—truly I don't care to discourage a young man. He has a violent death in his face; but I hope no danger of hanging.

Death and resurrection, no doubt, Valentine may expect at the hands of Angelica, but the multiple meanings are Congreve's, not Foresight's. We soon find Foresight, prompted by Scandal, inspecting his own face in a mirror to see whether he appears to be failing in health. While he is thus occupied, Scandal courts his wife, who observes, "Was there ever such impudence, to make love to me before my husband's face!" But the face of the husband sees only the husband's face in the mirror, and deciding it is a sick face, the husband retires to bed, leaving his cuckolder in possession of the field (III). He should perhaps have seen his horns sprouting in that mirror, but as Scandal had told him earlier in another context, "Either you suffer yourself to deceive yourself or you do not know yourself." What he is, Valentine describes well enough in his mad style: "His eyes are sunk and his hands shrivelled; his legs dwindled and his back bowed; . . . Ha! Ha! Ha! that a man should have a stomach to a wedding supper when the pigeons ought rather to be laid to his feet, ha! ha! ha!" (IV). With less physiognomy and more vision, Foresight might have seen his true face in the mirror: that of an old man with a young wife.

Later on in the play Foresight tries to read Tattle's physiognomy to discover if his allegation that he knows more secrets than Valentine is true. But as Tattle rightly points out, it is impossible to find out from his face what is going on in his heart (IV). Foresight fails to do just this in the final act after Prue tells him that she is going to marry Tattle (she thinks). Foresight wonders why he could not have predicted this marriage by his art. "Hum, ha!" he says to Tattle, "I think there is something in your physiognomy that has a resemblance of her." "I fancy you have a wrong notion of faces," says Tattle, who then declares, "I have a secret in my heart, which you would be glad to know" —the secret that he is going to marry Angelica. Foresight does not, in fact, know this secret, but neither, of course, does Tattle know it in the sense that it is true. Foresight's futile study of faces, like Tattle's self-deluding appetite for secrets, is symbolic of how difficult it is for characters in the play to know each other by means of outward signs.

It was particularly difficult to know Mrs. Foresight and Mrs. Frail by their faces, as Scandal and Ben discovered. Both of these women are highly sophisticated versions of the prude. The skill with which they keep their countenances is deftly brought forward when we get a brief glimpse behind them in the sisters' first scene together. Mrs. Foresight censures Mrs. Frail for visiting a scandalous place called the World's End.

> MRS. FRAIL.   The world's end! What, do you mean to banter me?
>
> MRS. FORESIGHT.   Poor innocent! You don't know that there's a place called the World's-End? I'll swear you can keep your countenance purely. You'd make an admirable player.
>
> MRS. FRAIL.   I'll swear you have a great deal of confidence, and in my mind too much for the stage.
>
> MRS. FORESIGHT.   Very well, that will appear who has most: You never were at the World's-End?
>
> MRS. FRAIL.   No.
>
> MRS. FORESIGHT.   You deny it positively to my face?
>
> MRS. FRAIL.   Your face! what's your face?
>
> MRS. FORESIGHT.   No matter for that, it's as good a face as yours.
>
> MRS. FRAIL.   Not by a dozen years' wearing. But I do deny it positively to your face then.
>
> MRS. FORESIGHT.   I'll allow you now to find fault with my face; for I swear your impudence has put me out of countenance. But look you here now—where did you lose this gold bodkin?—O sister, sister!
>
> MRS. FRAIL.   My bodkin?

MRS. FORESIGHT.   Nay, 'tis yours, look at it.
MRS. FRAIL.   Well, if you go to that, where did you find
this bodkin? O sister, sister! Sister every way.

(II)

It was easier to know these women carnally than to know what went
on behind their countenances. After proposing himself to Mrs. Foresight as a lover and finding her willing, Scandal concludes, "And now
I think we know one another pretty well" (III). But he does not. When
next morning he speaks fondly to Mrs. Foresight of "the pleasures of
last night . . . too considerable to be forgot so soon," he gets a fine
sample of a marble countenance. "Last night! and what would your
impudence infer from last night? Last night was like the night before,
I think." When Scandal asks her if they did not go to bed together last
night, she asks, "With what face can you ask that question?" But it is
she who possesses the astonishing face, and Scandal shakes his head in
disbelief: "This I have heard before," he says, "but never have believed." Never before had he met a woman who could deny that she
had done favors "with more impudence than she could grant 'em" (IV).
Ben experiences an equally baffling change of face in Mrs. Frail, Mrs.
Foresight's "sister every way." Because Ben knows he is "a little rough"
and that "he wants a little polishing," as his father says, he is surprised
when the town-bred Mrs. Frail takes his side. "Not at all," she counters,
"I like his humor mightily; it's plain and honest. I should like such a
humor in a husband extremely" (III). Since kind action normally follows kind words, and since seagoing men apparently expect people to
be what they seem to be, Ben is mightily taken aback by Mrs. Frail's
sudden about-face when she discovers that Valentine will inherit his
father's estate instead of him. Having undergone a "hurricane" from
his father for preferring Mrs. Frail to Prue, he expects to have her approbation, but instead he finds "the wind's changed." Suddenly Mrs.
Frail is full of prudish virtue and piety—the tragic actress, Mrs. Barry,
played the role originally: "And were you this undutiful and graceless
wretch to your father? . . . O impiety! How have I been mistaken!
What an inhuman merciless creature have I set my heart upon! O, I
am happy to have discovered the shelves and quicksands that lurk beneath that faithless smiling face!" But hers had been the smiling face
that covers quicksands, and Ben is glad to have discovered them. "Let

them marry you as don't know you: gad, I know you too well, by sad experience" (IV).

Both sons experience the inconstancy of a father who is continually altering his course to follow the vagaries of his interest. In the early acts of the play Sir Sampson believes that Valentine is "of all my boys the most unlike me" (II) and that Ben is a "chip of the old block" (III). But Sir Sampson tacks about suddenly when Valentine, because he is *non compos mentis*, is unable to sign the deed conveying his estate to Ben and Ben refuses to marry Prue. Then it is "Bless thee, Val, how dost thou do, boy?" and much ado to find ways and means to "make [Ben's] heart ache" (IV). These sudden shifts in direction lay open the selfish principle that activates Sir Sampson, giving Angelica puppet strings by which to manipulate him. Using her knowledge of his weaknesses, she makes it possible for him to experience the kind of "sudden eclipse" (Foresight's term) that he has caused others to undergo. "I have tried you . . . and know you," she concludes as the play concludes.

The minor characters, too, are subject to unmasking. Trapland, the scrivener, comes on the scene a proper man of business and leaves a lip-licking whoremaster (I). "Honest" Brief Buckram, the lawyer, serves "mad" Valentine as an excuse for a digression on the hypocrisy of the whole legal profession (IV).

Protagonistic characters are essentially one-faced or constant or plain-dealing unless forced into a mask of self-defense like Angelica, or tempted into one by despair like Valentine. Prue, though a plain-dealer in her lack of guile, is one only in default of the cleverness to be otherwise and does not have Congreve's full approval. Nevertheless, in one of the most delightful scenes in the play she functions as a foil to hypocrisy like the typical hoyden of Restoration comedy. When the counterfeit Tattle teaches her that her "words must contradict [her] thoughts," she asks, not quite believing, "Must I tell a lie then?" "Yes," he answers, "if you'd be well-bred. All well-bred persons lie." After several ridiculous attempts to say one thing and think another, Prue finds herself overjoyed at the novelty. "O Lord, I swear this is pure! I like it better than our old-fashioned country way of speaking one's mind." The fop teaches the hoyden how to be a prude in order that the fops and prudes in the audience may see how ridiculous they are. Prue learns her lesson too well, though. She had asked Tattle, "Must not you lie, too?" and he had replied, "Yes, but you must believe I speak truth." The poor girl does believe him and so pays for her eagerness to desert the "old-fashioned country way" (II).

Congreve invites us to compare Ben and Prue the first time their names are coupled, when Mrs. Frail jokes about the marriage between "the sea-beast" and "the land-monster. . . . The progeny will be all otters; he has been bred at sea, and she has never been out of the country" (I). They are both children of nature, animals, in fact. It is significant that Ben, who remains true to his origins, comes out better in the play than Prue, who does not. Ben serves Congreve as a plain-dealing norm, in effect, by which the other characters can be measured. He is one of 3 (of 11) country-bred fellows in the sample of plays who do not turn fop when they come into town. Since other characters (even Valentine) cannot appreciate him, Ben has to describe himself. " 'Tis but a folly to lie; for to speak one thing and to think just the contrary way, is, as it were, to look one way and row another. Now for my part, d'ye see, I'm for carrying things above board, I'm not for keeping anything under hatches" (III). To Mrs. Frail's doubts of his constancy he answers, "Flesh, you don't think I'm false-hearted like a land man! A sailor will be honest, tho'f mayhap he has never a penny of money in his pocket.—Mayhap I may not have so fair a face as a citizen or a courtier; but for all that, I've as good blood in my veins, and a heart as sound as a biscuit."

"And will you love me always?"

"Nay, an I love once, I'll stick like pitch" (III).

Because his principles are firm, Ben may be angered but he is never dismayed. The chance to make money does not turn him off course as it does his father. When Sir Sampson offers not to marry in order to improve Ben's inheritance, Ben says, "Pray don't let me be your hindrance. . . . Mayhap I have no mind to marry." Mrs. Frail's flattery—"such a handsome young gentleman"—fails to turn his head. "Handsome? he! he! he! nay, forsooth, an you be for joking, I'll joke with you" (III). And when Mrs. Frail deserts him, he is philosophical: "Mayhap I have a good riddance on you" (IV). Ben always presents the same face to the world—his own.

Scandal, because he is a product of civilization and understands the ways of the world, would never have become Mrs. Frail's property as Ben did, but even without Ben's simplicity he, too, loves "to speak his mind," a characteristic which is perhaps more remarkable in a person who is fully aware of the consequences of it. It is Scandal who says that wit is "always contriving its own ruin" (I). To fully understand his function in the play, it will be necessary to look outside its formal limits.

The prologue declares that in *Love for Love* Congreve intends to return to the rigorous satirical standard set by Wycherley in *The Plain Dealer*.

> [Nowadays] satire scarce dares grin, 'tis grown so mild,
> Or only shows its teeth as if it smiled.
> As asses thistles, poets mumble wit,
> And dare not bite, for fear of being bit.
> They hold their pens, as swords are held by fools,
> And are afraid to use their own edge-tools.
> Since *The Plain Dealer*'s scenes of manly rage,
> Not one has dared to lash this crying age.
> This time the poet owns the bold essay,
> Yet hopes there's no ill-manners in his play:
> And he declares by me, he has designed
> Affront to none, but frankly speaks his mind.

The relationship of *The Plain Dealer* to *Love for Love* is more than a similarity of intent. In *The Plain Dealer*, finding his plot too limited a vehicle for all he had to say, Wycherley used the device of having uninvolved characters walk across the stage to give Manly an opportunity to deliver lectures on the vices and follies of the personality type or calling represented by each character. Such lengthy satirical digressions are scarce in Restoration comedy, though short ones abound. Congreve uses Valentine's mad scenes for the same sort of satirical digression, and in this respect appears to be imitating *The Plain Dealer*. It is also apparent that his two male protagonists are modeled on Wycherley's, except that he has reversed their positions. Freeman, the sidekick, has become Valentine and Manly, the major figure, has become Scandal. In moral terms, Wycherley had given the lead to the pessimist: Congreve gave it to the optimist. Scandal, like Manly, refuses to believe that there are honest people in the world; he, too, is given an opportunity to satirize a series of characters in a description of his art gallery; and he, too, is converted in the last act. Thus, besides serving several internal functions, Scandal may be a reincarnation of Wycherley's plain-dealer.[35]

Scandal shows what Valentine could not, that merit and skepticism may coexist, and what Ben could not, that Plain-dealing can accompany sophistication. The comparison between Tattle and Scandal that the first act of the play so strongly urges us to make demonstrates both of these propositions. When Tattle's imminent arrival is announced, Scandal announces his departure, as if one room could not contain such diametrically opposed personalities. But Valentine pleads with him to stay: "You are light and shadow and show one another; he is perfectly thy reverse both in humor and understanding." Like Tattle and unlike Ben, Scandal understands the world, but unlike Tattle, he refuses to comply with it. Unlike Valentine and unlike Tattle, Scandal doubts the possibility of disinterested behavior in human beings, but his skepticism is actually more distinterested than Tattle's sham belief. Tattle and Scandal represent extreme responses to the knowledge that the world is corrupt. While Congreve prefers Scandal's response to Tattle's, he nevertheless prefers Valentine's compromise to either. This compromise is quite similar to Swift's famous position with regard to his fellow men that is laid down in his letter to Pope of September 29, 1725: "I have ever hated all nations, professions, and communities, and all my love is toward individuals: for instance, I hate the tribe of lawyers, but I love Counsellor Such-a-one, Judge Such-a-one: so with physicians—I will not speak of my own trade—soldiers, English, Scotch, French, and the rest. But principally I hate and detest that animal called man, although I heartily love John, Peter, Thomas, and so forth."[36] This passage works for *Love for Love* if we substitute womankind for mankind, and women's names for "John, Peter, Thomas, and so forth." Tattle pretends to love all womankind. Scandal loves none. Valentine loves one. Both Congreve and Swift attack the romantic notion that it is possible to love

---

[35] Davies believes that Scandal is another Manly (III:326).

[36] Jonathan Swift, *Gulliver's Travels and Other Writings*, ed. Louis Landa (Boston, 1960), pp. 493-94.

in general as Tattle pretends to. Tattle, too, appears to descend from *The Plain Dealer* and may be understood as Manly understood his double, Lord Plausible:

> LORD PLAUSIBLE. What, will you be singular then, like no-
>   body? Follow love and esteem nobody?
> MANLY. Rather than be general like you; follow everybody,
>   court and kiss everybody, though perhaps at the same time
>   you hate everybody.
>
> (I)

Scandal, like Swift and Manly, hates mankind because he "follows love" in his loyalty to Valentine. But he is wrong in his blanket rejection of womankind, because it does not allow for the possibility of a good woman in the singular. As Truth, Valentine hates mankind in his mad scene, but he loves both Scandal and Angelica.

Neither Tattle nor Scandal is what he seems to be, but the reasons for our mistaking their identity are different. Tattle wears a false face. Scandal wears his true face, but the world reads it wrong. Valentine says to him, "As you set up for defamation, he is a mender of reputations" (I). If the one is perfectly the reverse of the other as Valentine maintains, then Scandal is no more a defamer than Tattle is a mender of reputations. Congreve is not explicit about how Scandal may defame and not defame as he is explicit about how Tattle may mend and not mend reputations, but it appears from Scandal's behavior that like a true satirist his defaming attacks are general, not particular; that he "lashes the vice, but spares the name." When Tattle is accused of having told what ladies have done him favors, he maintains that he would "never have told particulars. . . . Perhaps I might have talked as of a third person, or have introduced an amour of my own in conversation, by way of novel; but never have explained particulars" (III).

Several episodes are devoted to proving that he does explain them, however. On the other hand, Scandal has the reputation of "a villainous character . . . a libertine in speech as well as practise." Women consider that "it is more dangerous to be seen in conversation with [Scandal] than to allow some other men the last favor" (III), but we have no instances of his divulging any particulars of his affairs. On the contrary, the "pictures" he collects and to which Valentine refers as "satires, descriptions, characters, and lampoons" turn out to be very general indeed. "Most are in black and white," Scandal says,

> And yet there are some set out in their true colors, both man and women. I can show you pride, folly, affectation, wantonness, inconstancy, covetousness, dissimulation, malice, and ignorance, all in one piece. Then I can show you lying, foppery, vanity, cowardice, bragging, lechery, impotence and ugliness in another piece; and yet one of these is a celebrated beauty and t'other a professed beau. . . . I have a beau in a bagnio, cupping for a complexion and sweating for a shape. . . . Then I have a lady burning brandy in a cellar with a hackney coachman. . . . I have some hieroglyphics too; I have a lawyer with a hundred hands, two heads, and but one face; a divine with two faces and one head; . . . I have a poet weighing words and selling praise for praise and a critic picking his pocket. (I)

No particulars are given here nor is it suggested that Scandal ever makes use of particulars. Mrs. Foresight accepts the proposition that his slanders against womankind are a good blind for their affair because no one would suspect an accuser of being a criminal (III), and her secret does prove to be perfectly safe with him. Nor does he violate the trust Valentine places in him as accomplice and confidant of his stratagems. He appears worse than he is.

Scandal is forever stating the unpalatable truth. He informs Trapland flatly that "he has been a whoremaster" (I). When Tattle says, "Scandal, I am yours—that is when you speak well of me," Scandal replies, "That is, when I am yours; for while I am my own or anybody's else, that will never happen" (I). When Mrs. Frail asks Tattle, Scandal, and Valentine which one will escort her to the exchange, Scandal's truthful reply affronts both her modesty and her vanity: "I will: I have a mind to your sister." "Civil!" is her ineffective reply to his bluntness (I). His courtship of Mrs. Foresight, partly before her husband's face, is equally insulting. She should submit to his advances, he claims, because (1) she has "purchased" a husband as a blind for love affairs, and (2) he is "neither deformed nor a fool." He knows her character so perfectly that it is futile for her to continue pretending to be nice any longer. And so impudence succeeds (III). But for such Plain-dealing, Scandal, as we have noted, has sacrificed his reputation. If, like Tattle, he said nice things, the world would overlook what he did in practice. But Scandal is all of a piece, one head with one face. And if his face frightens some people, the fear is in the eye of the beholder.

Angelica, says Valentine, "is harder to be understood than a piece of Egyptian antiquity or an Irish manuscript. . . . She is a medal without a reverse or inscription, for indifference has both sides alike" (IV). His ruse of madness having failed, Valentine concludes that what he had hoped was just a *mask* of indifference is actually Angelica's face. But Angelica does hint that she is wearing a mask. "Never let us know one another better [she says]: for the pleasure of a masquerade is done when we come to show our faces" (IV). But it is a mistake to give this much-quoted remark any final authority in the characterization of Angelica. She does not advocate double-dealing. To be sure, when provoked, she enjoys teasing Valentine. But when Valentine is contrite, she says, "I have done dissembling now . . . and if that coldness which I have always worn before you should turn to an extreme fondness, you must not suspect it" (V). Her final speech justifies this coldness as a countermeasure against his hypocrisy. Her mask of indifference, then, though it may have some superficial resemblance to the impenetrable countenances of Mrs. Frail and Mrs. Foresight, is not fraudulent but is a defensive strategy. That Angelica is a plain-dealer under normal circumstances is proved by the unprudish bawdiness of her dialogues with Sir Sampson and her Uncle Foresight. Being truly chaste, she permits no guilty feelings to drive her to false modesty, as when Mrs. Frail censures Prue for using the word *smock* (II). Angelica's frankness is also demonstrated by her assistance of Scandal and Valentine in the destruction of Tattle's pretenses to secrecy, by her appreciation of Ben as a "sea-wit" (III), and by the clear-headed realism with which she recognizes and faces the dangers to which she is exposed. Congreve demonstrates his confidence in her trustworthiness by having her state the morals of the play.

Valentine's "mad" ravings not only allow Congreve to insert a good deal of satire on things in general (the legal profession, politics of religion, the court, the City, false friends, woman) but they also provide a central symbol for the play. It is a masterstroke that the most striking and most central plot-element should also be an emblem of its central paradox: that Plain-dealing is madness and madness is Plain-dealing.

Plain-dealing is madness because wit is "always contriving its own ruin," as Scandal points out on entering the play. When in Act I Valentine is threatening to turn poet (meaning *playwright*), Scandal ironically objects. "Who would die a martyr to sense in a country where the religion is folly?" It is madness to speak plainly. So, when Valentine lashes the vices and follies of the age, he assumes a character appropriate to the occupation: a madman. It is assumed madness indeed, but in a great tradition: in a world of inverted values, plain-dealers like Hieronimo, Hamlet, Edgar, and Valentine must be mad.

In affairs of the heart, madness has another meaning, but that is a subject for the next chapter.

CHAPTER SIX

Love vs. Self-Love

In the following dialogue about women, is X a fop or a wit?

 x. The women of virtue are grown such idiots in love, they expect of a man, just as they do of a coach horse, that one's appetite, like t'other's flesh, should increase by feeding.

 y. Right . . . and don't consider that *toujours chapons bouilles* will never do with an English stomach.

 x. Ha, ha, ha! To tell you the truth, Charles, I have known so much of that sort of eating that I now think, for an hearty meal, no wildfowl in Europe is comparable to a joint of Banstead mutton.

 z. How do you mean?

 x. Why, that for my part, I had rather have a plain slice of my wife's woman than my guts full of e'er an ortolan duchess in Christendom.

 z. But I thought . . . your business now at Windsor had been your design upon a woman of quality.

 x. That's true . . . though I don't think your fine lady the best dish myself, yet a man of quality can't be without such things at his table.

 z. Oh! then you only desire the reputation of having an affair with her?

 x. I think the reputation is the most inviting part of an amour with most women of quality.

 z. Why so . . . ?

 x. Why, who the devil would run through all the degrees of

form and ceremony that lead one up to the last favor, if it were not for the reputation of understanding the nearest way to get over the difficulty?

z. But . . . since the world sees you make so little of the difficulty, does not the reputation of your being too general an undertaker frighten the women from engaging with you? For they say no man can love but one at a time.

x. That's just one more than ever I came up to, for, stap my breath, if ever I loved one in my life.

z. How do you get 'em then?

x. Why, sometimes as they get other people. I dress and let them get me. Or, if that won't do, as I got my title, I buy 'em.

z. But how can you, that profess indifference, think it worth your while to come so often up to the price of a woman of quality?

x. Because you must know . . . that most of 'em begin now to come down to reason; I mean, those that are to be had, for some die fools.

(II)

X, of course, is a fop: Lord Foppington, in fact, Cibber's famous role in his own play, *The Careless Husband* (1705). One knows he is a fop because comic heroes do not (1) admire themselves; (2) make love for the same reason that they eat, the gratification of appetite; and (3) seduce women of quality and reputation merely for the glory of having brought them down. Lord Foppington's philosophy is that of a perfect libertine. But we are told by recent academic critics that it is not the fops but the heroes of Restoration comedy who are libertines, natural men trying to exist in an artificial society.[1] And of course from Collier until today the notion persists that they are libertines in the simpler meaning of "unprincipled rakes." Nevertheless, as one realizes immediately when one reads Cibber's caricature of the libertine as Lord Foppington, comic heroes are better men than this. However promiscuous they may be, in

[1] Dale Underwood declares that the comic hero sees life as "a ruthless and self-seeking battle for survival, conquest, power, conducted beneath an urbane veneer of 'politesse'" (*Etherege and the 17th Century Comedy of Manners*, New Haven, Conn., 1957, p. 36). See also my n. 13, chap. III.

affairs of the heart they are less vain, less interested in self-gratification, and less eager for self-aggrandizement; they have more regard for the merits of their mistresses as people and their own obligations to them as lovers.

In love affairs Generosity implies a greater regard for the other person than libertinism allows. A brief survey of several contexts in which the word occurs shows some of the things expected of a generous lover. For instance a comic hero noted for "generosity" in *She Would and She Would Not* is also "stark mad—in love" (I), a state of maximum self-abandonment. In *Love Makes a Man* risking one's life for one's beloved and demonstrating constancy are called "a *generous* proof of the most faithful love" (V). Mirabell in *The Way of the World* had "too much *generosity* not to be tender of [a woman's] honor" (I). A woman need not fear rape in keeping an assignation if she can "trust [her lover's] *generosity*" (*Sir Patient Fancy*, III). On the other hand, a lover is "un-*generous*" who after obtaining a woman's favor will "pry into the gift," assert his rights, or behave jealously (*Lying Lover*, II). According to these passages, a male who feels a "generous" passion, then, is in love, willing to risk his life, careful to preserve his mistress's honor, does not use force to win her, and is not possessive after he has done so. Qualities such as these separate the hero of Restoration comedy from the libertine or unprincipled rake.

Another big difference, of course, is that libertines do not marry in the end. If they did it would be unjust, especially poetically unjust, for them to marry the splendid kind of woman usually matched with the hero of Restoration comedy. For this reason the libertine view of Restoration comedy always overlooks or attempts to discredit as a formula the ending of the plays.[2] But I shall try to show that the ending (besides being necessary to a comedy) is also the final confirmation of the hero's Generosity, the evidence of his capacity to give and hazard all he has for a fine woman in the ancient chivalrous way. The plays themselves are generous in a way. Written by men, about a world and for a world in which men can do pretty much what they please, they gallantly give the victory in the war between the sexes to the women, proclaim the

[2] Underwood maintains, for example, that the ending of *The Man of Mode* is "ambiguous" (*ibid.*, p. 92).

advent of peaceful cooperation, and celebrate the production of heirs and the continuation of society. And this is perhaps their principal ethical contribution, their most civilizing force.

Since, again, the affirmative side of Restoration comedy's argument is somewhat tacitly maintained, I shall begin with the negative side, the attitudes of blocking characters. They can be summed up under the three libertine characteristics we have observed in Lord Foppington: self-admiration, self-aggrandizement, and self-gratification.

Narcissism, of course, constitutes an insurmountable barrier to giving one's self generously in love, and the plays present it as such. The wig, the cane, the gloves, the fan, and the snuffbox swim before our eyes whenever we picture the Restoration stage in imagination. To these props we should probably add the mirror which, though not as decisive an indicator of period, is a common feature of the comedies and has greater moral import. Giving instructions to a would-be fop named Mockmode, a dancing master in *Love and a Bottle* tells his pupil to say "zauns" instead of "zoons," to call every man "Sir" and every woman "Madam," to take snuff and never sneeze, and to worship his own shadow in the glass (II). In this episode it seems almost as if Farquhar, in his debut as a playwright, is assuring his audience that he knows how to write a comedy. Gazing in a glass is indeed as proper for fops as not sneezing when they take snuff. Sir Philip Modelove (*Bold Stroke for a Wife*, II), Lord Foppington (*Relapse*, I), Saunter (*Double Gallant*, I), Modish (*Mulberry Garden*, I), Sir Fopling (*Man of Mode*, IV), Sir Courtly (*Sir Courtly Nice*, II, IV), Young Woudbe (*Twin Rivals*, III), Maiden (*Tunbridge Walks*, II, IV), Craffy (*City Politiques*, I), Lord Froth (*Double Dealer*, II), Cimberton (*Conscious Lovers*, III), Sir Timothy Shacklehead (*Lancashire Witches*, III), Bull Junior (*Plot and No Plot*, III), Sir Amorous Vainwit (*Woman Is a Riddle*, II), and Tickletext (*Feigned Courtesans*, I) all enjoy this pleasant occupation.

Among women the looking glass helps to identify a coquette or female narcissist. And so Donna Aurelia (*Evening's Love*, III), Lady Fancyfull (*Provoked Wife*, I), Mrs. Clerimont (*Tender Husband*, III), Melantha (*Marriage à la Mode*, III), Lady Outside (*Woman Is a Riddle*, II), Loveit (*Man of Mode*, II), Belinda (*Old Bachelor*, II, IV), and Lady Wishfort (*Way of the World*, III) are presented looking in mirrors. Although she does not appear on stage with a mirror, Lady

Faddle of *The Country Wit* makes "court to herself" (I). Hortentia of *Aesop* keeps to her chamber and converses with herself because she scorns everyone else (I). Maria of *The Fond Husband* calls herself nature's "masterpiece" (II). The female is at least as vain as the male.

In several plays a direct connection between self-admiration and incapacity to love is made. For instance, in *Love and a Bottle*, after associating Mockmode with the looking glass, Farquhar makes his narcissism the cause of his failure to win a lady. When his rival's appearance on the scene reminds him that he is supposed to be a lover as well as an elegant fellow, Mockmode reflects, "I was so in love with myself that I quite forgot her" (II). Crowne made this same point about a fop more effectively when he had Sir Courtly propose marriage to the wrong woman because he was so engrossed with his own face in the glass that he did not notice what lady he addressed (V). Etherege's Sir Fopling, who may be considered the archetypal if not the original fop, was just as happy studying himself in the mirror as conversing with company (*Man of Mode*, IV). This may explain why it is that when he composes a song to his mistress, it shows a greater interest in his own performance as a lover than in winning her.

> How charming Phillis is, how fair!
>   Ah, that she were as willing
> To ease my wounded heart of care,
>   And make her eyes less killing.
> I sigh, I sigh, I languish now,
>   And love will not let me rest;
> I drive about the Park and bow,
>   Still as I meet my dearest.
>   (IV)

Sir Novelty of *Love's Last Shift* is rejected as a suitor because he has "too great a passion for [his] own person to have any for [his] wife's" (III). Dapperwit fails to win Martha in *Love in a Wood* because she notices that he is so "wedded already to [his] thoughts" that he cannot propose to her (V). Modish and Estridge "can be in love with nothing but [themselves]" (*Mulberry Garden*, I). Addison knew the formula well enough to label Tinsel in his *Drummer* "too great a coxcomb to be capable of love" (IV). Witwoud and Petulant are "not capable" of admiring Millamant (*Way of the World*, II); Lord Foppington "knows not how to value a woman truly deserving" (*Careless Husband*, I); and Cimberton in Steele's otherwise revolutionary *Conscious Lovers* is still the traditional fop in his incapability, by virtue of self-love, of appreciating "the personal charms" of Lucinda (II).

Self-admiration chills an amour. An exemplary lover, it follows, is self-depreciating. True, the plain-dealer's predominant attitude is impudent self-confidence. But self-confidence is not inconsistent with modesty about one's talents and achievements. We see the same mixture of qualities in athletes. Thus Dorimant, who claims, "I fathom all the depths of womankind" (*Man of Mode*, III), may also say, "I am in my *nature* modest" (my italics, I).

Like Dorimant, most plain-dealing or witty heroes show their essential modesty despite their predominant air of impudence. One Wildish will not accept compliments on his wit and finds a fop's civilities "above [his] merit" (*Bury Fair*, I). Another Wildish admits his ineptness as a lover (*Mulberry Garden*, IV). A Don John refuses to accept compliments on his honesty (*Chances*). A Rashley and a Wittmore admit they are bad plotters (*Fond Husband*, III; *Sir Patient Fancy*, II). A Sir George Airy allows himself to be "humbled" by Miranda (*Busy Body*, II). A Horner (*Country Wife*) as cheerfully gives up his reputation for virility for strategic reasons as a Volatil (*Wife's Relief*) does his for courage. A Roebuck calls himself a fool (*Love and a Bottle*, I), and a Mirabell owns "frailties" (*Way of the World*, I). A Colonel Plume does not think himself qualified to marry Silvia (*Recruiting Officer*, III); a Ramble, a "brave universal lover" in *The Country Wit*, thinks, "If I were fifty Rambles bound together, I had not merit enough for [Christina's] love" (II, III); and a Manly "professes himself worse than he is" (*Plain Dealer*, I).

In the blunt, Manly, type of hero, the serious and simple one, self-depreciation may be exaggerated to nearly ridiculous proportions. Bellamy thinks he is "a damned ignorant and senseless fellow" (*Evening's Love*, IV), Carlos (a scholar) admits he has "little understanding" (*Love Makes a Man*, II), Truman does not think he deserves a woman's love (*Squire of Alsatia*, IV), Farewell claims he is not a wit (*Sir Courtly Nice*, IV), Leander calls himself "the greatest dunce in nature" (*Sir Patient Fancy*, I), Clerimont has a "humble opinion of [his] merit"

(*Double Gallant*, II), and Aimwell is just "humble" (*Beaux' Stratagem*, III). Of 4 characters named Worthy, 1 admits he has "more faults . . . than I know how to mend" (*Love's Last Shift*, III); another calls himself an "obsequious, thoughtful, romantic, constant coxcomb" (*Recruiting Officer*, I); another is ashamed for his sins (*Greenwich Park*, V). The last Worthy maintains his "unworthiness" (*Fair Quaker of Deal*, I). Characters with *love* in their names also suffer from inadequacy. Loveworth occasions his friend Reynard's remark that "men of greatest sense are always most doubtful of their merit" (*Tunbridge Walks*, I). Lovewell is "modest" (*Love and a Bottle*, I, IV), Morelove is "modest" enough to "spoil" any woman (*Careless Husband*, III), and Vainlove will not marry Araminta "'til I merit her" (*Old Bachelor*, III).

The female protagonist is modest, too. Heroines of plays by Wycherley, Congreve, Vanbrugh, Crowne, Ravenscroft, Behn, Betterton, Shadwell, Bullock, and Johnson doubt the power of their own charms. Helena of *The Rover* admits to "little wit" (III); Lady Easy of Cibber's *Careless Husband* "can't boast of [her] good qualities" (I); Hypolita of his *She Would and She Would Not* feels "as humble as an offending lover" (I). "Sir Anthony Love" in Southerne's play of that name, actually the courtesan Lucia in breeches, says she "neither desires nor deserves" marriage to the hero Valentine, who offers it (IV); and Dorinda of *The Beaux' Stratagem* doubts that she merits Aimwell (V).

Another feature of the foppish lover is that he thinks of Love as a form of self-aggrandizement. "To be capable of loving one doubtless is better than to possess a thousand," says Heartfree in *The Provoked Wife*. "But how far that capacity's in me, alas I know not" (V). The assumptions on which this statement is based, its hesitancy, the doubts expressed, and the words used all make it a typical plain-dealing remark, although the amount of meaning concentrated into its small compass is indeed somewhat extraordinary. The choice presented to the rambling hero of Restoration comedy is always the choice between one and a thousand, between loving and possessing, between constancy and promiscuity, between giving and taking. "Doubtless," or "I know not"—Heartfree's hesitancy to make an unequivocal affirmation also has the authentic ring of the comedies in general. But Heartfree and his fellows in other plays give promise, are "capable," as he says, may have the "capacity"—if the Liberality, Courage, and Plain-dealing they have exhibited signify anything—to entertain a "generous passion" for some one person. It is Violante of *Sir Courtly Nice* who provides this phrase when she affirms, in the face of evidence to the contrary, her belief that her lover is capable of a "generous passion" (II). It is precisely this passion that the pure rake or libertine, who wants to *possess* a thousand because he cannot give himself to one, knows nothing of.

Generosity excludes "the possession" of one partner by the other. We see, then, that the principle of self-aggrandizement operates in the realm of sex as it does in that of trade. One may set out to acquire a thousand women just as another sets out to make a thousand pounds. In Restoration comedy antagonistic characters of both sexes were capable of looking on members of the opposite sex as commodities to be owned and sold. In the language of the plays to make fools of people was to make "properties" of them (*Man of Mode*, V; *Constant Couple*, III). There is a kind of sexual relationship in which one partner enjoys the cruel excitement of having another human being absolutely in his power. Either the male or the female may seek to "use" or make a "property" of the partner.

Sometimes the female at least was almost literally a property, that is, if she were kept. Although Aimwell may say, "Of all the keepers I think those the worst that keep their money" (*Beaux' Stratagem*, I), keepers of women fare little better in Restoration comedy than misers. Casual keeping like that suggested as part of the past of plain-dealing protagonists in a number of plays is neither developed at length nor condemned, but the few habitual keepers who are substantially presented are severely censured. There are only 5 of these, but there is so much consistency in their treatment that more instances would probably not provide conflicting evidence. In all cases the would-be possessor gets his comeuppance by being possessed himself. Like Keepwell of *Bellamira*, they become the "incorrigible cullies" of mistresses who by fake tantrums and withholding of favors reduce their "owners" to the level of tail-wagging puppies who will perform almost any trick demanded of them to win a caress. The plays show the utmost disdain for them. Lord Drybone, for example, is "a filthy old fellow"

(*Country Wit*, I). Whatever relationship between the sexes the plays do advocate, they are certainly hostile to "keeping."

The pinchwife, who marries "to keep a whore to [himself]" as Horner so aptly puts it (*Country Wife*, I), is merely a keeper whose ownership of the erotic commodity he has bought is legally protected. There are more pinchwives (17) than there are keepers but they are not essentially different in character. In the first place they are worthless as husbands, ranging from 49 to 80 years old. Barnaby of *The Amorous Widow* (II) and Francisco of *The False Count* (I) are simply "impotent"; while others, like Sir Davy Dunce in *The Soldiers' Fortune*, "signify little or nothing" (III). Nevertheless, they lust after young girls and are wealthy enough to marry for sex instead of money. Since they have in effect bought their wives they think of them as property: "My opinion is, my wife's my slave" (Francisco, *False Count*, I). Pinchwife (*Country Wife*, IV) and Wiseacre (*London Cuckolds*, I) are of the same opinion. These latter two and Sir Solomon Single carry such barbarity to its extreme by instituting ridiculous wife-training programs for which the modern term *brainwashing* is the most convenient description. This kind of husband hides his "tender virgin" in a "private and remote quarter of the town," where she is to be "kept and educated" (*Sir Solomon*, I). As if she were a pet, she is trained to do tricks like standing sentry to her husband's nightcap while he is away on business, because she is to understand that this is part of a wife's duty (*London Cuckolds*, IV). The perverse old Pygmalion to whom she is wed at first seems to succeed because his Galatea, very young and fresh from the country, is indeed almost without form. But nature is a better teacher than he is, and a hoyden's healthy appetites soon find their proper object when chance puts a gallant in the way. "C'est une grande difformité dans la nature qu'un vieillard amoureux."[3]

The meanest, most cowardly way of making women one's property is to take possession of their good names. The reputation of having an affair may be for some characters better than having the affair itself. For this reason a woman may be in greater danger from being seen near a

---

[3] Jean de La Bruyère, *Les caractères de Theophraste . . . avec les caractères ou les moeurs de ce siècle* (Paris, 1700), II:100.

fop than from allowing some other men the last favor. *Love's Last Shift* goes to some lengths to show that Narcissa makes a mistake in allowing her name to be connected with that of the boastful Sir Novelty Fashion (IV). A courtesan refuses her favors to Jolly in *The Parson's Wedding* because "they say thy pleasure lies in thy tongue; and therefore, though I do not give thee leave to lie with me, yet I will give thee . . . a thing that will please thee as well. . . . Master Wild shall lie [with me] and you shall have leave to say you do." Master Wild, for his part, speaks for the whole of Restoration comedy in his comments on Jolly's mode of self-promotion: "Never to love, seldom enjoy, and always tell—Faugh, it stinks and stains worse than Shoreditch dirt" (IV).

There are 15 characters in 12 plays who aggrandize their reputations as lady killers by blackening those of their ladies. Sedley, in *The Mulberry Garden*, allows the outcome of the contest for the favors of the heroines to hinge on the fops' blabbing. In *She Would If She Could* his friend Etherege explained why this practice was such a crime against generosity: "A friend that bravely ventures his life in the field to serve me deserves but equally with a mistress that kindly exposes her honor to oblige me, especially when she does it as generously too, and with as little ceremony" (IV). The lady's generosity with her favors obliges the gentleman not only to keep the secret but to fight any man who claims to know it.

Although it is done so unobtrusively as to be almost unnoticeable to modern readers, Etherege's Dorimant significantly observes the doctrine of secrecy in *The Man of Mode*. In Act III, when Bellinda is in danger of exposing her secret by rashly beginning a tête à tête with Dorimant during a gathering at Lady Townley's, he warns her, "Softly! these are laughers." When she persists, he saves the situation by concluding their whispered confidences with a remark "aloud" that disguises the subject of their conversation. Later he lies to his friend Medley when Medley wants to know what he and Bellinda had been talking about (III), and in Act V he lies "aloud" again to disguise the subject of another private conversation with Bellinda, and finally he lies to Mrs. Loveit to put her off the secret, at which Bellinda gratefully remarks, "He's tender of my honor though he's cruel to my love." Dorimant cannot conceal his "famous" affair with Mrs. Loveit, because she herself has published it by her hysterics.

Dorimant is not an exceptional gallant. Roebuck declares that "the tongue is the only member that can hurt a lady's honor" (*Love and a Bottle*, II) and consequently minds his; Bevil thinks "a gentleman ought in honor to lie for his mistress" (*Epsom Wells*, III) and does. When Lodowick preserves Lady Fancy's good name, she can "see [he] is a man of honor and deserves a heart if I had one to give him" (*Sir Patient Fancy*, IV). But in *Tunbridge Walks* (1703) the code is beginning to deteriorate a bit, a phenomenon noticeable in other late plays. Loveworth, a protagonist of this play, somewhat cynically explains to the innocent Hillaria that there are exceptions to the rule of secrecy: "Real intrigues, Madam, we never discover; and only talk of favors in opposition to those ladies [coquettes] who pretend to a crowd of lovers and yet value themselves in having power to resist 'em all" (II). But 22 protagonistic characters in 15 plays bear out the rule that generous lovers do not toy with a lady's good name. We have already noted that protagonists are generous in their material support of women who have done them favors.[4]

If, in the battle of the sexes, the male makes a property of his partner by possessing her, the female may enjoy the same pleasure of absolute power by withholding her favors and thus reducing her lover to abject slavery. The name for this empire-building type of female is the *coquette*. Besides supplying numerous examples of this type, the plays supply a number of characters who may be described as *prudes*, but the characteristics of the two types are so often mixed that it is not practical to isolate them. The fact that neither term by itself can cover all the salient features of the type most frequently presented may result from loose usage of *coquette* and *prude* during the period; or it may be that the two behavior patterns are outward manifestations of one developing psychic condition (this was Pope's understanding of the terms in *The Rape of the Lock*); or it may be that both factors operate to obfuscate the clear distinctions between the words that we easily make today. A survey of the seventeenth- and eighteenth-century contexts in which *coquette* and *prude* occur produces little certainty as to their meanings. Although *prude* seems to retain its sense of a hypocritical squeamishness about sex, and *coquette* retains its attribute of building

---

4 See pp. 63–64.

empires over males, in practice either term may be applied to the other form of behavior, or to something less definite. Dryden, who is the first to use *coquette* in the set of plays with which we are concerned, applies the label to Aurelia in *An Evening's Love* (1668, III), although vanity is her only overtly described trait and by itself vanity would seem too broad a characteristic to need such a specific term. Voltaire entitles his version of *The Plain Dealer* "La Prude ou la Gardesse de la Casette," even though the original Olivia who inspires his title is as notable for the coquette's empire-building and enjoyment of male suffering as she is for the prude's squeamishness. The terms are little used during the seventeenth century, during which we are more likely to find the term *jilt* used for behavior like Olivia's, but in the early eighteenth century, particularly in Cibber's works, they seem well established, though the usage is still confusing. Thus, although Lady Betty Modish of *The Careless Husband* (1704) is accused of being a "coquet" in the usual sense of attracting multiple admirers and "the dear delight of seeing [them] in pain" (II), in a later passage the same motive is attributed to a woman designated as a "prude" (V).

Coquette is used to denote such variant types as Lady Fancyfull in *The Provoked Wife* (1697), who displays the full range of the attributes of the coquette and prude as they are commonly understood; as Hillaria in Baker's *Tunbridge Walks* (1703), who is proper enough except for her desire to marry a rich man and the pleasure she takes in having a duel fought over her; as Lady Outside of Bullock's *Woman Is a Riddle* (1716), whose "ambition," despite her pretense of grief for a deceased husband, "is to have a number of gallants" (II); and as Phillis, the cold-coy maid who apes quality in Steele's *Conscious Lovers* (1722). In *The Rape of the Lock* the word *prude* is used in a context that emphasizes the empire-building, mischief-making, and affectation we commonly associate with coquetry, as well as the ill humor of the prude. The terms seem to be almost interchangeable.

Perhaps one of the reasons that coquette and prude tend to blend in Restoration comedy is that, as Pope explains, prudery is a consequence of coquetry. We seem to be dealing with a widespread kind of female behavior, stemming from a single psychological and cultural basis but having several overt manifestations, any one of which indicates the presence of the whole complex. The salient cultural fact is that in a society in which the female is the vehicle for transmitting economic stability from one generation to the next, she may not have the disposal of herself. This being so, she may not encourage any man whom she cannot marry without exposing herself to censure as a loose woman, and it follows that she certainly cannot encourage more than one man. The definition of coquetry in the *Encyclopédie* (1757) is consistent with this hypothesis: "... c'est dans une femme le dessein de paroître aimable à plusieurs hommes: l'art de les engager & de leur faire espérer un bonheur qu'elle n'a pas résolu de leur accorder: d'où l'on voit que la vie d'un coquette est un tissu de faussetés, une espèce de profession plus incompatible avec la bonté du caractère & de l'esprit & honnêteté véritable que la gallanterie." Vanbrugh's Lady Brute (*Provoked Wife*) well describes and decries the psychological basis of this dated character flaw.

> Coquetry is one of the main ingredients in the natural com-
> position of a woman; and I, as well as others, could be well
> enough pleased to see a crowd of young fellows ogling and
> glancing and watching all occasions to do forty officious
> things: Nay, should some of them push on even to hanging
> or drowning, why—faith—if I should let poor woman alone,
> I should e'en be but too well pleased with it. . . . But after all,
> 'tis a vicious practise in us to give the least encouragement but
> where we design to come to a conclusion. For 'tis an unreason-
> able thing to engage a man in a disease which we beforehand
> resolve we never will apply a cure to. (I)

Protagonistic heroines of Restoration comedy are witty, gay, and frank, and though they may seek adventure and rebel against parental decisions made for them, they almost never compromise themselves by being "forward" with gentlemen or interesting themselves in more than one.

Perhaps because the conditions of courtship underwent little change from the sixteenth to the eighteenth century, one finds a good explanation in Castiglione's *Courtier* of the connection between the outwardly opposite qualities of prude and coquette. How can one character combine an attraction toward men with an aversion to sex? After pointing out how "vain greediness joined with the fondness and cruelty of women [moves them] to procure as much as they can to get them a great number of lovers," Castiglione's spokesman, noting the inconsistency between this "fondness and cruelty," goes on to consider the origin of the cruelty:

> To keep [men] still in afflictions and in desire, they use a certain lofty sourness of threatenings mingled with hope, and would have them to esteem a word, a countenance or a beck of theirs for a chief bliss. And to make men count them chaste and honest, as well others as their lovers, they find means that these sharp and discourteous manners of theirs may be in open sight, for every man to think that they will much worse handle the unworthy, since they handle them so that deserve to be beloved.[5]

This love of power that Castiglione speaks of is a major feature of the coquette-prude in Restoration comedy. Lady Lurewell is "one whose pride is above yielding to a prince" (*Constant Couple*, V). Lady Betty Modish, "one of the proudest beauties in Christendom" (*Careless Husband*, I), avers that "power in all creatures is the height of happiness" (II). Lady Dainty seeks "a conquest worthy of my sex's highest pride" (*Double Gallant*, V). Mrs. Woodly's "imperiousness" is remarkable (*Epsom Wells*, III). Lady Fanciful thinks "all men her captives" (*Provoked Wife*, I). Lady Brumpton explains her ascendancy in her own realm of admirers and justifies her efforts to expand her empire as part of a national trend: men, she says, "imagine themselves mighty things, but government founded on force only is a brutal power. We rule them by their affections, which binds them into belief that they rule us, or at least are in the government with us. But in this nation our power is absolute. Thus, thus, we sway [*playing her fan*]. A fan is the standard and flag of England" (*Funeral*, I). Lady Cockwood, the title character in *She Would If She Could* (1668), is a good example of this empire-building type of coquette. She is called a "jilt" and is the first character in this set of plays to carry coquetry so far as to delight in having a duel fought over her. Since there can be no greater proof of one's power over men than to be considered worth fighting for, co-

---

[5] Castiglione, *Courtier*, tr. Thomas Hoby (Everyman, n.d.), p. 253. I have modernized spelling and punctuation.

quettes, by encouraging duels or intriguing so that they will occur, can be hazards. Lady Lurewell (*Constant Couple*), Narcissa (*Love's Last Shift*), Miss Notable (*Lady's Last Stake*), Olivia (*Plain Dealer*), Angelica (*Rover*), and Hillaria (*Tunbridge Walks*) all cause duels or the threat of duels. In *Woman Is a Riddle* (1716) Lady Outside baldly declares, "'Tis a vast pleasure to have men fight about one" (II), as if she knows that this is a cliché for her type.

Castiglione's "lofty sourness" also pervades the coquette-prudes of Restoration comedy. Lady Flippant boasts, "I never did so mean a thing as . . . to love" (*Love in a Wood*, III), while she sets her cap for all comers; and she is echoed by Narcissa of *Love's Last Shift* and Bellinda of *The Old Bachelor*. Hypolita of *She Would and She Would Not* exhibited to her lover "a coldness unaccountable to sense" (I), for which she was eventually sorry. Lady Wealthy of *The Gamester*, Lady Lurewell of *The Constant Couple*, and Arabella of *The Fair Quaker of Deal* "hate mankind." Mrs. Marwood in *The Way of the World* "dissembles an aversion to mankind." Durfey's coquettes reach melodramatic proportions. In part I of his *Don Quixote* the icy coldness of Marcella actually caused the death of her lover. "What a strange, coy, wild, impertinent, unnatural thing hast thou been hitherto. Thou worest thy eyes as if thou wert a basilisk, destroying others still to please thyself" (pt. II, III). Apparently audiences disapproved of Durfey's allowing Marcella to go unpunished because in the preface of part II he called attention to the fact that he had corrected the omission "by punishing that coy creature by an extravagant passion here, that was so inexorable in the first part." His method of punishment was to have her fall in love with the best friend of the man whose passion for her had destroyed him. Since he can only hate her, she goes out of her mind, but not before he has given her a piece of his, calling her "a creature that can purr and then can squeak [i.e., cry rape]; that scratching can repulse the eager lover and yet be prompt and willing to engender" (II).

Of course this "aversion" is only a pose with all of Marcella's sisterhood. A tension builds up in them from the fact that they are altogether too fond of what they profess to despise, as Etherege and Congreve are telling us when they call their coquette-prudes "Loveit" and "Wishfort." Castiglione rightly interprets the coquette's pretended aversion as cover: "Thinking themselves with this craft safe from slander, oftentimes they lie nightly with the most vile men and whom they scarce know."[6] Such women are simultaneously exposed and punished in Restoration comedy when their lust can no longer be kept a secret. When the truth is out, her two lovers, Manly and Vernish, can read off Olivia in *The Plain Dealer* without ceremony: This lady, who once would spit at the mention of a lover, is at last simply:

MANLY.   A mean, jilting—
VERNISH.   Traitorous—
MANLY.   Base—
VERNISH.   Damned—
MANLY.   Covetous—
VERNISH.   Mercenary whore.

(V)

Perhaps the most outrageous coquette-prude is the Angelica Bianca created by Mrs. Behn in *The Rover*. Here we find a Spanish lady of high birth and irresistible beauty who sells herself for 1,000 crowns a month to prove her aversion to mankind by ruining her lovers financially. When, inevitably, her natural desires conquer her ambitions, she falls in love with the penniless Rover and pays *him* for the favor. But as soon as he has had her, he loses all interest and she joins the ranks of his cast mistresses. Thus Venus punishes all who defy her.

In addition to Castiglione's way, coquetry may generate prudery in Restoration comedy when the coquette, in hopes of binding an admirer to her more firmly, makes the mistake of granting the last favor. Of course the young man tires of easy game, and the coquette, instead of blaming herself, vows to "hate mankind" forever and devotes herself to "revenge" on the "perfidious villain." Lesser slights, real or fancied, can produce the same result. The classic example is Loveit in *The Man of Mode*, whose Phaedraesque rants are echoed by scores of chagrined young ladies in these comedies. Mrs. Loveit, we are sometimes told by Dorimant's detractors, was "spitefully" treated or used with "extreme brutality" by Dorimant.[7] As John Dennis's contemporary interpreta-

---

[6] *Ibid.*
[7] L. C. Knights, "Restoration Comedy: The Reality and the Myth," *Explorations* (London, 1946), p. 139; John Wain, "Restoration Comedy and Its Modern Critics," *Preliminary Essays* (London, 1957), p. 17.

tion of the play proves, when women fall, it is mainly their own fault; and Mrs. Loveit is just another fool being exposed on the stage for the instruction of young ladies in the audience who might make the same mistake. Loveit, says Dennis, "is a just caution to the fair sex never to be so conceited of the power of their charms or their other extraordinary qualities as to believe they can engage a man to be true to them to whom they grant the last favor, without the only sure engagement [marriage] . . . that they shall not be hated and despised by that very person whom they have done everything to oblige."[8]

A woman in this position feels immense chagrin because she senses what she cannot admit to herself, that it was not her own special charms or accomplishments that made the man attentive but something that scores of girls could have managed, even common street girls. She feels that she has been his "property" and she is enraged at him because it is too humiliating to put the blame where it really belongs: "Ungrateful, perjured man!" "Devil, monster, barbarian! I could tear myself in pieces. Revenge, nothing but revenge can ease me. Plague, war, famine, fire. . . . With joy I'd perish to have you in my power but this moment" (*Man of Mode*, II). "Revenge," cries Loveit, and the cry echoes throughout the theatres. "Revenge," cries Flareit of *Love's Last Shift*. "Revenge," cries Mrs. Woodly of *Epsom Wells*. "Revenge," cry Lady Touchwood (*Double Dealers*), Clarinda (*Double Gallant*), Lady Flippant (*Love in a Wood*), Lady Loveall (*Parson's Wedding*), Aurelia (*Cutter of Coleman Street*), Maria (*Fond Husband*), Lady Fancyful (*Provoked Wife*), Corina (*Revenge*), Lady Cockwood (*She Would If She Could*), Mrs. Termagant (*Squire of Alsatia*), Arabella (*Fair Quaker of Deal*), Louisa (*Love Makes a Man*), Lady Wronglove (*Lady's Last Stake*), Mrs. Haughty (*Quaker's Wedding*), Melinda (*Recruiting Officer*), Angelica (*Rover*), and Lady Wishfort (*Way of the World*). "Ungrateful perjured villain," screams Mrs. Raison of *Greenwich Park*. "Base perfidious wretch," echoes Mrs. Haughty of *Quaker's Wedding*. "Ungrateful wretch," "traitor," "perfidious man," "devil incarnate," "unworthy wretch," shrieks Mrs. Termagant of *Squire of Alsatia* and falls into a fit.

But perhaps the most violent tirade comes from the pen of Durfey,

8 John Dennis, "A Defence of Sir Fopling Flutter," *Critical Works*, ed. Niles Hooker (Baltimore, 1943), II:249.

whose Maria responds to her rejection in the following Phaedraesque heroics: "My love refused! 'Tis death to the dull fool; death, double death; damnation too, 'tis likely. But why did I name it love? There's no such word; for with this breath I banish it forever, and in my breast receive obscure revenge, my heart's delightful darling! Oh, the pleasure in that slender word revenge!" (*Fond Husband*, II). The empire-building is over, but perhaps if the cast mistress cannot win back her property, she can spoil someone else's.

Lest the unhappy girl's tantrums be received as merely a normal reaction to her predicament, Etherege, Shadwell, and Congreve each introduce into one of their comedies a second cast mistress whose sensible response to her plight shows how the ill-humored one should have responded. In *Man of Mode* Bellinda, diametrically opposed to Loveit, blames herself for giving in to Dorimant—"I knew him false and helped to make him so"—and holds no grudge for what has happened. "Take no notice of me," she says to her seducer, "and I shall not hate you" (V). Shadwell in like fashion balances a self-condemning Lucy against Mrs. Termagant in *The Squire of Alsatia*. This girl receives the news that her seducer is to marry another with a courageous, "Heart, do not swell so. This has awakened me and made me see my crime. Oh, that it had been sooner!" (V). While Mrs. Fainall of *The Way of the World* is not so unbelievably heroic in tone, she does admit, in contrast to the vengeful Mrs. Marwood, to loving "with indiscretion" and "without bounds"; so far is she from hating Mirabell that he can make her "privy to his whole design" for winning Millamant (II).

Insofar as *The Relapse* may be considered a continuation of *Love's Last Shift*, Berinthia of the former and Flareit of the latter may be considered still another set of good and bad cast mistresses. Berinthia, like Mrs. Fainall, helps her seducer, while Flareit attacks her cooling lover with a sword. Fainlove in *The Tender Husband* helps her erstwhile lover reclaim his wife from extravagant courses. None of these friendly cast mistresses is punished for her slip. In return for services rendered, their one-time lovers protect their reputations (*Man of Mode, Way of the World, Relapse*), provide a generous settlement (*Squire of Alsatia*), arrange advantageous marriages (*Tender Husband, Way of the World*), or help the girl to make a new amorous liaison (*Relapse*). Even for the girl who slips, then, there is a viable alternative to revenge.

One can avoid the "gnome's embrace" and follow Clarissa's advice to coquettes in *The Rape of the Lock* to "keep good humor still whate'er we lose."

There are 65 coquette-prude types in the set of plays under discussion, far the largest group of female blocking characters. Nevertheless, the plays censure only 43 of them (66 percent), principally the earlier ones.[9] Although as late as 1717 Cibber in *The Non-Juror* calls the coquette a "hateful character," the principal female protagonist is identified as a "coquette" and he defends her with copious quotation from Pope's praises of Belinda before her fall in *The Rape of the Lock* (I) and omits from her characterization the quality of prudish hypocrisy. In the later plays the waters are muddied by the fact that initially reprehensible characters are allowed to reform in the end and are forgiven. If harmless after all, coquetry can be attractive, and sentimentalism provides a way of letting us enjoy it without actually approving of it.

Normally, however, the way of self-aggrandizers, especially when they are male, leads to disaster in Restoration comedy. A similar fate awaits another kind of selfish type—the Yahoo—whose motivation is simply gratification of lust. This position is well occupied by Surly in Crowne's *Sir Courtly Nice*. In the second act Surly defines himself in a catechism:

> Q. Hast thou no concern for any beast but thyself?
> SURLY. Yes, bird, for many things for my own sake; for witty men whilst they drink with me, handsome whores whilst they lie with me, dogs, horses, or cattle whilst they belong to me; after that, I care not if the wits be hanged, the whores be poxed, and all the cattle bewitched. . . .
> Q. Have you no love for anything?
> SURLY. I have appetite.
> Q. Have you no love for women?
> SURLY. I have lust.
> Q. No love?

[9] I have made a more thorough analysis of coquette-prudes in an article entitled "The Coquette-Prude as an Actress's Line in Restoration Comedy during the Time of Mrs. Oldfield" (*Theatre Notebook*, XXII (1968):143–56), parts of which are included in this chapter. My attempt there was to find out if the coquette-prude type was recognized as a specialty in the theatres. Apparently it was. Elizabeth Barry and, after her, Christina Horton were the principal specialists in that line.

SURLY. That's the same thing. The word love is a fig-leaf
to cover the naked sense, a fashion brought up by Eve, the
mother of jilts: ... you may import whatever lewdness you
will into [women's] commonwealth if you will wash it
over with some fine name.

For this philosophy, after having been gulled unmercifully, Surly is
hustled off the stage with a box on the ear from the leading lady.
G. W. Knight (possibly following J. W. Krutch) in his recent book,
The Golden Labyrinth, makes the error of attributing these brutal
sentiments to Crowne.[10] This response is one more instance of the
power of an entrenched critical attitude to disarm even the most prac-
ticed judgment.

Surly's most important descendant is Heartwell, the title character
of Congreve's *Old Bachelor*, who thinks love is "drudgery," uses wom-
en like "physick" for his health, "hates the sex," advocates lust instead
of love, and boasts that he is perfectly invulnerable to feminine charms
(I). The aim of the play is to prove that this defiant position is un-
tenable and wrong. It does so by turning Heartwell into Heartsick by
causing him to fall in love with and (he thinks) marry a young lady
who turns out to be a whore. Into this category also falls a sort of booby
named Blunt, in *The Rover*, who maintains he is immune to love. He
prefers "a clap" to "an amour" and would rather buy his sexual satisfaction than take the trouble of wooing a woman for it (I, II). For this
unpopular attitude he is gulled and disgraced by a clever prostitute.

To this group should be added perhaps some of the debauched and
faithless husbands of fine wives, of which the most famous are Loveless
of *Love's Last Shift* and Sir John Brute of *The Provoked Wife*. In Cibber's play Loveless's outrageous infidelity is called "blind, ungrateful,"
and "lewd" (I); Sir John, having married "because he had a mind to lie
with" Lady Brute, has reverted to drinking and whoring by the time
Vanbrugh's play begins. Riot of *The Wife's Relief or the Husband's
Cure* is a repetition of Loveless, even to the device (in this case prevented from conclusion) of his cuckolding himself. In Richmore of *The
Twin Rivals* Farquhar created a rake of truly melodramatic proportions, but this sinister character does not really constitute an indictment

---

[10] G. W. Knight, *The Golden Labyrinth* (New York, 1962), pp. 140–44; J. W.
Krutch, *Comedy and Conscience after the Restoration* (New York, 1949), p. 197.

of the typical hero of Restoration comedy as Farquhar apparently intended it to because, in attempting rape, he loses all claim to kinship. But Richmore is not an innovation, heralding a new morality;[11] he is only the worst in a succession of rakes held up to contempt or ridicule in Restoration comedy. Durfey had presented a rapist in *Don Quixote*, pt. II (1694)—a "damned wolf or satyr" named Diego (I). Vanbrugh had experimented a year earlier than Farquhar with the same sort of uncomical material in *The False Friend*, which actually is described as "A Comedy" on the title page. The villain of that play is a Don John who, "by a general attack" on all the ladies and resolving "to love nothing," like Heartwell of *The Old Bachelor*, keeps his heart his own (I). For this and for attempting to rape his friend's wife, death—nothing less— is Vanbrugh's penalty.

Typical of the phrasemaking that too often passes for criticism of Restoration comedy is the remark made in a symposium on English stage comedy in 1954 to the effect that the Elizabethans had succeeded in grading sex "into love and lust," but that in Restoration comedy sex was allowed to "subside into unity again."[12] The truth is that love and lust were very carefully dichotomized in these plays. Just as we have failed to see the difference between a wit and a rake, we have failed to distinguish two kinds of sex in the plays.

Lust is presented as something brutal, disgusting, and bad; and protagonists are consistently credited with a capacity for something finer, something more generous, something harder to define, something generally called "love" which is specifically not lust. The attitude toward the baser passion often sounds downright Victorian. A fop disgustingly prefers "simple fornication" to love (*Mulberry Garden*, IV); a witwoud who tries to cuckold his father is "a monster" (*City Politiques*, I); another, discussing his appetite for his intended wife in a conceit involving sauce and meat, sets a protagonist's "teeth on edge" (*Country Wife*, IV); an old man who wants to buy a young wife is described as a "goat" (*Aesop*, II); another old man's "blood boils" with lust for his pretty ward (*Busy Body*, III).

In women lust is uglier. Lady Touchwood's "violent passion" leads

<hr>

[11] William Archer, editor of the Mermaid *Farquhar* (New York, 1959), seems to feel that *Twin Rivals* is a radical departure from Restoration moral laxity (p. 22).

[12] *English Institute Essays, 1954* (New York, 1955), p. 105.

her to attempt to "ravish" Mellefont (*Double Dealer*, I); Lady Kno-well has "salacious appetites" (*Sir Patient Fancy*, IV); Olivia in *The Plain Dealer* can be described only in terms of a "goat or monkey" (IV): "the raging flame of inconsiderate lust" motivates Mrs. Haughty (*Quaker's Wedding*, V); Truman must undergo the "most lewd dal-liance" with Ruth in order to subvert her authority as governess to the heroines of *The Squire of Alsatia* (IV); and "intemperance" is a mild word for the passion that moves Louisa to throw herself at Carlos in *Love Makes a Man* (IV). Such lust motivates 84 antagonistic characters.

The persistent notion that these plays encourage what the facts show they in truth condemn has caused us to ignore the very large group of young ladies in them whose purity is unchallengeable and the large number of young men whose intentions are unquestionably honorable. What are we to make of characters like the hero of Cowley's *Cutter of Coleman Street* (1661) who spurns his mistress when he mistakenly be-lieves she has tried to seduce him, saying, "I little thought to see upon our love, / That flourished with so sweet and fresh a beauty, / The slimy traces of that serpent Lust" (III); or of characters like Sir Harry Fillamore of Mrs. Behn's *Feigned Courtesans* (1678) who sees "a vast difference between an innocent passion and a poor faithless lust" (I); or of the "frozen virgin" Violante in *Greenwich Park* (1691) who de-clares, "Love ne'er made whores; conveniency and lust [do]. Love's pure and chaste, the beauty of the mind, if so allowed" (II); or of ladies like Florinda of *The Rover* (1676) who has fallen in love with Belville out of regard for his "merit," not his virility (III)?

Chaste young women and well-intentioned young men are hardly ever missing from a comedy: we find them even in the sordid atmo-sphere of a *Kind Keeper* (1677) or a *Bellamira* (1687). The former contains Mrs. Pleasance, a young lady who in the midst of wholesale fornication is horrified to be offered 50 guineas for her favors and de-livers a lecture that causes the proposer of the fee to realize, "I have another kind of love to this girl than to either of [my compliant mis-tresses]" (IV). *Bellamira* presents a young lady who, though she is mis-takenly raped by a young man, is by him pronounced afterward as innocent as she was before and desired as a bride. One may have to grant that in the latter case Sedley and his audience were perhaps more interested in the rape than in the conversion of the lover, but the conversion cannot be ignored. Moving to more familiar ground, we all remember *The Country Wife* because of Horner and the salacious china closet scene, but we give little weight to the subplot of the play which relates the courtship by a Harcourt—whose intentions are always honorable—of an Alithea—whose behavior never departs from the requirements of modesty and virtue. And in *Man of Mode*, however questionable the conduct of Dorimant, Loveit, and Bellinda may be, Young Bellair and Emilia are simply young people in love who want to get married.

Perhaps we ignore the many innocent lovers in Restoration comedy because they seem irrelevant to what seem to be the main concerns of the plays. But there are so *very* many of them (144 in 64 plays) that perhaps instead we should adjust our conception of these main concerns. How can this virtuous group exist side by side in the world of the comedies with the plain-dealing and cynical heroes and heroines? Perhaps characters like Harcourt and Alithea and like Young Bellair and Emilia occur because they enable the dramatists to repeat in individual plays the complementarity of attitudes that is produced by tragedy and comedy on the stage. Whereas tragedy presents an ideal world, comedy presents the real or imperfect world. Thus Dryden can say, "Admiration would be the delight of [tragedy], and satire of [comedy]."[13] We look up to the characters of tragedy and down on those of comedy. The strong contrast between these two worlds appears to have so greatly fascinated Restoration audiences that a number of tragicomedies were produced—some highly successful—in which the (to us) unmixable worlds existed side by side.

In one play, *Marriage à la Mode*, Dryden takes a keen delight in the irony reflected by one world on the other. He makes Melantha in the comic plot punctuate all her remarks with the oath, "Let me die." On her lips the phrase has sexual connotations, which are strengthened by a poem in Act IV about sexual dying. Also in the comic plot love is discussed in military imagery. Palamede must kiss all night in his own defense; Rhodophil, the husband, is an "old knife," in danger of having "no edge left"; Palamede thinks of challenging his mistress to a duel to "decide the difference betwixt the two sexes." In the heroic plot real

[13] John Dryden, *Essays,* ed. W. P. Ker (Oxford, 1926), I:120.

swords are wielded in deadly earnest, and when Leonidas declares, "I'll die with her" and "If sword and poison be denied me, I'll hold my breath and die," he is not speaking in metaphor. Thus the comic plot serves to elevate the heroic one, while heroic gestures increase the triviality of comic antics.

Complementarity is probably only one reason for combining plots which are to some critics so diametrically opposed in attitude that the critics find it difficult to believe that the same audiences could enjoy both. In the conclusion of these tragicomedies, however, the playwright deliberately merges the two worlds by having the promiscuous, fun-loving, plain-dealing comic hero participate heroically in the heroic action of the other plot. The point is obvious: despite the comic hero's unprepossessing appearance, he has a Great Soul underneath. To an audience descended from the Cavaliers the playwright is in effect saying, "Your external glory has faded but this is what you are really like underneath." As for difference in values, I believe that it should not be hard to show that Generosity energizes tragedy even more clearly than it does comedy.

The set of plays under consideration contains 13 of these tragicomedies, the last (*The Wife's Relief*) being staged first in 1711. Perhaps Charles Johnson who wrote it hoped to capitalize on the popularity, in the early part of the century, of *The Comical Revenge, The Spanish Friar,* and *Love Makes a Man,* all of which exploited the dual motifs.

The Harcourt-Alithea and Young Bellair–Emilia plots of plays like *The Country Wife* and *The Man of Mode* appear to be vestiges of the heroic plots of these tragicomedies. In the name of unity the heroic accents are dulled, but the more serious pair of lovers still provides a contrast which intensifies the comic action. But, more important, when the comic pair in the final act show that they, too, are capable of love, the effect is similar to the joining of the two plots of a tragicomedy in the final act. Underneath these exteriors lie generous hearts.

Although sometimes the differences are greater and sometimes less, it is possible to distinguish two pairs of lovers—one more heroic and the other more comic—in 26 ostensibly unmixed comedies. The contrast between the two types of lovers is often consciously developed, as it is in *The Beaux' Stratagem* where Aimwell's and Dorinda's "romantic" temperaments are pitted against Archer's and Mrs. Sullen's cynical realism in friendly debates; but in most plays one feels that the two pairs exist merely in obedience to a convention whose purpose or potential use has never been considered. Sometimes only the males are contrasted, the females remaining undifferentiated, as is the case with Constant and Heartfree in *Provoked Wife*; sometimes it is the females who are contrasted, while the males are undifferentiated, as is the case with hoydenish "wild and witty" Gatty and the reserved "sly and pretty" Ariana in *She Would If She Could* (II). In fact in this play there is so little difference between the males that Etherege brackets them together in the *dramatis personae* as "honest gentlemen of the town," and they behave as if the bracket remains in place throughout the play.

The plain-dealing or witty protagonist is considerably more complex than his more heroic counterpart. Toward the world he is a wit, a debunker of pretentiousness, a railer against hypocrisy and fraud. Toward womankind he is an "atheist," an "infidel," who strongly doubts the possibility of an enduring relationship with a member of that sex. In a wasteland of doubt he seeks the regenerative faith that heroic characters in the plays exhibit. For this reason he is promiscuous, wandering restlessly from girl to girl. Vanbrugh describes his course of life perfectly in *The Relapse*:

> A man sees perhaps a hundred women he likes well enough for an intrigue, and away; but possibly, through the whole course of his life, does not find above one who is exactly what he could wish her; now her, 'tis a thousand to one, he never gets. Either she is not to be had at all (though that seldom happens, you'll say), or he wants those opportunities that are necessary to gain her. Either she likes somebody else much better than him or uses him like a dog because he likes nobody so well as her. Still something or other Fate claps in the way between them and the woman they are capable of being fond of; and this makes them wander about from mistress to mistress like a pilgrim from town to town, who every night must have a fresh lodging and's in haste to be gone in the morning. (V)

The plain-dealing girl is a wit also, hates pretense also, and doubts protestations of sincerity emanating from men.

There are 159 of these, male and female, in 71 plays, amounting to just a few more than there are of the heroic type. But the fact that they occupy nearly twice as many leading roles makes theirs the dominant attitude toward love. (On a scale of five, 64 percent of the plain-dealers have roles of first importance, but only 38 percent of the heroic type occupy roles of first importance.) That it is an essentially generous attitude must now be demonstrated.

The difference between the plain-dealing and heroic types of love, as I have suggested, is usually expressed in terms of faith and doubt. Upon entering the stage in *The Man of Mode*, the more heroic character, Young Bellair, defends his faith against the plain-dealing Medley in a dialogue that most felicitously defines the opposing doctrines. The argument arises because Young Bellair's engagement to Emilia has prevented him from giving his friends as much of his time as was his custom.

> MEDLEY.   Gentle Sir, how will you answer this visit to us to your honorable mistress? 'Tis not her interest you should keep company with men of sense who will be talking reason.
>
> YOUNG BELLAIR.   I do not fear her pardon; do you but grant me yours for my neglect of late.
>
> MEDLEY.   Though y'ave made us miserable by the want of your good company, to show you I am free from all resentment, may the beautiful cause of our misfortunes give you all the joys happy lovers have shared ever since the world began.
>
> YOUNG BELLAIR.   You wish me in heaven, but you believe me on my journey to hell.
>
> MEDLEY.   You have a good strong faith, and that may contribute much towards your salvation. I confess I am but of an untoward constitution, apt to have doubts and scruples, and in love they are no less distracting than in religion. Were I so near marriage, I should cry out in fits as I ride in my coach, "Cuckold, cuckold!" with no less fury than the mad fanatic does "glory!" in Bethlem.
>
> YOUNG BELLAIR.   Because religion makes some run mad must I live an atheist?
>
> MEDLEY.   Is it not [a] great indiscretion for a man of credit,

who may have money enough on his word, to go and deal with Jews, who for little sums make men enter into bonds and give judgments?

YOUNG BELLAIR. Preach no more on this text. I am determined, and there is no hope of my conversion.

(I)

As plain-dealer, Medley is typical in associating himself with reason, in comparing love to madness, in his atheism or lack of faith, and in his cock-of-the-walk advocation of promiscuity. Young Bellair reverses the usual context of "conversion," for it is normally the atheist who must be converted. The analogy to religious belief is common also. Love is "faith" in *The Comical Revenge, The Old Bachelor, She Would and She Would Not, The Double Gallant, Love for Love*, and *The Wife's Relief*, to mention several. The truly archetypal name for a heroine is that of Fidelia, assuager of the archetypal plain-dealer's doubts in Wycherley's play of that name.

Doubts about marriage are the universal earmarks of plain-dealers in these comedies. Sir Harry Wildair has his choice between fighting a duel and marrying. To show his courage, he marries. As marriage to Millamant approaches, Mirabell says, "Heaven grant I love you not too well" (*Way of the World*, V); and Millamant for her part fears, "If Mirabell will not make a good husband, I am a lost thing—for I find I love him violently" (IV). Heartfree "trembles" at the thought of courting Belinda (*Provoked Wife*, IV). Careless of *The Parson's Wedding* prays, "Lord deliver me from love" (II). Heroes of *The Squire of Alsatia, The Wife's Relief, The Soldiers' Fortune, Love in a Wood, The Gamester, The Feigned Courtesans, Epsom Wells*, and *The Double Dealer* also express fear of marriage. Careless of *The Careless Lovers* is an "atheist in love" (I). Jolly of *The Cheats* and Courtall of *She Would If She Could* are "infidels," like Scandal of *Love for Love*.

The promiscuity that follows from such doubts is best conveyed by a roll call of the plain-dealers: Ramble, "Brave Universal lover" (*Country Wit*, II); Young Valere, "the gay, the Rover, the unconquered Rambler" (*Gamester*, IV); Rover (*Rover*); Ramble (*London Cuckolds*); Ranger (*Love in a Wood*); Woodall (*Kind Keeper*); Atall (*Double Gallant*); Courtall (*She Would If She Could*); Careless (*Committee, Double Gallant, Double Dealer, Careless Lovers, Parson's*

Wedding); Wild (*Parson's Wedding*); Wildish (*Bury Fair, Mulberry Garden*); Wilding (*Quaker's Wedding*); Wildblood (*An Evening's Love*); Sir Harry Wildair (*Constant Couple*); Roebuck, "Wild as winds and unconfined as air" (*Love and a Bottle*, III).

It can be understood that anti-Puritan advocates of nature like the Restoration playwrights would sympathize with healthy animal appetites in the young male. Dennis went so far as to insist (in defense of Dorimant) that the Aristotelian-Horatian requirement of decorum in characterization dictated a certain amount of sexual intemperance in males up to a certain age. Chastity would be improbable.[14] Some writers went to considerable lengths to insure that their plain-dealing hero's promiscuity would be interpreted as harmless youthful high spirits, proper for his age. Dorimant, for instance, makes use of the appeal to nature when he justifies his keeping an assignation with Bellinda, although he is in love with Harriet, by saying, "I am not so foppishly in love here to forget I am flesh and blood yet" (IV). The laws of nature similarly excuse the infidelity of Valentine in *Sir Anthony Love*, who tells himself indulgently, "I may be a lover, but I must be a man" (III). One of Shadwell's plain-dealing heroes is excused by his uncle for being "given to women" because "all young fellows . . . are" (*Squire of Alsatia*, I). In Dryden's *Kind Keeper* "drinking and wenching" are passed over as "the slips of youth" (I).

If we object to this promiscuity, we should observe that the ladies in the plays do not. Their attitudes may probably be taken as a sign of the audience's attitude. Only a prude would object. Somewhat enviously, Ariana says in *She Would If She Could*, "The truth is, [the men] can run and ramble here and there and everywhere, and we poor fools rather think the better of them" (I). One of the ramblers she speaks of defends himself on the same grounds: "Whatsoever women say, I am sure they seldom think the worse of a man for running at all. 'Tis a sign of youth and high mettle, and makes them rather piquée who shall tame him" (III). Bevil and Rains of *Epsom Wells* tell their ladies the same tale: "the wilder we are, the more honor you'll have in reclaiming us" (II). The Rover's "unconstant humor," says Hellena, "makes me love him" (*Rover*, IV); and Dorimant's wickedness makes him attractive to Loveit (*Man of Mode*, II). Betterton's Diana is rather too painfully ex-

14 Dennis, II:246–47.

plicit about the attractiveness of the unconstant humor in men: "I love a man that knows the way to a woman's bed without instructions" (*Revenge*, I). Although she can say this to a confidante, she is not about to let the man she speaks of know it. In a much later play the same idea is more ambiguously expressed: "I love a man that has some sparks of fire in him that will break forth sometimes and light me to his virtues" (*Quaker's Wedding*, II).

And what are these virtues that compensate for the inconstancy that accompanies them? They are the same heroic ones that the playwright assumes when he puts his comic hero in the heroic plot. Farquhar, perhaps because he comes on the scene in the midst of the Collier attack, undertakes to explain what had probably been taken for granted until his time. In *Love and a Bottle* Lovewell knows that Roebuck is better than he appears to be when he says to him, "I . . . esteem thy follies as foils only to set [thy virtues] off" (I); and his mistress knew what these virtues were when she said, "His follies are weakly founded upon the principles of honor, where the very foundation helps to undermine the structure" (III). In *The Recruiting Officer* the theory is refined; now the same high spirit that produces promiscuity produces virtues: the prudish Mellinda cautions her "mad" friend Silvia against setting her heart on wild Captain Plume:

> MELLINDA. Thou poor romantic Quixote! Hast thou the vanity to imagine that a young sprightly officer that rambles o'er half the globe in half a year can confine his thoughts to the little daughter of a country justice in an obscure part of the world?
> SILVIA. Pshaw! what care I for his thoughts? I should not like a man with confined thoughts; it shows a narrowness of soul. Constancy is but a dull, sleepy quality at best— they will hardly admit it among the many virtues; nor do I think it deserves a place with bravery, knowledge, policy, justice, and some other qualities that are proper to that noble sex.
>
> (I)

When a play contains a wild hero like this, the chances are very good that he will be tamed in the course of the dramatic action by a young lady made of similar substance. It happens this way in 54 plays. To qualify for this high mission, the young lady must walk a knife-edge on either side of which lies a precipice of moral destruction. Her precarious position is well conveyed by Steele's attempt in his *Lying Lover* to describe how she seems to her bewitched gallant: "As he that is not honest or brave is no man so she that is not witty or fair is no woman. . . . To come up to that high name and object of desire, she must be gay and chaste, she must at once attract and banish you. I don't know how to express myself, but a woman, methinks, is a being between [men] and the angels. She has something in her that at the same time gives awe and invitation" (I). If invitation exceeds awe she is either seduced and cast off like the rest of the easy wenches or she causes a nasty misunderstanding for which she may be condemned as a coquette. If awe exceeds invitation she will be condemned as a prude. Only by walking the narrow path between these pitfalls can she reach the elevation above common womanhood which enables her to become a beacon to lead her hero out of his wilderness of meaningless affairs.

A certain wildness is the main attractive force, expressed as a sort of giddiness, a heedlessness of strict rules of propriety. For instance, Gatty (*She Would If She Could*), Arabella (*Wife's Relief*), Hellena (*Rover*), and Harriet (*Man of Mode*) are explicitly "wild"; Miranda (*Woman Is a Riddle*), Hippolita (*Gentleman Dancing Master*), Cornelia (*Feigned Courtesans*), Harriot (*Funeral*), Lucia (*Epsom Wells*), and Hillaria (*Careless Lovers*) are "mad"; Maria (*Non-Juror*) is "giddy." Although this giddiness may extend to enjoying "any mischievous design," as it does with Sylvia of Otway's *Soldiers' Fortune* and many others, it does not extend to giving encouragement when the girl does not intend to "come to a conclusion." A typical prank is accosting one's lover in disguise to see how he will behave when he thinks one is someone else. In the pranks and counter-pranks that make up a plot, the girl nearly always succeeds in outwitting the man. Besides giving this proof of her wit, she also shows all the marks of Generosity in the forms of Liberality, Courage, and Plain-dealing that have been identified previously. By this good-humored playfulness she avoids the coquette-prude's coldness.

While she fans the lover's flame by her plaguiness, she holds him off, not by the prude's contempt or bragging aversion, but by withholding every token of favoritism. She is, like Steele's Harriot, "hard to make particular" (*Funeral*, II). Etherege's Harriet, we remember, refused even to talk to Dorimant after it became impossible for her to avoid noticing that his general remarks on love had taken a definite turn in her direction: "Men grow dull when they begin to be particular," she said, turning away (*Man of Mode*, III). At the same time, Harriet is defying her mother by talking to Dorimant at all, and it is thus possible for her to be noteworthy for wildness (I, III, IV) and a certain "coldness" (IV) at the same time. This warring of elements goes on around a good number of plain-dealing heroines.

When Dorimant feels himself falling in love with Harriet, he fears that she "may revenge the wrongs I have done her sex" (IV). Enduring his lady's coldness may not be a sufficient penance for a hardened unbeliever like Dorimant; he may have to pass further tests before she can be sure he is worthy to be her husband. As one lady puts it, "A true lover is to be found out like a true saint, by trial of his patience" (*Soldiers' Fortune*, IV). Therefore Harriet will accept Dorimant only after he has paid suit to her in the country, for she knows that "all beyond High Park's a desert to [him] and no gallantry can draw [him] farther" (V). Etherege's heroines had made similar conditions in *She Would If She Could*. Noticing this pattern also in Wycherley and Dryden, Professor Anne Righter in a recent essay on Wycherley sees it as a conventional feature of Restoration comedy.[15] Indeed it was a necessary part of female strategy and for good reasons: "If we run into the world [says Steele's Harriot], that youth and innocence which should demand assistance does but attract invaders. . . . How do I see that our sex is naturally indigent of protection" (II). A girl runs a greater risk in love than a man. Julia of *Sir Solomon* was also quick to see this when she considered marrying Young Single against his and her father's refusal to recognize the match.

> Since thou art doomed to poverty
> By a mad father's harsh decree
> And since my sentence is the same
> From mine, if I admit thy flame;
> Single, 'twill just in me appear

---

[15] In *Restoration Theatre*, eds. John Russell Brown and Bernard Harris (London, 1965), p. 76.

To try well what must cost so dear:
No common test is fit to prove
The truth and firmness of thy love;
Since thou with nothing com'st to me,
And I leave all to follow thee.

(III)

Male impudence arouses a streak of female contrariness. "There is not so impudent a thing in nature as the saucy look of an assured man, confident of success," says Millamant (*Way of the World*, IV). It is a look, indeed, that dares the lady to daunt it, though Gatty's black threats are certainly overdone in *Bury Fair* when she says to Wildish, "Tremble, for I will make thee such an example as shall be a terror to thy sex, and revenge all the insolencies committed upon mine" (II). In the beginning of *Careless Lovers* Hillaria was declared "an enemy to love" (II), but Careless ought not to have felt aggrieved, for she was really trying to win him by applying the principle of Arabella in *Wife's Relief*, who realized that "if we would have the fellows pray, we must keep 'em fasting" (II). "The truth is," Careless's friend Lovel points out, "she played the tyrant with thee; but you deserve that and more" (V). Whenever a heroine who is actually in love pretends she is not, or refuses to be "particular," she is testing, waiting to see how much the man will sacrifice for love. On this assumption 49 heroines in these plays test their lovers. Measures more specifically designed to reveal the lover's qualifications are taken by other heroines in 15 plays.

If she does not drive him away by her coldness or lose his respect by melting, the young man, reduced to a helpless condition by conflicting awe and ardor, is ripe for conversion to a religion of which she is the deity. He is now ready to make what Heartfree calls "a great leap in the dark" (*Provoked Wife*, V), to give up his bachelor freedom and the pleasures of rambling. Since he is a plain-dealer, a rational man who knows all about human frailty and the fragility of love, he can do so only by taking leave of his senses. Therefore, when Archer teaches a landlord's daughter the art of love, he tells her that "a lover must embrace his ruin and throw himself away" (II). Archer would never do such a thing himself—Farquhar in *Beaux' Stratagem* is here less sentimental than his predecessors, not more so—but his friend Aimwell would. In the last act, just when the fair Dorinda yields her hand to him in marriage, Aimwell has qualms about the stratagem he has used to win her. He finds that he "prefers the interest of [his] mistress to [his] own" and confesses that he is not Lord Aimwell as he has pretended to be, but Lord Aimwell's younger brother, thus "throwing himself away." But blessed are the meek: his mistress will marry him without a penny; even that is not ultimately necessary because his older brother promptly dies.

Aimwell's profitable madness is by no means unique, for all heroes who are in a strict sense madly in love marry heiresses. *Greenwich Park* teaches that "the flame which reason rules has interest in it" (II). Vanbrugh's *Aesop* pronounces that love and wisdom cannot go together. An antagonistic character in *Wife's Relief* thinks "a lover is . . . a sort of obstinate Rhodomontado wretch that declares war against all his senses; a little inclined to poetry, very lazy, and always talks in blank verse" (IV). Oronces (*Aesop*), Lionel (*Bellamira*), Young Reveller (*Greenwich Park*), Lovewell (*Love and a Bottle*), Reynard (*Tunbridge Walks*), Wilding (*Quaker's Wedding*), and Don Philip (*She Would and She Would Not*) are duly "mad." In this context it is not difficult to see that Manly's insane love for Olivia after she jilts him in *The Plain Dealer* is not a reprehensible intemperance as some critics insist,[16] but Wycherley's demonstration of Manly's heroic capacity to entertain a generous passion for a lady.

Of course, love is a gamble, as the leaden casket affirms in Shakespeare's *Merchant of Venice*. In Restoration comedy the idea of the lover's throwing himself on the mercy of Fortune is also current. So Roebuck of *Love and a Bottle* declares, "Woman's our fate" (V). Alithea, as we have noted, sums up *The Country Wife* with the statement that "women and fortune are truest still to those that trust them" (V). *The London Cuckolds* might seem to be a strange place to find instruction in this doctrine, but Ravenscroft has plotted even this bawdy play around a moral. The contrast he sets up between the two heroes requires us to accept the proposition, stated in Act I, that "love like riches comes more by fortune than industry." Ramble carefully plans his seductions and continually fails to achieve them. Townley, who is not interested in scoring points like Ramble, twice succeeds by accident just where Ramble's elaborate designs fail. Both times, quite signifi-

---

[16] Manly's "madness" is discussed on pp. 99–100.

cantly, Ramble fails because he takes thought for how he is going to escape instead of giving his single-minded attention to the lady. When at last he does succeed, it is only after Townley has convinced him of his fault, and it happens by chance. His escape, of course, fails. Townley never worries about the future and takes an interest in the young wives as people rather than as conquests. Furthermore, since the antagonistic old husbands treat their wives as property and since Ramble "hoards women" and pursues them as a "business" (I), the play seems by means of Townley's success and their failure to condemn acquisitiveness and recommend Generosity even for cuckold-makers.

In *Mulberry Garden* Sedley makes the point that lovers must trust Fortune by contrasting the old man Forecast with three mad pairs of lovers, one in prose and two in heroic couplets. Forecast opposes the marriage of one daughter to a Cavalier because the Puritans are then in power. His forecasting puts him precisely on the wrong side when the king is restored in Act V; and for their foolhardy loyalties, the young people at this point inherit the earth. The lesson is reinforced by a debate between two fathers over the best way to bring up daughters. Forecast is for keeping his daughters "under lock and key" and training them in "huswifery" (I), while Everyoung lets his daughters ramble. Forecast and the plain-dealing hero Wildish discuss these policies:

> FORECAST. These young wenches, Mr. Wildish, have less forecast than pigeons; so they be billing, they look no farther; ne'er think of building their nests, nor what shall become of their little ones.
>
> WILDISH. Sir, I think they're in the right; let 'um increase and multiply, and for the rest, trust him that set 'um a work.
>
> (II)

Indeed, viewed overall, Restoration comedy presents a grand pattern of the old trying without success to gather everything to themselves, while it instead falls to the generous young, who are intently engaged in throwing everything, including themselves, away. Rashley's speech against consideration in Durfey's *Fond Husband* also describes a conflict between generations:

> Damn consideration [he says] 'tis a worse enemy to mankind than malice: let impotent age consider that is fit for nothing but dull tame thoughts of what he has been formerly; let the lawyer and the physician consider, what quibbles and what potions are most necessary; and let the sly fanatic consider how to be securely factious. But let the lover love on, whilst all his thoughts and senses are employed in the dear joys of rapture . . . without one grain of dull consideration. (V)

Freedom from consideration may produce merely carelessness or inconsiderateness in a young man, but it also prepares him for making final commitments like marriage, which require not self-gratification, not self-aggrandizement, not self-admiration, but self-immolation. So, to give an inconsiderable example, we find that Wilding in *Quaker's Wedding*, for many years nothing more than "an agreeable rake," under the influence of Annabella begins to spout strange speeches: "Follies I have promiscuously shown, vices alternately have swayed me, but till now, never till now was I ever warmed by virtuous constancy or felt the sacred fire of real love." His mistress is understandably dubious. "Are you really so mad . . . to put it into my power to be revenged of you?" He is: "I leave my fate to you" (V). These lines show Restoration comedy in 1703 at the point where its main ideas are becoming clichés, and people like Wilkinson can assemble plays mechanically from the ready-made materials, without thinking. This brief passage contains reference to the hero's period of unconstant libertinism, the analogy of love to religion, his throwing himself away, his madness, his trust in Fortune, and his surrender, received like Dorimant's as "revenge for the wrongs [he] has done her sex."

"I leave my fate to you," Wilding says, almost like a soldier reciting a memorized order of the day. Perhaps he has learned the speech from Young Single of Caryl's play *Sir Solomon* (1669). Single's mistress, having just heard his rival's suit for her hand, turns to him like King Lear turning to Cordelia and says, "Now, Sir, what have you to say in your own behalf to counter-balance the perfections of such a competitor?" He answers simply, "Madam, I am nothing but what you please to make me" (IV). Or perhaps he was imitating Elder Worthy of *Love's Last Shift*, who in the same position told his mistress, "I am your slave; dispose of me as you please" (II). Or perhaps Congreve's Valentine or Mirabell had shown the way by giving up strategic positions and placing themselves at the mercy of their opponents in the final acts of *Love for Love* and *Way of the World*. Wilkinson's Wilding was by no means a novelty.

There is precedent also for the "farewell to vice and folly" aspect of Wilding's speech. Bellamy gives a crude but truthful physiological explanation for the rambling hero's change of heart in Dryden's *Evening's Love*, declaring that "constancy and once a night come naturally upon a man towards thirty" (III). In the preface to the same play Dryden also gives the critical grounds for the conversion of plain-dealing heroes. Assuming that instruction is the purpose of comedy, it follows that playwrights do not "make . . . vicious [protagonists] happy, but only as heaven makes sinners so; that is, by reclaiming them first from vice. For it is to be supposed they are, when they resolve to marry; for then, enjoying what they desire in one, they cease to pursue the love of many."[17] Whether nature or art is the cause, heroes of Restoration comedy do reform, though sometimes, as in the case of Dryden's *Wild Gallant*, we have to wait until the epilogue for the news. There we are told "The Wild Gallant has quite played out his game; / He's married now and that will make him tame." Despite some evidence to the contrary, Beatrix assures us in the text of *Evening's Love* that her suitor Wildblood will "degenerate into as tame and peaceable a husband as a civil woman would wish to have" (V). Woodall of Dryden's *Kind Keeper* reforms after accepting the truth of what Mrs. Pleasance tells him about his amorous adventures with two women of their acquaintance: "The [one] can afford you but the leavings of a fop; and to a witty man, as you think yourself, that's nauseous; the [other] has fed upon fool so long, she's carrion too, and common into the bargain. Would you beat a ground for game in the afternoon, when my Lord Mayor's pack had been before you in the morning? . . . Your two mistresses keep both shop and warehouse; and what they cannot put off in gross, to the keeper and the husband, they sell by retail to the next chance customer. Come, are you edified?" (IV). Woodall is. The meanness, futility, and boredom of libertinism are reasons for abjuring it.

[17] Dryden, I:143–44.

Some such reasoning as this encourages Wycherley's Ranger to adopt "another kind of love" for Lydia in *Love in a Wood*. As Summers observes in the introduction to the play in the Nonesuch edition, love "in a wood" can mean love in a state of madness. If the metaphor is intended, the literal forest of trees, St. James's Park, in which all the characters get lost becomes a symbol of the chaos in the mind of the undisciplined Ranger. In the park Wycherley crisscrosses his pairs of lovers in a series of dismaying adventures not unlike those that occur in *Midsummer Night's Dream*. After one futile chase, Ranger pauses to take stock of his life up to that point and chart a new course: "Lydia, triumph; I now am thine again. Of intrigue honorable or dishonorable and all sorts of rambling I take my leave. When we are giddy, 'tis time to stand still: why should we be so fond of the bypaths of love, where we are still waylaid with surprises, trapans, dangers, and murdering disappointments?" (IV). Ranger's revulsion from promiscuity here gives us a clue to his meaning in the paradoxical final lines of the play, in which he refuses to think of matrimony as loss of freedom.

> ... the bondage of matrimony? No—
> The end of marriage now is liberty,
> And two are bound—to set each other free.
>
> (V)

Marriage sets one free from the endless maze, madness, or wood of unlimited sexual adventure. The bonds-freedom paradox is raised also in Wycherley's poem "To Love," where he affirms that love not only has the power to chain us to "wedlock's yoke" but also allows us to "triumph in [those] chains."[18]

Ranger's reason for turning over a new leaf is echoed in a much lower key by Merryman in *Bellamira*, who breathes a sigh of relief at the prospect of marrying his ward Thisbe: "I should have killed myself with whoring and drinking," he reflects, "but now I will beget sons and daughters till threescore" (V). Shadwell, too, gives a practical reason for reform, leaving room for the idea of constancy being a special capacity of a chosen remnant. "All men of wit reclaim," according to

---

[18] William Wycherley, *Complete Works*, ed. Montague Summers (Soho, 1924), III:38–39.

a character in *Bury Fair*, "and only coxcombs persevere to the end of debauchery" (I). The monotonous chase tires Ravenscroft's Careless, too. "Why do all the great wenchers at last forsake all their mistresses for a wife?" asks his friend Lovel. "For we find most of them marry at the long-run; nay generally they prove the best husbands: and the reason is they have experimented the folly of that lewd course of life." Careless, having just been jilted by two whores, is ready to listen to wisdom of this sort: "I had never so good an opinion of marriage as now; for this dog trick that these two jilting jades shewed me in leaving me so much in the lurch has lessened them in my esteem, to the degree of honest women" (*Careless Lovers*, V). Thus prepared, he is ready to marry Hillaria, who has proved her superiority to other girls by dealing plainly with him and by defeating him in a battle of wits.

Other conversions more closely follow the religious analogue in spirit, and some are too early in the period to be discounted as incipient sentimentality. Two occur in the 1670s, one in the 1680s, three in the 1690s, and one in the first decade of the eighteenth century. In 1673, for example, we have Alonzo in *Dutch Lover*, who customarily falls in love as often as he sees a new face and winces at the mention of marriage, discovering in the first act that one look at Euphemia "changes nature in me." Ranger of *The Country Wit* (1675), who comes on the scene with the attitude that "the world is nature's house of entertainment, where men of wit and pleasure are her free guests, tied to no rules or orders" (II), changes his tune after meeting Christina. "The enjoyment of other women," he now says, "gives me not so much delight as a smile from her" (III). Constancy is difficult for one made of flesh and blood as he is, but in Act IV we find him struggling hard to achieve it: "I must now either repent and become downright plodding lover to Christina or in plain terms lose her. I must either forsake all the world for [her] or her for all the world. . . . Well, I cannot bear the loss of Mrs. Christina! I had rather endure marriage with her than enjoy any other woman at pleasure. I must and will repent and reform." Wellman (*Revenge*, 1680) has been converted before the curtain rises, but he lets us know that a superior woman helped him rise above the flesh: "In troth I loved [my whore] dearly once, till my soul showed me the imperfections of my body and placed my love on a more worthy object" (I). Young Reveller of Mountfort's *Greenwich Park* (1691) does not always appear to be under Mountfort's control, but at one point his creator clearly intends for him to give evidence of being converted. After a drinking bout he descends on his mistress with fire in his eye, only to say, "What the devil ails me! Or does the devil govern me! My blood's quite altered and those loose desires which never liked but for conveniency, are changed to real passion; my wanton drunkenness turned to a sober admiration, and I begin to fear I'm growing a dull, insipid, constant lover!" (III). Forthwith he begins to speak blank verse. Perhaps in imitation of the relapses of other heroes (Dorimant, *Man of Mode*; Ramble, *Country Wit*) or perhaps due to a lapse of Mountfort's attention, Young Reveller is soon equally in love with another girl; but finally he marries the one who has altered his blood.

The conversions of Loveless, "roused" from a "deep lethargy of vice" by Amanda in *Love's Last Shift* (V), and of Worthy, whose "gross desires of flesh and blood [are] in a moment turned to adoration" by the same Amanda in *The Relapse* (V), are not, in the context of the almost universal pattern of conversion in Restoration comedy, epoch-making as conversions. The initial depravity of Cibber's Loveless, the tearfulness and extent of his regeneration, and the fact that his wife is the agent are the novel features of *Love's Last Shift*. Worthy's conversion in *The Relapse* is an innovation because Amanda is the first superior wife of an unappreciative husband who refuses to cuckold the wretch and because Worthy therefore is the first potential cuckolder who becomes a worshipper of his mistress without hope of consummation, licit or illicit.

Roebuck's change of heart in *Love and a Bottle* is couched in language that seems emulative of the mawkish passages of these two successful plays. In the lines that conclude the play, the once "wild, roving" plain-dealer belies his character in these terms:

> I have espoused all goodness with Leanthe,
> And am divorced from all my former follies.
> Woman's our fate. Wild and unlawful flames
> Debauched us first and softer love reclaims.
> Thus paradise was lost by woman's fall;
> But virtuous woman thus restores it all.

In the same year Farquhar caused the same sort of overwrought moral revolution in Sir Harry Wildair of his *Constant Couple*, but almost immediately thought better of it. Perhaps audiences could not bear to see so successful a creation destroyed before their eyes. In the first edition of the play Sir Harry utterly changes his breezy manner when confounded by the pure Angelica: "Ha! Her voice bears a commanding accent! Every syllable is pointed. By Heavens, I love her. I feel her piercing words turn the wild current of my blood and thrill through all my veins."[19] These heroics were probably hooted off the stage, for the edition dated the next year contains a revision of the scene in which the same confrontation produces a bawdy song, humming, whistling, and nervous bows, as Sir Harry comes to realize that the situation calls on him as a man of honor either to fight a duel over Angelica or marry her. "I must commit murder or commit matrimony! Which is best, now, a license from Doctor's Commons or a sentence from the Old Baily? If I kill my man, the law hangs me; if I marry my woman, I shall hang myself.—But damn it! cowards dare fight; I'll marry! That's the most daring action of the two. So, my dear cousin Angelica, have at you" (V).

Flippant conversions like this second choice of Farquhar's are more in keeping with the spirit of Restoration comedy, if more difficult to write. Wildish of *Mulberry Garden*, who is held up as a shining example of Plain-dealing against a whole tribe of "whining" lovers, manages to convey to the audience the fact that he feels an emotion toward Olivia that he has never felt before, without embarrassing references to his soul or her divinity. As with Sir Harry, in the new situation he finds himself at a loss as to how to proceed. "I was to blame no earlier to use myself to these women of honor, as they call 'um; for now, like one that never practised swimming, upon the first occasion I am lost" (IV). One of the most pleasant conversions is the one that occurs to Willmore in the final moments of *The Rover*. Like Sir Harry and Wildish he stays in character while indicating a new attitude, but instead of publishing the news in the standard soliloquy, Mrs. Behn makes it arise out of a battle of wits in which the girl, Hellena, raises before our eyes the respect that causes the change in his attitude, which is manifest only as an alteration of course.

19 *Farquhar*, ed. William Archer, Mermaid ed. (London, n.d.), p. 135.

WILLMORE. I am parlously afraid of being in love, Child.
. . . Come—my bed's prepared for such a guest all clean
and sweet as thy fair self; I love to steal a dish and a bottle
with a friend, and hate long graces. Come, let's retire and
fall to.

HELLENA. 'Tis but getting my consent, and the business is
soon done. Let but old gaffer Hymen and his priest say
amen to't, and I dare lay my mother's daughter by as proper a fellow as your father's son, without fear of blushing.

WILLMORE. Hold, hold, no Bugg words, child. Priest and
Hymen: prithee add hangman to 'em and make up the con-
sort. No, no, we'll have no vows but love, child, nor wit-
ness but the lover: the kind deity enjoins naught but love
and enjoy. . . . Marriage is as certain a bane to love, as lending money is to friendship. . . .

HELLENA. [But supposing I conceive] what shall I get? A
cradle full of noise and mischief, with a pack of repentance
at my back? Can you teach me to weave inkle to pass my
time with? . . .

WILLMORE. I can teach thee to weave a true love's knot
better.

HELLENA. So can my dog.

WILLMORE. Well, I see we are both upon our guard, and I
see there's no way to conquer good nature but by yielding.
Here, give me thy hand: one kiss and [farewell]—

HELLENA. How like my page he speaks. I am resolved you
shall have none, for asking such a sneaking sum. He that
will be satisfied with one kiss will never die of that longing.
Good friend Single-kiss, is all your talking come to this? A
kiss, a caudle! Farewell, Captain Single-kiss.

WILLMORE. Nay, if we part so, let me die a bird upon a
bough, at Sherrif's charge. By heaven, both the Indies shall
not buy thee from me. I adore thy humor and will marry
thee, and we are so of one humor, it must be a bargain.
Give me thy hand. [*kisses her hand*] And now let the blind
ones, Love and Fortune, do their worst.

(V)

The relationship here established, based as much on mutual regard as
on sexual attraction, is not unlike a friendship. It was friendship that

finally bound the second Constantia and Don John in Buckingham's *Chances* (V). Wycherley in a poem "Upon Friendship Preferred to Love" objected that while friendship joined souls, love joined bodies only. But many lovers, he admitted, were also friends.[20] "Friend is all the ties that nature seeks," declared a character in *The Parson's Wedding*, the earliest play of this set. One way to end the war between the sexes, apparently, is to shake hands.

Plain-dealing wits appear in 68 plays: in 12, they function only as cuckolders; in 2, they are not involved with women; in 42, they undergo conversions like those described.[21] In the 12 remaining plays, the plain-dealers marry without showing signs of conversion. About them, audiences might think as they pleased. Given these figures one might suppose that audiences would supply the conversion by force of habit when the dialogue did not. A man who has already demonstrated his generosity by his Liberality, Courage, and Plain-dealing must be capable of throwing himself away.

The ethical content of Restoration comedy can be summed up in the meanings of the word *generosity* when that word is applied to the various activities of life that the plays are concerned with. By rewarding generous actions, the comedies tell us what we ought to be. What do they tell us about what we are? By deflating moralistic, religious, and romantic pretensions they remind us that we are fallen humanity. The typical plot of the Wildair tamed is a warning to all who think they are outside nature. The comedies seem to say—when Harriet makes Dorimant visit her in the country, when the Rover settles for Hillaria—"amor vincit omnia." The spectacle they present over and over again of weak woman humbling strong man, of softness overcoming hardness, of impetuous virility quenched by female calm, is a repetition of the great joke about Mars and Venus that provoked the laughter of the gods. When a Careless, a Ramble, or a Wildish is caught in the net of responsibility, baited with the very delicacy that he has so

---

[20] Wycherley, *Works*, III:43–44.

[21] David S. Berkeley counts 23 "penitent rakes" in Restoration comedy. His figure differs from mine because he has read a different set of plays, finding 15 "persistent rakes" in plays I had not selected. Since he and I have 8 "rakes" in common, apparently his definition of penitent rake is close to my definition of converted plain-dealer, though in one case (Carlos, *The False Count*) a character whom he chooses to call a rake I find too heroic to be classed as a plain-dealer. ("The Penitent Rake in Restoration Comedy," *Modern Philology*, XLIX (1952):223–33.)

often consumed with impunity, what is there left to say about his many victories in the sex war? Man is a social animal. The family is his natural state. Egoism and libertinism are the denial of our nature, not marriage. While Restoration comedy prudently attends to the preservation of the species by making sure that mothers will be supported, that children will have fathers, and that estates will have heirs, it enjoys a huge laugh at the expense of the brave little fellows who thought that they could defy the law of kind.

When, provided with a set of standard attitudes toward the most common acts, situations, and characters of love in Restoration comedy, we again approach *Love for Love* to see how it fits into the total picture, the first thing we notice is its title. Running true to form, Congreve has put a moral there, too, and what is more, "to that moral [he has] invented the fable" (*Double Dealer*, dedication). He did not coin the phrase, because it appeared fifteen years earlier in *The Revenge*, where it seems to be already a part of the language. In that play, speaking of a courtesan of whom he has been very fond, Wellman says women "are no ungrateful persons; they'll give love for love" (I). In a poem probably composed after Congreve's play, but again in the context of prostitution, Wycherley writes,

> If love's a blessing, (as it is) you say
> We for it ought not then to pay, but pray. . . .
> Nothing but pleasure can reward delight,
> Nothing but satisfaction do love right;
> Nothing but smile for smile and kiss for kiss
> But look for look or aught but joy for bliss
> Or love for love a true requital is.[22]

Cibber may have been thinking of Congreve's title when in 1700 he has Carlos of *Love Makes a Man* advocate "love for love" on the principle that "the sole delight of love lies only in the power to give" (II). These citations of the phrase make it clear that to give love for love is not to give it for money or for anything else material. It is to give it for nothing. Congreve probably means several other things by his title, but he means this, too.

22 Wycherley, *Works*, III:62.

The play is undoubtedly constructed to give instruction on the subject of Love. Love is the reason Valentine is in conflict with his father,
a conflict made objective in the final act when his father becomes his
rival for Angelica. For the "privateers"—Mrs. Foresight, Mrs. Frail,
Tattle, and the two old men—love legalized as marriage is a profit-
making device. The love of Valentine and Angelica provides the forward movement of the plot, while Ben's courtship of Prue, Prue's affair
with Tattle, Mrs. Frail's dalliance with Ben, Tattle's and Sir Sampson's
attempts to marry Angelica, and Mrs. Frail's attempt to marry Valentine provide the delaying action. For antagonistic characters, and even
temporarily for Scandal and Valentine, love is the means, and money or
power is the end. As the plot unfolds, each fold reveals that what appeared to be love was something else, until finally what appeared to
be something else (Valentine's deception) proves actually to have
been hidden love. Not until Act V does anyone give love for love.

Originality in the modern sense of creating works of art never before
seen or thought of, out of materials never before used, to say things
never before dreamt of, would have been incomprehensible to Restoration playwrights, who devoted their creative energy almost entirely
to the exploitation of forms and materials they accepted as given to
express conclusions they considered foregone. The task of the comic
poet was to invent variations on existing themes, not to invent new
ones. It may be interesting, therefore, as we survey *Love for Love* in
this final connection, to watch how Congreve uses the available stock
of ingredients for comedy.

Normally, the mirror would be used to make a comment on the fop's
or the coquette's narcissism, but Congreve in *Love for Love* gives it
instead to the two old men, in whose hands it appears perhaps more
ridiculous. When Foresight, the old physiognomist, inspects his face
to see if he looks sick, as has been suggested by his wife and Scandal
to get rid of him, the power of suggestion overcomes the testimony of
his own eyes, which tell him he is perfectly healthy. Nothing but un-
toward self-interest could have caused him to discover illness in a
healthy face. The picture Congreve makes on the stage of old Foresight studying his face while Scandal makes love to his wife is a
visual image of Foresight's egoism. Later another mirror serves to
emphasize the folly of Sir Sampson when he sets his mind on follow-

ing Foresight's unwise course and marrying a young wife. To show how much vanity an old man must have to think himself a fit mate for a girl, Congreve has Sir Sampson preen himself in a mirror before proposing to Angelica (V).

The coquettes, Mrs. Frail and Mrs. Foresight, show their self-admiration by taunts instead of by mirrors as is the rule. "Your face! what's your face?" "No matter for that, it's as good a face as yours." "Not by a dozen years' wearing" (II).

The fop shows his incapacity to entertain a generous passion in the conventional way, by acting as the lady's rival for his own love. Tattle proposes to Angelica by praising himself as a "complete and lively figure, with youth and health and all his five senses in perfection" (IV). How can she resist him? In contrast, we hear Scandal propose himself to Mrs. Foresight in the blunt hero's depreciatory way: "I have no great opinion of myself, yet I think I am neither deformed or a fool" (III). Ben's modesty also registers well when he responds to Mrs. Frail's blandishments. When she calls him handsome, he thinks she must be joking; and when his father proposes that he marry Prue, he says, "Mayhap the young woman mayn't take a liking to me" (III). Valentine's modesty is conveyed by the down-at-heels existence he unabashedly leads at the beginning of the play. Angelica is quite clearly more important to him than a high style of life. The remonstrances of Jeremy and Scandal show just how much his position on the social scale has fallen. Valentine, however, is quite gay about his miserable existence, if not about Angelica's coldness.

The use of people as properties, as utensils for the gratification of lust, or as tools for acquiring power or wealth is a dominant theme in *Love for Love*. Perhaps it is *the* dominant theme. Beginning at the least reprehensible level, we see Scandal, one of the "Atalls" of Restoration comedy—his taste extends even to Valentine's bastard's nurse (I)—exploiting Mrs. Foresight. The point of her failing to recognize him the morning after as her lover of the night before may be that it is she who has exploited him, not he who has exploited her. Perhaps a recognition of the futility of such "conquests" prepares Scandal for his conversion in the last act. If so, he would repeat the pattern of promiscuity, revulsion, and conversion that we have noted in *Love in a Wood* and *Kind Keeper*. Since Scandal's main function is to debate against Valentine's affirmation of love, Congreve skimps Scandal's own adventures. But by putting the bits Congreve gives us into the contexts supplied by other plays, we can see him as a plain-dealer still exploring the wilderness, but showing by his appreciation of Angelica the capability of a generous passion.

Prue wants a man as a child wants a toy—Robin the Butler will do, he is handsome (V)—and is a long way from being capable of a generous relationship with a man. Mrs. Frail, who requires a husband both to secure her reputation and to provide her with cash, is motivated entirely by self-aggrandizement. She talks about Ben to her sister like a very shrewd businesswoman: "You have a rich husband and are provided for; I am at a loss and have no great stock either of fortune or reputation; and therefore must look sharply about me. Sir Sampson has a son . . ." (II). Later, when Ben's fortune fails to materialize, her sister, with whom she is in partnership, makes "a bargain with Jeremy . . . to sell his master to us" (IV). Whatever appearances of love these two may occasionally project, profit or power always motivates them.

Sir Sampson makes love to Angelica for self-aggrandizement also: to revenge himself on his son, to acquire her property, to take possession of a pretty bauble, and to create by this act the illusion that his youthful virility persists. Foresight has purchased his wife for much the same reasons, but, says Mrs. Foresight, "I cannot say that he has once broken my rest since we have been married" (III). Tattle makes the meanest use of women, by making a property of their good names. Congreve is at some pains to develop the idea that reputations are commodities by creating the situation in which Tattle, to prevent Scandal from telling Mrs. Frail that he has told tales about her and him (undoubtedly false), confesses himself willing to pay an interesting price for Scandal's secrecy.

> SCANDAL.   Come, then, sacrifice half a dozen women of good reputation to me presently. Come, where are you familiar? And see that they are women of quality, too, the first quality.
> TATTLE.   'Tis very hard. Won't a baronet's lady pass?
> SCANDAL.   No, nothing under a right honorable.

(I)

Tattle brags of his ability to keep secrets in order to create the notion that he has secrets to keep. Angelica brings out this aspect of his psychological structure by suggesting that it is not in his "power" to name any ladies who have committed indiscretions with him. "Not in my power, madam! What, does your ladyship mean that I have no woman's reputation in my power?" "Ouns, why you won't own it, will you?" says Scandal (III). The point is that this is a kind of power that Tattle is only too glad to own.

The affair between Scandal and Mrs. Foresight probably takes place because it is conventional to have two pairs of lovers, one comparatively heroic and the other of a more plain-dealing sort. But Congreve has reversed the normal importance of the two couples, so that the plain-dealing pair seems an almost vestigial remnant of the past. In this play the believers in love have the primary roles and the nonbelievers the secondary roles. This is exactly the opposite of the situation in *The Man of Mode*, for example. To be sure, Valentine and Angelica are heroic only in contrast to the other pair. As soon as we consider them along with leading couples in other plays, they lose their heroic proportions. Valentine's promiscuous past and his hesitancy to put himself in his mistress's hands, and Angelica's doubts about his trustworthiness and her consequent testing, are marks of the skeptical plain-dealer. In this particular variation on the theme of love on two levels, Congreve generates more sympathy for Angelica and Valentine, the typical suspicious mistress and hesitant lover, by showing what total doubt and mistrust amount to in Scandal and Mrs. Foresight. Because he does not compare it with something "higher," Congreve thus writes a better apology for the plain-dealer's way.

In the final lines of the play, when Scandal is converted, the difference between him and Valentine is stated in terms of doubt and belief just as we have seen it expressed in numerous other plays. Valentine has "zeal and faith"; Scandal has been "an infidel" (V). But it is evident that Valentine had not become one of the faithful until he met Anglica. In the first act we have the visit of his bastard's nurse, asking for maintenance. And Valentine himself testifies that he has those "high-mettled appetites" which are standard equipment for plain-dealing heroes. "I am of myself a plain, easy, simple creature and to be kept at small expense," he tells his stingy father, "but the retinue [of appetites] that you gave me are craving and invincible; they are so many devils that you have raised, and will have employment" (II).

Because Valentine's period of probation is a long one, Congreve begins his play long after he has met Angelica, and so we miss the heroine's usual conversation with a maid or a confidante about the hero's wild but attractive ways, which gives the author a chance to apologize for them. But Valentine's rambling disqualifies him as a candidate for a chaste maid's hand no more in this play than in any other. Nevertheless, his bad record must be taken into account because it explains Angelica's wariness. Her problem is to create constancy in a man who has never found a woman worthy of it before. To convince him that she is indeed a prize worth his giving up his freedom for, she must walk the perilous knife-edge between "awe and invitation" that so often brought success to heroines in other plays. Angelica invites, like the rest, by a manner that is giddy, gay, and witty but never "particular." In the scene in which she teases Old Foresight about his occult practices and his wife's gadding until he lends her his coach so that she can go gadding herself, we are exposed to the good humor, plain speech, sharp wit, high spirits, and independence of mind that must have attracted Valentine to her in the first place. When she appears on stage with Valentine for the first time, we are exposed to the awe-inspiring coldness of manner by which she fends off particularity.

> ANGELICA. You can't accuse me of inconstancy; I never told you that I loved you.
> VALENTINE. But I can accuse you of uncertainty, for not telling me whether you did or not.
> ANGELICA. You mistake indifference for uncertainty; I never had concern enough to ask myself the question.
>
> (III)

So much for invincible Valentine. Angelica keeps him forever in that ticklish position he describes to Scandal, having no great reason "either for hope or despair" (I).

This is the limbo he must remain in if she is to be allowed to make up her mind about him free of the pressures that would exist if she showed him particular favors. If she were overly warm she might, like Prue, find herself engaged in an extramarital affair, guaranteeing to her as it did to Prue that she will "be hated and despised by that very person whom [she has] done everything to oblige." Or if she, as Mrs. Frail did Ben, encouraged him to hope for "un bonheur qu'elle n'a pas resolu de [lui] accorder," she would earn his contempt as a jilt, in the same way that Mrs. Frail earned Ben's. Until she is ready to marry him, only an attitude of perfect indifference gives her freedom of choice, and under the circumstances, the fact that it must be a pose is excusable. It is a necessary strategy in a world in which all men are to be considered guilty until proved innocent. We recall that Tattle told Prue, while teaching her the way of the world, that both the lover and his mistress always lie (II). But Prue had to learn her lesson from experience; indoctrination was insufficient for her.

To avoid these pitfalls, Angelica must wait patiently for incontrovertible evidence that Valentine loves her. His attempt to undermine her defenses and win a declaration of love from her by pretending that he has gone out of his wits for love of her casts grave suspicion on his motives. She will not give him love for a trick. Instead she gives him "trick for trick" (IV), rejects him as unfit on account of madness, and pretends she will marry his father.

A lover must "embrace his ruin and throw himself away." This is exactly what Valentine finally finds the courage to do, for Angelica's strategy is well calculated to engender the madness that is true love. When Valentine pretends to be mad, the allusion is not only to Hamlet, whose madness also had method in it, but to the conventional and specifically *un*-methodical madness of the typical lover of Restoration comedy. Since Valentine's madness is counterfeit, it will not do for Angelica. Before she visits her "madman," Angelica has received a proposal from Tattle who, as we remember, boasts that he has his "five senses in perfection." "O fie, for shame! [she cries] Hold your tongue; a passionate lover and five senses in perfection! When you are as mad as Valentine, I'll believe you love me, and the maddest shall take me" (IV). She requires a mad lover, someone mad enough to give and hazard all he has for her. Is Valentine really mad? She tricks him into revealing his sanity. Then he becomes her property instead of she his, a justifiable return for his deceit. Thus armed, she concludes as she leaves him in a state of immense chagrin, "I am not the fool you take me for; and you are mad and don't know it" (IV).

He was mad to think of making her "play the fool" for him, certainly, but perhaps he is also madder—that is, more in love—than his tactics would suggest. Now, suddenly, everyone in the play who thinks he is perfectly in his wits is mad and does not know it. Sir Sampson prepares to marry Angelica (he thinks) for good, sensible, selfish reasons. But Ben says his father's mad, "horn mad" (V). Tattle, whose five perfect senses have led him into Jeremy's trap where he is to capture Mrs. Frail on the assumption that she is the 30,000-pound frigate Angelica, talks mysteriously of his new plans to Old Foresight and daughter Prue; and the bemused old man, who had just begun to accept the fact that Tattle was to marry Prue instead of Ben, thinks, "He's mad, child, stark wild." When in a howling fit of disappointment Prue wants to marry the butler, Foresight calls for the rod and prays, "Heaven keep us all in our senses!—I fear there is a contagious frenzy abroad. How does Valentine?"

For his part, while all the sane characters are madly attending to their own interests, Valentine has gone mad indeed. He now finally embraces his ruin and throws himself away. His methodical madness had indeed been catching, but methodical, designing, acquisitive madness is madness indeed. Only the true madness that chooses lead caskets is the true sanity that earns the money and the girl. He who will save his life must lose it. To drive the point home, when Valentine declares himself ready to sign the deed irrevocably surrendering his birthright, Congreve has Scandal say, " 'Sdeath, you are not mad indeed, to ruin yourself?" The prodigal has returned. He kneels and says, "I yield my body your prisoner, and make the best on't." And now Angelica, who was to have been his property, whom he had expected to give him *all* for love, gives him love for love.

Plays on Which This Study Is Based

Aesop (Vanbrugh). In *Dramatic Works*, ed. Dobrée and Webb (Nonesuch Press, Bloomsbury, 1927).

The Amorous Widow, or The Wanton Wife [Betterton]. London, 1706.

Amphitryon (Dryden). In *Dramatic Works*, ed. Summers (Nonesuch Press, Bloomsbury, 1932).

The Beaux' Stratagem (Farquhar). In *Farquhar*, ed. Archer, Mermaid ed. (London, n.d.); *Restoration Plays*, Modern Library ed.

Bellamira, or The Mistress (Sedley). In *Poetical and Dramatic Works*, ed. Pinto (London, 1928).

A Bold Stroke for a Wife (Centlivre). Ed. Stathas (Lincoln, Nebr., 1968).

Bury Fair (Thomas Shadwell). In *Works* (London, 1720).

The Busy Body (Centlivre). In *Works* (London, 1761).

The Careless Husband (Cibber). Ed. Appleton (Lincoln, Nebr., 1966).

The Careless Lovers (Ravenscroft). London, 1673.

The Chances (George Villers, Duke of Buckingham). In *Works* (London, 1715), vol. II.

The Cheats (Wilson). In *Dramatic Works*, ed. Maidment and Logan (Edinburgh, 1874).

City Politiques (Crowne). Ed. Wilson (Lincoln, Nebr., 1967).

The Comical History of Don Quixote, Part the Second (Durfey). In *Works* (London, 1694).

The Comical Revenge, or Love in a Tub (Etherege). In *Dramatic Works*, ed. Brett-Smith (Oxford, 1927).

The Committee (Howard). In *Dramatic Works* (London, 1722).

The Confederacy (Vanbrugh). In *Vanbrugh*, ed. Swain, Mermaid Series (New York, 1949).

The Conscious Lovers (Steele). Ed. Kenney (Lincoln, Nebr., 1968).

The Constant Couple, or A Trip to the Jubilee (Farquhar). In *Farquhar*, ed. Archer, Mermaid ed. (London, n.d.).

The Country Wife (Wycherley). Ed. Fujimura (Lincoln, Nebr., 1965).

The Country Wit (Crowne). In *Dramatic Works* (Edinburgh, 1874).

Cutter of Coleman Street (Cowley). In *Representative English Comedies*, ed. Gayley and Thaler (New York, 1936).

The Double Dealer (Congreve). In *Complete Plays*, ed. Davis (Chicago, 1967).

The Double Gallant (Cibber). In *Dramatic Works* (London, 1754).

The Drummer (Addison). London, 1716.

The Dutch Lover (Behn). In *Works*, ed. Summers (London, 1915).

Epsom Wells (Thomas Shadwell). In *Works* (London, 1720).

An Evening's Love, or The Mock Astrologer (Dryden). In *Dramatic Works*, ed. Summers (Nonesuch Press, Bloomsbury, 1931).

The Fair Example, or The Modish Citizens (Estcourt). London, 1706.

The Fair Quaker of Deal, or The Humours of the Navy (Charles Shadwell). Dublin, 1757.

The False Count, or A New Way to Play the Old Game (Behn). In *Works*, ed. Summers (London, 1915).

The False Friend (Vanbrugh). In *Dramatic Works*, ed. Dobrée and Webb (Nonesuch Press, Bloomsbury, 1927).

The Feigned Courtesans, or A Night's Intrigue (Behn). In *Works*, ed. Summers (London, 1915).

The Fond Husband, or The Plotting Sisters (Durfey). London, 1678.

The Funeral, or Grief à la Mode (Steele). In *Steele*, ed. Aitken, Mermaid ed. (London, 1926).

The Gamester (Centlivre). In *Works* (London, 1761).

The Gentleman Dancing Master (Wycherley). In *Works*, ed. Weales (New York, 1967).

Greenwich Park (Mountfort). In *Six Plays* (London, 1720).

The Kind Keeper, or Mr. Limberham (Dryden). In *Dramatic Works*, ed. Summers (Nonesuch Press, Bloomsbury, 1932).

The Lancashire Witches, or Tegue O'Divelly the Irish Priest (Thomas Shadwell). In *Works* (London, 1720).

The Lady's Last Stake, or The Wife's Resentment (Cibber). In *Works* (London, 1754).

The London Cuckolds (Ravenscroft). In *Restoration Comedies*, ed. Summers (London, 1921).

Love and a Bottle (Farquhar). In *Complete Works*, ed. Stonehill (None-such Press, Bloomsbury, 1930).

Love for Love (Congreve). Ed. Avery (Lincoln, Nebr., 1966).

Love in a Wood, or St. James's Park (Wycherley). In *Complete Plays*, ed. Weales (New York, 1967).

Love Makes a Man, or The Fop's Fortune (Cibber). In *Works* (London, 1754).

Love's Last Shift (Cibber). In *Plays of the Restoration and Eighteenth Century*, ed. MacMillan and Jones (New York, 1931).

The Lying Lover, or The Lady's Friendship (Steele). In *Steele*, ed. Aitken, Mermaid ed. (London, 1926).

The Man of Mode, or Sir Fopling Flutter (Etherege). Ed. Carnochan (Lincoln, Nebr., 1966).

The Man's the Master (Davenant). In *Works* (London, 1673).

Marriage à la Mode (Dryden). In *Dryden*, vol. I, ed. Saintsbury, Mermaid ed. (London, n.d.).

The Mistake (Vanbrugh). In *Dramatic Works*, ed. Dobrée and Webb (Nonesuch Press, Bloomsbury, 1927).

The Mulberry Garden (Sedley). In *Poetical and Dramatic Works*, ed. Pinto (London, 1928).

The Non-Juror (Cibber). In *Works* (London, 1754).

The Old Bachelor (Congreve). In *Complete Plays*, ed. Davis (Chicago, 1967).

The Parson's Wedding (Killigrew). In *Restoration Comedies*, ed. Summers (London, 1921).

The Pilgrim (Vanbrugh). In *Dramatic Works*, ed. Dobrée and Webb (Nonesuch Press, Bloomsbury, 1927).

The Plain Dealer (Wycherley). In *Plays of the Restoration and Eighteenth Century*, ed. MacMillan and Jones (New York, 1931).

A Plot and No Plot (Dennis). London, 1694.

The Provoked Wife (Vanbrugh). Ed. Zimansky (Lincoln, Nebr., 1969).

The Quaker's Wedding (sometimes *Vice Reclaimed, or The Passionate Mistress*) (Wilkinson). London, 1703.

The Recruiting Officer (Farquhar). Ed. Shugrue (Lincoln, Nebr., 1965).

The Relapse (Vanbrugh). In *Plays of the Restoration and Eighteenth Century*, ed. MacMillan and Jones (New York, 1931).

The Revenge, or A Match in Newgate [Betterton? Behn? See van Lennep correspondence in *TLS*, January 28, 1939]. London, 1680.

The Rover, or The Banished Cavaliers (Behn). Ed. Link (Lincoln, Nebr., 1967).

She Would and She Would Not, or The Kind Impostor (Cibber). In *Works* (London, 1754).

She Would If She Could (Etherege). In *Dramatic Works*, ed. Brett-Smith (Oxford, 1927).

Sir Anthony Love, or The Rambling Lady (Southerne). In *Works* (London, 1721).

Sir Courtly Nice, or It Cannot Be (Crowne). In *Restoration Comedies*, ed. Summers (London, 1921).

Sir Martin Mar-all (Dryden). In *Plays*, ed. Loftis (Berkeley, Calif., 1966).

Sir Patient Fancy (Behn). In *Works*, ed. Summers (London, 1915).

Sir Solomon, or The Cautious Coxcomb (Caryl). London, 1671.

The Soldiers' Fortune (Otway). In *Complete Works*, ed. Summers (Nonesuch Press, Bloomsbury, 1926).

The Spanish Friar, or The Double Discovery (Dryden). In *Dryden*, vol. II, ed. Saintsbury, Mermaid ed. (New York, 1950).

The Squire of Alsatia (Thomas Shadwell). In *Plays of the Restoration and Eighteenth Century*, ed. MacMillan and Jones (New York, 1931).

The Surprisal (Howard). In *Dramatic Works* (London, 1722).

The Tender Husband (Steele). Ed. Winton (Lincoln, Nebr., 1967).

The Twin Rivals (Farquhar). In *Farquhar*, ed. Archer, Mermaid ed. (London, n.d.).

Tunbridge Walks, or The Yeoman of Kent (Baker). London, 1764.

The Way of the World (Congreve). Ed. Lynch (Lincoln, Nebr., 1965).

The Wife's Relief, or The Husband's Cure (Johnson). London, 1712.

The Wild Gallant (Dryden). In *Plays*, ed. Swedenberg *et al.* (Berkeley, Calif., 1962).

A Woman Is a Riddle (Bullock). London, 1717.

Index

A Note on the Author

BEN SCHNEIDER grew up in the Boston suburb of Winchester, Massachusetts, and went to college at Williams in the western part of the state, concentrating in English. After World War II, during which he was a radar man in the Army Signal Corps stationed in the Pacific, he obtained the Ph.D. at Columbia, specializing in English Romantic poets. His studies for the degree included a year as a research student at St. John's College, Cambridge, for the purpose of gathering material on Wordsworth's undergraduate days at St. John's.

After teaching at the University of Cincinnati, the University of Colorado, and Oregon State College, he came to Lawrence University in 1955, where he now teaches eighteenth-century English literature and Romantic poets. He is at present engaged in a project to convert *The London Stage*, a calendar of events at the London theatres from 1660 to 1800, into a computer-accessible information bank for theatre historians. Besides articles on Wordsworth and the London stage, he has published *Wordsworth's Cambridge Education* (1957).

UNIVERSITY OF ILLINOIS PRESS